MW01196868

LUMINOUS AWARENESS

A Guidebook to Natural Awakening in Life and in Death

PEMA DÜDDUL

Timeless Awareness Publications

www.timeless-awareness.com

© 2022 by Pema Düddul

Cover design: Jamyang Tenphel at Independent Author Services

Interior design: EbookPbook.com

All rights reserved. No part of this book may be reproduced in any form or by any means, electronic or mechanical, including photocopying, recording, or by any information storage and retrieval system, without permission in writing from the publisher.

978-0-6483972-9-8

First Edition

National Library of Australia Cataloguing-in-Publication entry:

Düddul, Pema. 1968–
Luminous Awareness/Pema Düddul.
9780648397298 (pbk.)
Non-Fiction—Philosophy & Religion
Non-Fiction—Self Help and Personal Development

DEDICATION

Dedicated to my Heart Teacher, Kyabje Dudjom Rinpoche, Jigdral Yeshe Dorje, and to my other beloved teachers: Ngakpa Karma Lhundup Rinpoche, Dungse Namgay Dawa Rinpoche and Jetsunma Tenzin Palmo.

Dedicated also to my Dharma companion and partner in life, Jamyang Tenphel, whose love, support and inspiring example made the writing of this book possible.

CONTENTS

ACKNOWLEDGEMENTS

Thanks to Casey Kemp, past editor at Shambhala Publications, for encouraging me to write and publish this book. It was not my idea but I am glad that I did it. Thanks also to my beta readers and Dharma friends: Debra Beattie, Leonie Bury, Annette Keenan, and Wendi Forbes, whose feedback was invaluable. Last, but by no means least, thanks to Jamyang Tenphel, whose wise advice shaped the contents of this book in numerous beneficial ways.

Awareness without feature,

Without end,

Luminous all around:

Here water, earth, fire, & wind

Have no footing.

Here long and short

Coarse and fine

Fair and foul

Name and form

Are all brought to an end.

With the cessation of the activity of the dualistic mind

Each is here brought to an end.

~ Siddhartha Gautama, the Buddha, from the Kevatta Sutta

LUMINOUS
AWARENESS

CHAPTER ONE

OUR TRUE NATURE

In your nature you are the Buddha. Take that nature as the path.

Enlightenment is our nature. In our true nature we are all perfect; exactly as we are, without modification or change. In our inner or fundamental nature we are all no different to the Buddha, pure and flawless. As Siddhartha Gautama, the Buddha himself, said:

> Look to your own nature which is intrinsically pure and rouse yourself.
> Look to the purity on which the world is founded and correct yourself.
> Look within and find happiness.[1]

These words of the Buddha are the essence of the vast and precious treasury of wisdom that is Buddhism. They point to the profound truth that our true nature is complete or perfect exactly as it is, at one with all and completely boundless. The Buddha is not saying we have to engage in all kinds of austerities or spiritual practices to "make" ourselves pure, but to look within and recognize the inherent purity that is already there. The Buddha is also saying that this true nature of ours, this inherent purity, is the foundation or ground of all other things, of the whole universe. In the final line of this beautiful verse the Buddha is saying that once we recognize these two things, the inherent purity of ourselves and the inherent purity of all that exists, we will find happiness. Once again, the Buddha is not saying we need to make

---

[1] Dhammapada, translated by Anne Bancroft, Vega Books, 2002, verse 379.

or fabricate happiness, to do or acquire things to become happy, he is saying by looking inward we find the inherent happiness that is already there. He is saying that happiness (or joy, love and contentment) is in fact the radiance or light of our true nature.

What does the Buddha mean by rouse and correct ourselves? And how exactly do we look to our true nature? The answer to these questions is what this book is all about. In essence, we can discover our true nature by doing some simple Buddhist practices outlined in these pages, such as meditation, and we can rouse and correct ourselves by adopting a certain philosophical worldview as well as an ethical approach to life. In the practice-focused Buddhist traditions of Tibet these three simple actions are often called View, Meditation and Conduct. The view is the fundamental Buddhist philosophy, worldview or perspective. The meditation is the practice or path. The conduct is ethical living.

To begin then, let's correct our view of ourselves and the world by gaining an understanding of who, or rather what, we truly are. One of the most important philosophical texts for Tibetan Buddhism, the *Uttaratantra*, contains the following passage:

> The Absolute is one undifferentiated whole. The potential of Buddhahood exists in every living being. Therefore, for ever and anon, all that lives is endowed with the Essence of the Buddha.[2]

The truth of Buddha Nature illuminates the non-truth of the way we see the world and ourselves. We are not separate from others or from the vastness of the universe. We are neither superior nor inferior to any other being, human or non-human. All living beings are utterly equal and precious. More to the point, all beings are no different in their nature to the Buddha. The true

---

[2] *Uttaratantra*, Verse 27, quoted in *Buddha-Nature: The Mahayana Uttara Tantra Shastra Maitreya's Root Text and Asanga's Commentary, Commentary by 13th Zasep Tulku Rinpoche*, Zuru Ling Tibetan Buddhist Centre, Vancouver, BC Canada, p. 163.

nature of our mind is Buddha mind. As the great Chan master Huang Po said, "The Mind is Buddha; Buddha is the Mind; which is infinite void, without boundaries, without name and form."[3] Echoing this, Padmasambhava, who established tantric Buddhism in Tibet around 750 CE, described the true nature of mind thus:

> In its true state the mind is naked, immaculate, clear, without duality, transparent, empty, timeless, uncreated, unimpeded; not realizable as a separate entity, but as the unity of all things.[4]

In a very similar vein, Mipham Rinpoche (1846–1912), a great philosopher practitioner of the Nyingma or ancient tradition of Tibetan Buddhism, describes the true nature of mind in this way:

> Mind's nature is indivisible emptiness and clarity,
>
> Inexpressible and indestructible, like space.
>
> In seeing it, there is no separate one who sees;
>
> There is but a single, all-encompassing sphere.
>
> Even looker and looking are one and the same.
>
> This view of seeing all at once is unsurpassed,
>
> A centerless, limitless, exceptional experience.[5]

These descriptions of the true nature of mind make it quite clear we are not what we think we are. We are not limited, small, constrained by our

---

[3] Huang Po, *The Zen Teaching of Huang Po on the Transmission of Mind*, translated by John Blofeld, Shambhala Publications, 1994, p. 118.

[4] Quoted in Ian A. Baker, 'Embodying Enlightenment: Physical Culture in Dzogchen as revealed in Tibet's Lukhang Murals', *Asian Medicine*, Vol. 7, 2012, p. 227.

[5] 'The Nature of Mind' by Mipham Rinpoche, translated by Adam Pearcey, 2016, with the assistance of Alak Zenkar Rinpoche, https://www.lotsawahouse.org/tibetan-masters/mipham/nature-of-mind

bodies and thoughts, separate and apart from each other. We are the exact opposite of that. The term "indivisible emptiness" is an attempt to describe the inexpressible, the truth of the vast, luminous openness—ungraspable and unbound by the constraints of the self—that is at the heart of all beings and all things. Khenchen Palden Sherab Rinpoche, a great contemporary master of the Nyingma tradition, described the true nature of mind in this way:

> Infinite and uncreated, the true nature of mind is great emptiness or the inconceivable openness known as dharmakaya. Great emptiness is not blank, empty space, a void or nothingness. It is very luminous, clear and full. Brightness and clarity shine forth spontaneously. This unceasing luminosity of the true nature is known as sambhogakaya. The mind is always active, radiating a world of transformations. Due to its inertia, it never stays the same for two instants. Each spark or radiant moment of manifest existence is non-separate from the original state of the true nature. Each spark is the union of emptiness and clarity. That radiance manifesting as point instants of space/time is known as nirmanakaya.[6]

Beyond the chatter of our ordinary mind, beyond the thoughts, feelings and sensations that we believe to be ourselves, there is something greater, something beyond words and concepts, beyond everything we currently know. As this greater reality is beyond words and concepts, Buddhism helps us grasp it by dividing this greater reality into different aspects, what are known as the Dharmakaya, Sambhogakaya and Nirmanakaya aspects. Kaya means "body" and refers to the living presence of enlightened mind, how enlightenment is embodied in all things. It also refers to the being of the historical Buddha

---

[6] Venerable Khenchen Palden Sherab Rinpoche, 'A Modern Commentary on Karma Lingpa's Zhi-Khro teachings on the peaceful and wrathful deities', transcript by the Venerable Khenpo Tsewang Dongyal Rinpoche. Full text here: https://holybooks-lichtenbergpress. netdna-ssl.com/wp-content/uploads/A-Modern-Commentary-on-Karma-Lingpas-Zhi-Kro-Teachings-on-the-peaceful-and-wrathfull-deities.pdf

(Shakyamuni) and all other Buddhas, including the many masters who have achieved enlightenment. There are generally three inseparable aspects of the Buddha: Dharmakaya (mind)[7], Sambhogakaya (speech or energy) and Nirmanakaya (body). These are also the three aspects of the true nature of our own minds: spacious awareness (Dharmakaya), luminosity or clarity (Sambhogakaya), and movement or compassion (Nirmanakaya). Our minds are one with the Buddha in their boundless awareness, penetrating luminosity and limitless compassion. We don't really need to know or use these terms as, in essence, they are words for three aspects of the same absolute truth and it is that truth, our perfect nature, which we should primarily be focused on, and not through mere words or concepts but through direct experience.

Ultimately, that which is beyond our ordinary monkey mind, the absolute truth, is a boundless spacious awareness. Maitreya-natha (270–350 CE), one of the founders of the Yogachara tradition of Buddhist philosophy, describes our fundamental or natural awareness in this way:

> Awareness is devoid of both apprehender and apprehended, in all their various forms. Free from subject and object, by its very own nature awareness is a mere indescribable luminosity.[8]

This luminous awareness has only one expression – limitless and unbiased love and compassion for all sentient beings, without bias or restraint. In other words, our true nature is Bodhicitta. *Bodhi* means awake and *citta* means mind, so Bodhicitta is the awakened compassionate mind that yearns to free all beings from suffering. What is the mind awake to? It is awake to the truth of our ultimate nature and the ultimate nature of reality. It is awake to the truth

---

[7] Dharmakaya is also another word or synonym for Buddha Nature, the true nature of mind, and the ultimate or absolute nature.

[8] Maitreya-natha quoted in *Distinguishing Phenomena from Their Intrinsic Nature: Maitreya's Dharmadharmatavibhanga with Commentaries by Khenpo Shenga and Ju Mipham*, translated by Dharmachakra Translation Committee, Shambhala Publications, 2021, p.27.

of *Shunyata* (or emptiness, which we'll discuss a little later) that is co-emergent or one with boundless compassion and unfettered love. As Kyabje Dilgo Khyentse Rinpoche once taught 'compassion is the expression of emptiness' and emptiness or Shunyata is the ultimate nature of everything.[9]

Lama Lena, a Western-born Dharma teacher, equates Bodhicitta with transcendent love and describes it thus:

> Love is the light that connects all life to all life. Giving birth and mating; dying and doing it again; loving again and again throughout time and space. You have loved, will have loved, every single living being there is. Don't throw them away. Don't ever discard them. They are your parents and your children, your teachers and your students, the bugs in your gut, your friends and your enemies, turn upon turn, as the wheel turns. Do not abandon that light which is beyond love, which is the very life force of the universe, which permits it to be more than just a big, dead ol' nothing. It's also called Bodhicitta.[10]

It is because Bodhicitta is our true nature that the development of selfless compassion and kindness are the heart of all Buddhist practice. What is Buddhist practice? It is the methods that lead us to recognize the true nature of our minds, our Buddha Nature, and connect us with the ultimate nature of all things. These methods can be summed up as: 1. recognizing the ultimate truth; 2. giving rise to love, and; 3. embodying compassion through action. There is nothing else to Buddhism bar the wisdom and joy these three bring. Tulku Thondup Rinpoche hints at this when he writes:

---

[9] Dilgo Khyentse Rinpoche, *The Heart of Compassion: The Thirty-seven Verses on the Practice of a Bodhisattva*, translated by the Padmakara Translation Group, Shambhala Publications, 2007, p.104.

[10] Lama Lena, *Bodhicitta and the Meaning of the Bodhisattva Vows*, Livestreamed teaching, May 6, 2021. Viewable on YouTube: https://youtu.be/bpiHsnNL_tw

Loving Kindness is the thought of wishing joy for all beings and the whole universe—without limits and conditions – and putting that wish into practice. Loving-kindness is love, but it is pure love, love that is totally open, universal, having no limits, unconditional – a love that has no attachment, no ego-centeredness, no self-centeredness. Meditation on loving-kindness is a training on the thoughts and deeds that benefit others. It is a practice that opens our heart with love to all, causing our life to blossom with feelings of boundless peace and joy.[11]

We are motivated to practice these methods that connect us to truth, love and compassion not just for ourselves but for the sake of all sentient beings. When we abide in the true nature of all boundless compassion arises naturally, along with the wisdom to know *how* to benefit sentient beings and the capacity to do what is necessary to help them. Practice makes us kinder, more compassionate, wiser and more capable beings. Bodhicitta is the ground or starting point for this transformation. It is our true nature. It is the path or practice itself and it is also the fruit, the awakened state; the state of uninhibited joy and love that is free of all suffering. How amazing that this sublime state is our ultimate reality!

What is a direct experience of our ultimate nature like? The nineteenth century Tibetan master and yogi, Shabkar Tsokdruk Rangdrol (1781-1851), describes his experience of the true nature of mind in this way:

Like the sun shining in a clear autumn sky, the luminous emptiness that is the true nature of mind was laid bare. In a state without center, without limits, empty like space, all phenomena— forms and sounds—were present in spontaneity, vivid as the sun, moon, planets and stars. Mind and phenomena blended completely in a single taste.[12]

---

[11] Tulku Thondup, *The Healing Power of Loving-Kindness*, Shambhala Publishing, 2021, p. 3.

[12] *The Life of Shabkar: The Autobiography of a Tibetan Yogin*. Edited by Constance Wilkinson and Michal Abrams. Translated by Matthieu Ricard, Jakob Leschly, Erika Schmidt, Marilyn Silverstone and Lodrö Palmo. Snow Lion Publications, 2001, p. 175.

That is our true nature and the ultimate nature of all. *That* is what Buddhism is designed to reveal for us. To be without limits, to be at one with everything, to experience our world as vivid luminosity, why wouldn't we want to abide permanently in that state? Only a profoundly deluded being would reject the opportunity to become one with that Great Perfection.

When we learn that this luminous perfection is the true nature of mind and our natural state, the first question that arises for us is: If this is true then why aren't we all enlightened already? It is quite simply because we are not aware of our true nature and have not had a direct experience of it. Even if we have been told what that true nature is we don't have confidence in it. We doubt it. We also have not practiced enough to have glimpsed the truth of it for ourselves. It is only practice—specifically meditation and the methods that awaken the heart—that grants us that direct experience. If we have received some Buddhist teachings we may intellectually accept that our true nature is this luminous non-dual awareness, this perfect enlightenment (or Bodhicitta). If we are honest with ourselves however we do not really believe this. We certainly do not *feel* the truth of it. We feel quite the opposite. We feel imperfect, flawed, not good enough, perhaps even broken or damaged. Rather than feeling amazed by our inner perfection, we mostly feel rather disappointed with ourselves. But this is a delusion. In fact everything we think about ourselves and the world is a delusion. The purpose of the Buddhist path is to crack open and remove that delusion.

The quickest way to be free of delusion is to develop certainty about our true, primordially perfect nature. We are not our negative thoughts and feelings. We are not our self-loathing nor our egocentrism. These things are fleeting distractions that obscure our ultimate nature, which is Bodhicitta. As esteemed Western-born Buddhist nun Jetsunma Tenzin Palmo explains:

In Buddhism, greed and anger, these very negative emotions which disturb the mind, are called adventitious defilements. Adventitious means that they're not innate. They come and they go, they're not part of our inherent nature. They're our second nature, they're not first nature. So therefore, our first nature is something very good, and that's why whenever we cultivate goodness in our hearts—kindness, compassion, thoughtfulness, concern for others—it reverberates with something very deep inside us which is our true nature.[13]

These adventitious negative emotions are the bulk of our suffering. They taint our experience of the world and damage our relationships with others. The suffering of negative emotions is universal. We are all weighed down by it. This is made clear in the First Noble Truth of Buddhism, which says that all experience is permeated by suffering or dissatisfaction. This dissatisfaction is the heart or source of those negative emotions. Why are we dissatisfied? Why do we suffer? Why are we unhappy? The answer is given in the Second Noble Truth. It is because we treat as permanent things that are impermanent. Because we relate to that which is utterly dependent as though it were independent. We treat as separate things that are connected. We treat that which is fluid and dynamic as though it were fixed and solid, and we see that which is insubstantial as substantial. We give meaning to meaningless things and treat what is meaningful as though it were nothing. We want what we cannot have, and do not want to take ownership of that which we have earned through our negative actions. We refuse to take responsibility for what we think, feel and do and constantly deceive ourselves about who and what we are. We live in a daydream of rainbows, illusions and mirages and behave as though it were all utterly real. We see delusion as truth and fear the actual truth because it undermines everything we are attached to – especially our fabricated sense of self. Worst of all we cherish ourselves and only pretend to care about others. In short, each and every moment we

---

[13] Jetsunma Tenzin Palmo [Facebook post] 26 June 2021. Available at: https://www.facebook.com/jetsunmatenzinpalmo (Accessed: 26 June 2021)

choose suffering and unhappiness as our sole inheritance because we do not have the courage to face the truth of things.

Though we need to be honest with ourselves and face that most of our suffering is a result of our ego-centrism and fear we need not berate ourselves for it. That is just a waste of time. Besides, there is a way out, a way to be free. That way is described in the Fourth Noble Truth and can be summarized as a life lived ethically and frugally, with love and kindness toward all beings as our sole motivation, and with daily meditation and contemplation as the method for dissolving our self-cherishing and opening our hearts. The fruit of this kind of life is liberation from suffering, awakening to our true nature, which is enlightenment. This awakening is guaranteed in the Third Noble Truth, which is that liberation is possible for all; that with the opening of our hearts we will finally know the absolute truth.

The surest way to open our hearts and have direct experience of our Buddha Nature, the true nature of mind, is to practice, specifically to practice meditation and give rise to love, joy and compassion. Merely knowing intellectually that we have Buddha Nature is not nearly enough. As Khenpo Karthar Rinpoche makes clear:

> Simply knowing that we possess Buddha Nature … is not sufficient to bring about awakening. If we know this but do not practice, it will not change anything. After all, this has always been our nature. We have always possessed Buddha Nature, or sugatagarbha, but we have not yet attained Buddhahood. Just its being there is not enough … The only point of studying Buddha Nature is to be inspired to practice Dharma, because it is the practice—not the knowledge—that reveals our Buddha Nature and enables us to attain Buddhahood.[14]

---

[14] Khenpo Karthar Rinpoche, *Karma Chakme's Mountain Dharma: Volume Three*, KTD Publications, Woodstock, NY, 2008, pp. xviii – xix.

If you wish to awaken to your true nature in the simplest way possible, so that you might be free of suffering and help others to be free, then this book and the approach it describes are for you. If, on the other hand, you are not inspired by simplicity but rather are drawn to all the bells and whistles (and drums and trumpets) of traditional Buddhist rituals then this book is not likely to appeal to you. This book is about liberation in this lifetime via a straight-forward, uncomplicated and direct route. This route is described in the Buddhist teachings on the bardo states. These bardo states occur in life—in-between thoughts, emotions and moments of perception—and in the process of dying in-between death and rebirth. The bardo teachings reveal thousands of opportunities for deep awareness each and every day and, most importantly, an opportunity for total awakening and liberation from all suffering at the time of death. If that sounds good to you, read on.

A Heart Wish

This book is intended to be everything a person interested in practicing the bardo teachings with simplicity and heart would need, covering the essentials from the very start of the path to the very end. It is my heart-felt wish that everyone, no matter their religion or background, has the opportunity to engage with the bardo teachings, which are the doorway to liberation in this very lifetime. *Luminous Awareness* is my small contribution to helping that happen. This book lays out a path of simple, unrestricted practices leading to the exact same result as the revered (and usually secret) Dzogchen tradition – total awakening in one lifetime.

In this time of strife and trauma nothing is more important than the wish for awakening and liberation from suffering for ourselves and all others. Bardo practice is a complete path in itself, encompassing Sutra, Mahayana, the heart essence of Tantra and also the most sublime teachings – Dzogchen. There is nothing else that is needed. Bardo practitioner or not, we don't need to chase after "higher" practices or teachings. The highest teachings and practices are designed to reveal our true nature, our natural state. As our true nature is already with us all we need do is relax and practice the fundamental methods explained in this book. Realization will come. We don't need to worry about when it will come, we just practice. There is a famous aphorism from the Chan tradition of unknown origin: *Before enlightenment, chop wood, carry water. After enlightenment, chop wood, carry water.* I have my own version of this: *Before enlightenment, serve others, be kind and compassionate. After enlightenment, serve others, be kind and compassionate.* Our goal is to awaken to our true nature in order to better serve others, not to become some special or holy being. So we practice and serve and continue to practice and serve, enlightenment or no enlightenment.

We live in a time of great upheaval, crisis and change. The suffering of others is undeniable. The world needs us all to step up. This is why when my fellow Buddhists ask me "What can we do to help?" I respond by suggesting we should take whatever practical measures we can to alleviate the suffering of others *plus* our practice, especially our meditation. It should not be either or. Making it so is succumbing to yet another dualistic choice that is characteristic of samsara (the illusory realm of cyclical suffering) and is a result of not understanding the true nature of things, our interconnected reality. That being said, our practice should be our main priority as it will transform us into beings who know what practical steps to take that will actually help others.

Spiritual practice and meditation make us less prone to negative or harmful emotions like anger and hatred. Buddhist meditation, with its emphasis on Shunyata and impermanence, severs anti-social behaviors like greed, selfishness and bigotry at the root. Put simply, by transforming ourselves through practice we affect a broader social change by ensuring that all of our actions are helpful, which means we actively benefit those around us. By transforming ourselves, we transform the world, making it a saner, more compassionate place.

Without practices like meditation and the unique Buddhist methods for awakening the heart, we can only achieve fleeting, partial kindness prone to bias, which is not truly or deeply beneficial. More to the point, meditation is not separate to or other than true compassion. Meditation *is* true compassion, lasting unbiased compassion, not just ordinary kindness. This is what we need right now. This is what we as Buddhists can do in times of upheaval and crisis. We can practice, we can meditate, we can awaken our hearts. This is what we as Buddhists should do. It is our responsibility and obligation.

Of course we must help others in any way we can, but we must do our practice as well. Meditation and other practices aimed at recognizing our true nature are the only effective ways to deeply transform the world. Change must start with us, with a peaceful inner revolution. Even while the world literally burns around us we must sit in meditation. Help others, of course, but also sit. We must find the calm and stillness that leads to the flowering of unbridled and wise compassion; only then will we actually know how to help in meaningful, lasting ways. This is the true revolution we need. Fight injustice, yes, we must if we have the capacity, but we must also sit. Rescue animals, yes, we must if we can, but we must also sit. Give support to those who are suffering, yes, if we have the means we must, but we must also sit in meditation. Help and then sit. Sit and then help. These two should always be together. Traditionally, it is said that these two, meditation and compassion, wisdom and skillful means, are as inseparable as the two sides of our hands. As Tsoknyi Rinpoche so eloquently describes:

> Without calmness of mind, it's very hard to have a sense of delight. Without this sense of delight, there is no genuine compassion. If we're totally preoccupied with our own experience—how I feel, what my problem is, and so forth—there is no chance at all for us to care about how others feel. There is simply no room for compassion.[15]

---

[15] *Fearless Simplicity: The Dzogchen Way of Living Freely in a Complex World*, translated by Erik Pema Kunsang & Marcia Binder Schmidt, Rangjung Yeshe Publications, 2003, p. 55.

To sideline practice and meditation in times of crisis in favor of social engagement or activism is like watering a plant in a basement. The plant will survive for a while, but in the end it will die from lack of light. The plant is our chance for enlightenment in this lifetime. The sun is our practice or meditation and the water is ordinary acts of kindness or activism. Helping others in practical ways will keep us going for a while, but eventually we'll burn out and even our ordinary kindness will wither. As our kindness withers we are even more cut off from true compassion and so the likelihood of our realization will wither as well. Only practices such as meditation and the other practices described in this book, all motivated by selfless altruism, will give rise to the true compassion that endures, the unbound compassion that is the expression of our true nature or Bodhicitta.

The bardo practices are among the surest methods to connect us to that true nature, to awaken Bodhicitta; the experience of which is a source of resilience, compassion and joy. So we must sit and help, help and sit. Acts of kindness and practice or meditation together lead to the full flowering of Bodhicitta, the awakened compassionate mind otherwise known as enlightenment. We need that enlightenment to save the world. The quicker beings realize their true nature, the quicker the world will change, especially if they awaken in large numbers. In my humble opinion there is only one guaranteed way to get to that mass awakening – through Buddhist practice motivated by selfless altruism.

In this book I show how to make bardo practice the heart of our lives *right now* so that we can awaken our limitless potential. My hope is that this guidebook and the practices it describes will be of benefit to those who read it by making them better able to serve others. Of course, I also hope that through these bardo practices we will all awaken to our enlightened nature. I will close this chapter with a wonderful poem about our true nature and the true nature of mind by Nyoshul Khen Rinpoche (1932-1999), a revered Tibetan master:

Profound and tranquil, free from complexity,

Uncompounded luminous clarity,

Beyond the mind of conceptual ideas;

This is the depth of the mind of the Buddhas.

In this there is not a thing to be removed.

Nor anything that needs to be added.

It is merely the immaculate

Looking naturally at itself.[16]

---

[16] Nyoshul Khen Rinpoche quoted in Don Farber, *Portraits of Tibetan Buddhist Masters*, Motilal Banarsidass, 2018, p. 30.

CHAPTER TWO

THE SWIFTEST WAY OUT: THE BARDO TEACHINGS

Every moment of every day is a window into your true nature – Bodhichitta.

To be permanently free of obscuring emotions, to escape the cycle of suffering and pain, we need to experience directly the "luminous emptiness" that Shabkar described in the quote shared in the previous chapter. The teachings and practices around what are called the after-death, or bardo, states, which are derived from the *Bardo Thodol* (known in the West as *The Tibetan Book of the Dead)*, are among the surest and simplest methods for doing that, for awakening to our true nature. In fact, as I noted earlier, the bardo practices constitute a complete path with no need for anything else.

The *Bardo Thodol* is a *terma* text revealed by Karma Lingpa (1326–1386), a great Tibetan visionary. The word *terma* translates roughly as 'hidden treasure'. This means that the text was originally composed by Padmasambhava, known reverently as Guru Rinpoche, who established Buddhism in Tibet around 750 CE, but it was concealed or hidden because Padmasambhava believed that the Tibetan population were not ready to receive it at that time. Centuries later it was "rediscovered" by Karma Lingpa, when he was just fifteen years old. Visions and dreams led Karma Lingpa to a cave at the top of a mountain in central Tibet where the terma was concealed. Its title (*Bardo Thodol*) has been translated as *Liberation through Hearing during the Intermediate*

State. The title points to the profound opportunity that exists in the bardo moments – that of total liberation.

What is liberation? Liberation is freedom from the pain caused by disturbing emotions and release from the confines of the dualistic mind. Liberation is freedom from the limitations imposed by misunderstanding who, or rather what, we truly are. It is a permanent release from the bonds of the deluded self. Liberation is freedom from the suffering of cyclic existence (samsara) and awakening to our true nature (and thus reaching nirvana). Nirvana or liberation is not a place or realm of existence, such as a "pure land" or heaven, which we reach after death. It is a state that is realized in this very life. In fact, it is a quality of our true nature. According to the early teachings of the Buddha (the Sutrayana) liberation is achieved by knowing (and feeling) the truth of three profound aspects of reality: impermanence (anicca), suffering or dissatisfaction (dukkha) and the fact of non-self (anatta). All of these are brought into stark relief in the bardo teachings.

To wake to our true nature and be free of all suffering sounds magnificent but also rather intimidating and unachievable. In reality it is very simple and totally achievable. My partner Jamyang Tenphel, following the example of his guru, the great Drukpa Kagyu master Kyabje Togden Amtrin, puts it this way:

> Samsara is simply perceiving your reality through the lens of the self. When that lens is removed we experience everything as luminous awareness. It's not complicated.[17]

The great Dzogchen master Tulku Urgyen Rinpoche (1920 – 1996) said much the same thing:

---

[17] Jamyang Tenphel, *The Awakening Heart: Contemplations on the Buddhist Path*, Timeless Awareness Publications, 2023, no page, Kindle Edition.

Samsara is mind turned outwardly, lost in its projection. Nirvana is mind turned inwardly, recognizing its nature.[18]

This verse from Tulku Urgyen Rinpoche is an eloquent rendering of a much older teaching from the Eighth Century master Sri Singha, the wellspring of the original Tibetan Buddhist lineages, who taught his disciple Padmasambhava that:

In general, all phenomena belonging to samsara and nirvana are, from the very beginning, spontaneously perfected as the essence of awakened mind. However, because of failing to realize and not knowing this to be just how it is, sentient beings circle among the three realms and continue to wander among the six abodes.[19]

The *Bardo Thodol* itself says much the same thing:

By not seeing your own mind is actually the Buddha, nirvana becomes obscured. With respect to samsara and nirvana, [the difference is simply due] to ignorance or to awareness respectively … If you come to perceive them as existing somewhere other than your own mind, this is surely an error.[20]

The *Bardo Thodol* is the best-known sacred text of the Nyingma tradition, the oldest of the Buddhist lineages in Tibet. As a text belonging to the Nyingma tradition, a large part of it is concerned with Dzogchen, the tradition of teaching and practice known as the Great Perfection, the most revered teachings in the Tibetan Buddhist system. Dzogchen is a tradition of simplicity and pragmatism that rejects complicated practices or rituals

---

[18] Tulku Urgyen Rinpoche quoted in Jonathan Cott, *On the Sea of Memory: A Journey from Forgetting to Remembering*, Random House, 2005, p. 170.

[19] Sri Singha quoted in Erik Pema Kunsang, *Wellsprings of the Great Perfection: The Lives and Insights of the Early Masters*, Rangjung Yeshe Publications, 2006, p. 334.

[20] Padmasambhava, *Self-Liberation through Seeing with Naked Awareness*, translated by John Myrdhin Reynolds, 2000, Snow Lion, p. 23.

and scholarly pursuits, such as debate, in favor of unpretentious meditation practice. It is both a part of the tantric Buddhist path and completely separate from it.

The *Bardo Thodol* was one of the first Tibetan Buddhist texts to be translated into English (in 1927) and has been popular in the West ever since. It is a guide through the *bardos*, which are the intermediate states between death and our next rebirth, between sleep and waking and between obscured mental states (dualistic thinking) and meditative states of clarity and bliss. The *Bardo Thodol* is the most widely read book about Tibetan Buddhism in the West. Its popularity is due in large part to the human fascination with the mysteries of dreams and death. His Holiness the Fourteenth Dalai Lama points to this when he writes:

> Always and everywhere, humans have faced two major life passages in which our habitual mind seems to dissolve and enter a radically different realm. The first passage is sleep, humanity's constant companion; transitory and filled with the dream life that has enchanted cultures from the beginning of history. The second is death, the grand and gaping enigma, the final event that organizes so much of individual existence and cultural ritual.[21]

As well as describing the experiences we will have as we die and after death, the *Bardo Thodol* is a profoundly practical guide to similar states or moments we experience in our everyday life. These in-between or bardo states that occur throughout our daily life are like windows into enlightenment, portals to Bodhicitta. The wisdom contained in the *Bardo Thodol*, and the bardo teachings in general, illuminate the ways that enlightenment is already present in our lives but obscured by our dualistic or deluded mind. Enlightenment

---

[21] Dalai Lama, *Sleeping, Dreaming, and Dying: An Exploration of Consciousness*, Wisdom Publications, 2002, p. 3.

seems so far away from where we are now. In reality it is tantalizingly accessible. These in-between or transitional mind states occur most strongly in dreaming, meditation and dying, but also in the space between each and every thought, each and every moment.

Although the bardo teachings primarily come from Tibetan Buddhism, there is mention of the intermediate states in some of the early sutras. These sutras use the word "antarabhava" to refer to the period or state between death and rebirth. Antara translates as "in-between" and bhava as "state". One of these early sutras (Silasutta, SN 46.3) describes achievement of enlightenment after death but before rebirth as one of seven ways practitioners can reach liberation. It reads:

> If one does not attain final knowledge early in this very life or by the time of death, then with the utter destruction of the five lower fetters[22] one becomes an attainer of nirvana in the interval.[23]

The bardo tradition in Tibet draws its inspiration from this sutra and from the *Wisdom of the Hour of Death* sutra, a later or Mahayana sutra, in which the Buddha provides concise advice on how to approach death and dying. The heart of this sutra is contained in the following paragraph:

> As for wisdom of the hour of death, you should cultivate the perception of insubstantiality since all phenomena are naturally pure. You should cultivate the perception of great compassion since all phenomena are contained within Bodhicitta. You should cultivate the perception of referencelessness since all phenomena are naturally luminous. You should cultivate the perception of utter non-attachment since all things

---

[22] The principal of the five lower fetters is our deluded sense of self, referred to in the sutras as "Self-identity views", which means to believe in the inherent existence of a self, to believe we exist independently, separately and permanently.

[23] For a translation of the full Silasutta see: https://legacy.suttacentral.net/en/sn46.3.

are impermanent. You should cultivate the perception of not searching for Buddhahood elsewhere since the mind is wisdom when realized.[24]

Here we have all the themes I will cover in this book: the centrality of compassion to the path; the impermanent and empty nature of the self and all things (referencelessness); the importance of renunciation and the true nature of the mind (Buddha Nature). We will return to these notions—and to the truth of the luminous and pure nature of everything—over and over again, for they are the essence of the bardo teachings as well as the essence of the entire Buddhist path. Although this sutra is focused on the time of death, it applies to all other bardos as well, to the glimpses of pure spacious awareness between each thought in meditation, between dreams and waking, in fact between each moment of our lives.

This book is not intended to be a comprehensive discussion of all the bardo teachings and their many associated practices. It is intended to be a distilled discussion of the most essential elements of the bardo teachings for those who want to engage with these teachings simply, in a way that is meaningful and beneficial to them, and who want to engage with them *right now*. This book is for those who want to dive into the bardo practices without having to undertake arduous preliminaries that can take years, or having to seek multiple empowerments that can be costly and have substantial pre-requisites. We can begin our journey to awakening in this very moment, wherever we are, whatever our life conditions might be and no matter what we believe about ourselves. We certainly shouldn't think we need to travel to far off places like the Himalayas or become different people to who we are now. In fact, to do so is a mistake. As Chogyal Namkhai Norbu Rinpoche,

---

[24] *The Noble Mahāyāna Sūtra The Wisdom of the Hour of Death*, translated by Lowell Cook (2018). See the full sutra here: https://www.lotsawahouse.org/words-of-the-buddha/sutra-wisdom-hour-of-death

who was the first Lama to widely disseminate the Nyingma and Dzogchen teachings in the West, explains:

> Every teaching is transmitted through the culture and knowledge of human beings. But it is important not to confuse any culture or tradition with the teachings themselves, because the essence of the teachings is knowledge of the nature of the individual. If someone does not know how to understand the true meaning of a teaching through their own culture, they can create confusion. Sometimes, Western people go to India or Nepal to receive initiations and teachings by Tibetan masters living there, maybe in some monasteries. Once there, they are fascinated by the special exotic atmosphere, by the spiritual "vibration". Maybe they stay a few months, and when they go back home they feel different from the people around them. Maybe they dress differently, they eat Tibetan food, they behave in some peculiar manner, and they think that this is an important part of their spiritual path. But the truth is that to practice a teaching that comes from Tibet, there is no need to try to become like a Tibetan. On the contrary, it is crucial for practitioners to integrate that teaching into their own culture to keep it alive within themselves.[25]

Enlightenment transcends time, place, culture, language and identity. To think it is elsewhere in some other place or intrinsically part of some other culture is a fundamental error. That being said, we certainly do need teachers, and for many of us those teachers have been from cultures other than our own. In my case they have mostly been Tibetans. It is in honor of those teachers that I use the Tibetan names they gave me, but in no way does this imply that I believe we need to become quasi-Tibetans to awaken to our true enlightened nature. Tibetan culture is rich, magnificent and precious, but

---

[25] Chogyal Namkhai Norbu, *Dzogchen: The Self-Perfected State*, Shambhala Publications, 1996, p. 25.

the only Tibetan cultural characteristic I truly value is the Tibetans' deep devotion to the Buddha Dharma.

Nothing Else is Needed

I received instruction on the bardos from a number of Buddhist teachers, most notably Ngakpa Karma Lhundup Rinpoche, whose down-to-earth and insightful guidance and deep devotion continuously reminds me of the importance and profundity of the Dharma. The written instructions of my heart teacher, Kyabje Dudjom Rinpoche, Jigdral Yeshe Dorje (1904 – 1987), one of the greatest meditation masters of the Twentieth Century, have also been deeply important to my understanding of the bardos and how to apply the teachings simply and with heart. If I know anything at all about this topic it is solely due to my teachers' kindness. Everything written here is based on my study and practice. Any errors in this work are wholly due to my own imperfect understanding. Only the Buddhas are perfect, so I hope you will forgive these imperfections.

In writing this book I drew substantially on teachings I've received over many years. The most recent of these teachings turned out to be the most influential and transformative. This was a teaching on a pith instruction called *Refined Essence of Oral Instruction* given by Ngakpa Karma Lhundup Rinpoche.[26] Like the *Bardo Thodol*, the *Refined Essence of Oral Instruction* comes down to us from Padmasambhava, this time through the visionary Dorje Lingpa (1346-1405). It is revered as a condensed instruction that brings all Dharma teachings into one. It approaches the bardos from a distinctly uncomplicated perspective. I also drew on *Self-Liberation through Seeing with Naked Awareness*, a core part of the *Bardo Thodol*, which focuses on discovering the true nature of mind and is a classic text of the Dzogchen tradition.[27]

---

[26] Given on Zoom to a group of Western students in the midst of the Covid pandemic.

[27] I received the transmission for this text from Ngakpa Karma Lhundup Rinpoche.

Finally, I drew on teachings I've received multiple times on a pithy text by Longchenpa (1308 – 1364), *Crucial Advice: A Complete Set of Instructions for the Bardos.*[28]

The bardo practices are a seamless bridge between Sutra, the early teachings of the Buddha, Mahayana (the teachings focused on compassion), tantra or Vajrayana and the Dzogchen approach. These practices provide the foundation and fertile ground for realization to bloom, with no other practices required. Let me repeat that in a slightly different way for the sake of clarity – bardo practice is a complete path in itself that leads to the realization of the self-perfected natural state (Dzogpachenpo).

Ngakpa Karma Lhundup Rinpoche said about *Self-Liberation through Seeing with Naked Awareness*, the heart of the *Bardo Thodol*, that no other teaching is needed at all. If we have the transmission for that text, read it often, contemplate its meaning and apply the meaning to daily practice, then that is more than enough to free us. That is a sure path to liberation. Bardo practice, especially as it is taught here in this book, does not require supplementation with any other methods. The path of bardo practice will lead to recognition of our true nature and enlightenment. This is expressed beautifully by Kyabje Dudjom Rinpoche:

> It has been said that the whole of the Buddha's doctrine could be summarized in the teaching on the six bardos. The Buddha Dharma is vast and profound, and the many approaches of the various vehicles and cycles of teaching comprise an inconceivable wealth of instruction. For those who wish to attain the primordial citadel of Buddhahood in the course of a single human life, the practice of these teachings is presented within the framework of the six bardos.[29]

---

[28] Longchenpa, *Crucial Advice: A Complete Set of Instructions for the Bardos,* Translated by Adam Pearcey (2010). See full text here: https://www.lotsawahouse.org/tibetan-masters/longchen-rabjam/complete-set-instructions

[29] Dudjom Rinpoche, *Counsels from My Heart*, Shambhala Publications, 2001, p.59.

As Dudjom Rinpoche pointed out in the quote above, there are six bardos (see table below). There are spiritual practices associated with each of these bardos. Meditation is the foundation of all of these practices. Some of the practices are associated with more than one bardo, as the table below illustrates.

Table 1: The Bardos and their Practices

Bardo	Practice
Bardo of this Life	Shamata, Illusory Form Yoga and Guru Yoga
Bardo of Dreaming	Dream Yoga and/or Guru Yoga
Bardo of Samadhi (meditative absorption)	Shamata (simple awareness)
Bardo of Dying	Phowa and/or Guru Yoga
Bardo of Luminosity	Guru Yoga and/or Phowa
Bardo of Becoming (rebirth)	Illusory Form Yoga and Guru Yoga

I will cover all of these practices in detail later in the book. For now, here are some brief definitions. Shamata or Calm Abiding meditation is simple silent sitting. Illusory Form Yoga is learning to recognize the ways our dualistic minds distort our perception and fabricate our realities. Phowa is the transference of consciousness at the time of death to a pure land or Buddha realm. Guru Yoga, as we will see in the next chapter, is recognizing the true nature of mind as the guru.

CHAPTER THREE

AWAKENING TO WHAT WE TRULY ARE

One's own fundamental awareness, naked and unadorned, is the true guru.

I will explain the practices for each bardo in detail as our discussion progresses. For now, I will take some time to briefly outline Guru Yoga as it is widely misunderstood and criticized in the West, due to a large number of guru-related scandals. The essential thing we need to know about Guru Yoga is contained in its Tibetan name, *Lamai Naljor*, which Ngakchang Rinpoche defines in this way:

> Lamai Naljor (Guru Yoga in Sanskrit) is the most important practice of Tantra. It is also the most important practice of Dzogchen. The word *Lama* has the meaning not only of the external teacher but also of the individual's own realized nature. The word *Naljor* has the meaning of union. *Lamai Naljor* therefore means the practice of unifying; with the mind of the teacher and recognizing that the mind of the teacher and one's own enlightened nature are identical.[30]

Guru Yoga, then, is getting to know our true or ultimate nature. Guru Yoga is awakening to what we truly are. Revered master Yanthang Rinpoche

---

[30] 'Interview with Ngakchang Rinpoche', *Arobuddhism*, https://arobuddhism.org/q-and-a/lamai-naljor.html

described Guru Yoga as the heart of the Nyingma, the heart of the Vajrayana, and the heart of Dzogchen.[31] Like the bardo practices, the practice of Guru Yoga is considered a complete path in itself. Longchenpa makes this clear when he writes:

> Lamai Naljor is the essence of the path itself, so the realization of the unconditioned nature is born in the mind, and one becomes liberated. Therefore, Lamai Naljor is more profound than all other paths.[32]

In contrast with this profound view, Guru Yoga is often presented as merely serving a spiritual teacher (*Lama* in Tibetan). This is a leftover of the feudal system in Tibet, where Buddhist masters occupied similar positions to the feudal nobility. The high Lamas or masters were equivalent to the highest ranked aristocrats. This has meant that service to the teacher is interpreted literally, as performing the functions of a servant. Thus we see Dharma students cooking for the teacher, driving the teacher around, even cleaning the teacher's house or doing their laundry. These things are acts of gratitude and respect, but they are not likely to lead to the recognition of the true nature of mind in this lifetime. If this is the only or main way we are serving the Dharma then something has gone wrong. True service to the Dharma (and the teacher) is to dedicate our entire lives—every day, every hour, and every minute—to the practice, mostly to practice on the cushion. Of course, anything can be practice if we are mindful, but to be truly mindful we first need to spend hundreds of hours on the meditation cushion. In most cases literal service to the teacher is not functioning as Guru Yoga. It is generosity and kindness motivated by gratitude and respect, which is good, of course, but not why we have a teacher. We have a teacher to help us recognize the

---

[31] Yangthang Tulku quoted in Chodrak Gyamtso (Director) *Domang Yangthang*, Rayonner Films, 2022. See full film: https://youtu.be/sKxjoZzEAKI

[32] Longchenpa quoted in in Thinley Norbu, *A Cascading Waterfall of Nectar*, Shambhala Publications, 2006, p. 165.

true master inside us, our boundless hearts, and awaken to what we really are. Our goal in Guru Yoga, and indeed in all practice, is to meet and abide in our fundamental nature. As Kyabje Dudjom Rinpoche so beautifully explains:

One's own awareness, fresh and uncontrived,

Is the primordially present ultimate Lama

From whom you have not been separated for even an instant.

This meeting with the original abiding nature—how amazing![33]

On the surface this quote seems clear enough, but what does it really mean? It is both very simple and deeply profound – our own fundamental awareness is the guru. When we are aware of looking at the sky, the awareness of looking is the guru. When we are aware of hearing a sound, our awareness of hearing is the guru. When we delight in a beloved's touch, our awareness of the touch and of the delight is the guru. On the outer level, when we say this awareness is the guru it doesn't mean some abstract guru, but our actual guru, the human teacher we have taken into our hearts. For me this is Kyabje Dudjom Rinpoche, which means my ever-present fundamental awareness is Dudjom Rinpoche himself. Our heart teacher is thus ever present, always with us, not separate from us, never abandoning us or leaving us alone. They are always there, always underpinning every experience with the radiance of love, compassion and joy.

On a deeper level our own awareness, our own basic capacity of being aware, is also the absolute guru, which we call Buddha Nature or Bodhicitta, the awakened loving mind. At all times our unadorned awareness is both our heart teacher and our enlightened nature. This is the truth of what we are. It is our sense of "me" that is false. It is the sense of being a separate, isolated, independently existing entity that is completely fabricated. The presence of

---

[33] Dudjom Rinpoche, *Wisdom Nectar: Dudjom Rinpoche's Heart Advice*, Snow Lion, 2005, p.117.

the absolute guru, primordial non-dual awareness, is the ultimate truth of every single moment.

Guru Yoga is about recognition of and coming to directly experience this ultimate truth. It is not about obedience to a human teacher nor about becoming a slave to that teacher's whims. It is a meditative practice not an outer show of subservience. Guru Yoga is about spiritual autonomy not spiritual servitude. I cannot stress this more – fawning over teachers and abandoning critical thinking in favor of some kind of celebrity guru fandom is the opposite of Guru Yoga. Much is made of the idea that the essence of Guru Yoga is seeing the teacher as a perfect Buddha. His Holiness the Dalai Lama himself cautions us not to do this blindly:

> It is frequently said that the essence of the training in Guru Yoga is to cultivate the art of seeing everything the guru does as perfect. Personally I myself do not like this to be taken too far. Often we see written in the scriptures, "Every action seen as perfect." However, this phrase must be seen in the light of Buddha Shakyamuni's own words: "Accept my teachings only after examining them as an analyst buys gold. Accept nothing out of mere faith in me." The problem with the practice of seeing everything the guru does as perfect is that it very easily turns to poison for both the guru and the disciple. Therefore, whenever I teach this practice, I always advocate that the tradition of "every action seen as perfect" not be stressed. Should the guru manifest un-Dharmic qualities or give teachings contradicting Dharma, the instruction on seeing the spiritual master as perfect must give way to reason and Dharma wisdom.[34]

Furthermore, seeing the teacher as a Buddha is not something we should fake or force. It needs to come naturally based on experience – direct experience

---

[34] Quoted in Rob Preece, *Preparing for Tantra: Creating the Psychological Ground for Practice*, Shambhala Publications, 2011, no page, eBook.

of the guru's positive, stainless qualities over many years. At no point should we act as though we see our teacher as a Buddha when in our hearts we do not. That is just fooling ourselves and playing a deceptive game.

In this current moment, when there have been so many instances of so-called gurus abusing their students, having sex with their students, misappropriating funds and otherwise behaving badly, we need to be very careful in choosing a teacher. Guru Yoga with a living teacher can be very dangerous if we make the wrong choice. No spiritual teacher should ever harm their students nor engage in sexual relationships with them. This is just unethical. If they do these things they have broken their commitment or samaya with the Buddha himself and with the whole spiritual community or Sangha. This is why in the Nyingma school the teachers at the heart of our Guru Yoga practices are all fully-enlightened beings from the past – Padmasambhava, Yeshe Tsogyal, and Shakyamuni Buddha, among others. The fact that these teachers are no longer alive adds a level of safety and enables us to truly trust the practice. As Jamyang Tenphel has made clear:

> If living teachers have let us down, or we are afraid they might, we can look to the instructions and blessings from masters of the past. The masters of the past cannot let us down. We can safely look, with devotion, to them.[35]

Any historical master for whom we feel respect and admiration will do. This means we can begin on the path whether or not we have a close relationship with a living master. As the great yogi Togden Shakya Shri once taught:

> If you have devotion and faith toward the master, there is not even a hair tip's difference if the master is alive or not. Understand that whenever

---

[35] Jamyang Tenphel, *The Awakening Heart: Contemplations on the Buddhist Path*, Timeless Awareness Publications, 2023, no page, Kindle Edition.

you make a request to a master, you will always spontaneously receive his [or her] blessing.[36]

This makes it very clear that Guru Yoga focused on a master from the past is equally effective as that with a living teacher. I will return to this idea a few more times as we explore the bardo practices because there is a persistent misunderstanding that we need a living teacher for all stages of the path. The truth is we don't really need a living teacher until the later stages of our practice. More to the point, practicing Guru Yoga with the object of our devotion being an enlightened master from the past is a powerful way to connect with our true nature deeply and safely, right here and right now.

It must be said that the student can also corrupt the student-teacher relationship. The authentic need for a teacher at certain stages of the path is distorted by some students into a kind of spiritual fandom, where so-called practitioners chase after relationships with high Lamas and jostle for position as their closest student, effectively competing with their fellow practitioners and being envious of any who seem to be closer to the Lama than them. This is absolute poison. It is the opposite of what true devotion is – openness and relaxed surrender. Devotion has nothing to do with how close or not we are to the teacher. Jetsunma Tenzin Palmo makes this point clearly when she notes about the student-teacher relationship:

> Sometimes people feel … that they can't get to see them [their Lama] enough. They don't get to have an intimate relationship and so forth, but actually the important thing is not the intimate relationship. The important thing is our devotion, our openness. The Lama is always open. A genuine Lama, as they say, is like the sun shining. But if we close all the doors and windows and draw the curtains, we cannot complain because

---

[36] *Togden Shakya Shri: The Life and Liberation of a Tibetan Yogin*, by Kathog Situ Chokyi Gyatso, translated by Elio Guarisco, Shang Shung Publications, 2011, p. 159.

it's dark. So, if we open up our curtains and open the windows wide, the sun will come pouring in because the sun's always there.[37]

Opening the windows and curtains is a metaphor for letting go of our presumptions and expectations and surrendering into open-heartedness. All that being said, the quality needed to fuel Guru Yoga is devotion. In English this word has a lot of connotations, some of them quite negative, especially the notion of "blind devotion", which is highly dogmatic. The Tibetan word translated as devotion is *mögü*. It means respect and longing. This longing is the wish to be united with wisdom, with the ultimate nature of all. It has nothing to do with mere adoration of a person. Although our devotion often causes us to feel deeply emotionally connected to the teacher who shows us precisely how to unite with wisdom, those emotions aren't the point of Guru Yoga. They can bring a lot of energy to our practice but are not the result we want. The point of Guru Yoga is merging with profound wisdom and boundless compassion. Guru Yoga is becoming one with Bodhicitta.

When we practice Guru Yoga our solitary spark of devotion merges with the boundless flame that is the compassion of the teacher and our mind and the guru's mind become one. It's not a game or trick or conceptual fabrication. It's real and true. It's the absolute truth, it's the ultimate reality. It is a reality that cannot be encountered through intellectual learning. It can only be encountered through practice, through meditation and Guru Yoga. Khenpo Tsewang Dongyal Rinpoche explicitly links devotion, Bodhichitta and awakening when he teaches:

The path to enlightenment is grounded in devotion and bodhichitta. Devotion is faith in and loyalty to your spiritual potential and to the guides and inspiration that are leading you to its actualization

---

[37] Jetsunma Tenzin Palmo [Facebook post] 10 October 2022. Available at: https://www. facebook.com/jetsunmatenzinpalmo (Accessed: 10 October 2022)

– including the Buddha, Dharma and Sangha, Guru Padmasambhava and the lineage masters, as well as the teachings in both their theoretical and practical aspects. Bodhichitta is opening your own heart and mind to the hearts and minds of others, as well as fully developing your abilities, so that you will be an ever-active force of good in this life and lives to come.[38]

Rinpoche makes an important point about devotion here – it is not just focused on the teacher but to our own potential, our own hearts or Buddha Nature as well. Devotion, then, opens the heart and allows our own fundamental or natural goodness to flow to others in an unending stream of benefit. Apart from respect and longing, *mögü* has the qualities of openness to the truth and gratitude. Devotion is not blind, slavish or dogmatic. It is practical rather than ideological, and curious and discerning rather than unquestioning and obedient. There is nothing to fear in true devotion. What is there about respect, openness and becoming one with our own ultimate nature that is frightening? There is nothing frightening about that at all.

The most important thing with any spiritual practice like Guru Yoga, even simple meditation, is that we rely on a qualified guide or teacher. If we rely on a qualified teacher, we cannot go astray. No truly qualified or realized teacher will suggest that Guru Yoga is about obedience or servitude. Any person who considers themselves spiritually superior to others is unqualified to teach. Furthermore, true masters bend over backwards to make the teachings and practices as accessible as possible. No realized master would suggest that meditation or any other practice needs to be complex and difficult to be effective. In fact, quite the opposite is true. As Jetsunma Tenzin Palmo notes:

---

[38] Khenpo Tsewang Dongyal Rinpoche, *Inborn Realization: A Commentary on His Holiness Dudjom Rinpoche's Mountain Retreat Instructions*, Dharma Samudra, 2016, p. 217.

We always imagine that a practice must be extremely complex and difficult – otherwise, how can it work? But in actual fact, the essential practice is very simple.[39]

Simplicity in practice is often much more effective as it is a profound challenge to our habitual tendency to want to know and do more and more in order to adorn our needy ego with accomplishments. The nun and master Jetsun Khandro Rinpoche puts it this way:

Ignorance loves to articulate and express and be intelligent and we hunger, we always have this essence [of hunger to express our ego]. The bad habit that we have is we think unless it's very difficult it shouldn't be appreciated. So this whole "sweating it out" and doing the effort part of it becomes that which feeds into the ego's pretense of being wise.[40]

With that in mind, I'd like to reassure you at the outset that although the bardo teachings can seem quite complicated, in essence they are profoundly simple. In that spirit I will explain everything simply. Any unusual words or terms will be defined in a way that is easy to understand. The practices will be explained in easy to understand language. That being said, in Buddhism not knowing is not a problem. In fact recognizing and accepting that there is much we don't know is a sign of maturity, humility and intelligence. As Dzogchen Ponlop Rinpoche has noted 'It's better to know that you don't know than to think that you know.' Not knowing is the beginning of learning. Recognizing and accepting our not knowing is always a good thing.

In terms of meditation and other forms of practice, knowing too much can actually be a problem. Conceptual ideas about meditation can be a significant obstacle. That's why it's quite common in practice-focused traditions, such

---

[39] Jetsunma Tenzin Palmo [Facebook post] 20 September 2021. Available at: https://www.facebook.com/jetsunmatenzinpalmo (Accessed: 20 September 2021)

[40] See Jetsun Khandro Rinpoche's full discussion of this on Youtube: https://youtu.be/_3Cdzp5k4ZU

as the Nyingma and the Drukpa Kagyu, for teachers to give only a little of the theory and then let each person discover the depths of meditation for themselves. The practitioner then asks questions of their Dharma peers or teachers as experiences arise that they wish to understand. This avoids the common pitfall of people knowing a lot of meditation theory and mistakenly believing they have had the lofty experiences described in the texts—or have reached the more subtle levels of meditation the teachings define—and yet are merely the victims of a type of suggestion. Oftentimes those with a lot of information but little actual practice misidentify their ordinary and common experiences as higher meditational states.

So, in reality, it is better not to know too much. It is better to have a beginner's mind, as they say in the Zen tradition. As Shunryu Suzuki Roshi once taught: 'A mind full of preconceived ideas, subjective intentions, or habits is not open to things as they are'.[41] It is quite clear then that our focus should not be on learning all the Dharma concepts and terms, or becoming adept at philosophical debate or elaborate rituals, but rather on a few simple practices supported by the fundamental Buddhist view or philosophy. The *Bardo Thodol* helps us to identify which practices are most important.

---

[41] Shunryu Suzuki Roshi, Zen Mind, Beginner's Mind: 50th Anniversary Edition, Shambhala Publications, 2020, p. 77.

CHAPTER FOUR

WHAT IS A BARDO?

In-between every moment is nothing less than your true nature itself.

In Tibetan Buddhism, a *bardo* is an intermediate or transitional state, a liminal state between each moment; between each thought, between sleeping and waking, between gross and subtle levels of mind, a moment between moments. A bardo is also the intermediary state between life, death and rebirth, and the space between ignorance or samsara and awakening or nirvana. To quote Francesca Freemantle, a long term practitioner in the Kagyu tradition:

> Bardo can have many implications, depending on how one looks at it. It is *an interval, a hiatus, a gap*. It can act as a boundary that divides and separates, marking the end of one thing and the beginning of another; but it can also be a link between the two: it can serve as a bridge or a meeting place, which brings together and unites. It is a crossing, a stepping-stone, a transition (emphasis added).[42]

The word "bardo" has further connotations of stillness within or between movement. As Ngakchang Rinpoche notes:

> Etymologically, it [the word bardo] breaks down into 'bar', which means some kind of a movement or flow, like a stream; and 'do' which means

---

[42] See 'The Luminous Gap in Bardo', *Tricycle: The Buddhist Review:* https://tricycle.org/magazine/luminous-gap-bardo/

some kind of an island or rock in the stream. There is an area amidst movement; that is the idea here. It doesn't merely apply to the period after you're physically dead although everyone says: 'When you're in the bardo' as if we weren't in it now. ... So bardo has some meaning similar to gap, gestalt, time frame, or 'pool of temporal space'.[43]

The idea of an island of stillness within a stream of movement is profoundly important in the bardo teachings, because it points to present experience, the moment between past and future, to the immediacy that is being in the now which can open us to a direct and intimate encounter with our true nature. An island of stillness in a torrent of wild water is the analogy commonly used for the nature of mind, the "present nowness" as Dudjom Rinpoche called it that lies between our constant thinking, imagining and feeling. The true nature of mind is said to have three qualities – *stillness*, *clarity* and *movement*. Stillness is open spaciousness or Shunyata. Clarity is our fundamental luminous awareness (*rigpa* in Tibetan). Movement is Bodhicitta, which is boundless compassion co-emergent with the realization of emptiness, our true nature's sole expression. These three qualities are not separate but a unity, a state of perfection that is a complete and infinite oneness. This state cannot be discovered while the delusion of a separate self persists. The delusion of self must drop away for the ultimate nature to be revealed. The disturbing thoughts and emotions that we mistakenly label as our self are truly adventitious, which means they arise as a result of an external factor rather than being inherent to us. They come and then they go again. Likewise the self. In each and every moment the self comes into existence and then dissolves again. This happens so swiftly that we don't notice the coming and going. The self feels seamless and continuous to us. It is not. In the gap between the dissolution of each "self-moment" and the arising of the next

---

[43] See '*The Nine Bardos of the Aro gTér*': https://aroencyclopaedia.org/shared/text/n/nine_bardos_ar_eng.php

there is the ultimate nature. So tantalizingly close, yet completely obscured by the activity of the monkey mind.

The bardo teachings and practices help us to notice the gaps, the intervals, so that we can recognize our true nature. In a way, the bardos are nothing less than our true nature itself. In general, as already noted in Chapter Two, it is considered that there are six bardos. In some traditions however they talk about only four bardos (living, dying, luminosity and becoming or rebirth). In some they even divide it into eight or nine. Don't worry about this or get confused, this is not a problem. It is just evidence of the diversity of Dharma, of the different ways of thinking about and understanding the same thing. In this book, I will refer to:

1. the natural bardo of the present life;
2. the hallucinatory bardo of dreaming;
3. the bardo of meditative absorption or samadhi;
4. the painful bardo of dying;
5. the luminous bardo of ultimate reality; and
6. the karmic bardo of becoming or rebirth.

The main point to understand is that a bardo is a mind state, a more subtle mind state between the grosser mind states of the dualistic mind (the compulsive, thinking mind). This is even true of the Bardo of Living, which is the bardo between birth and death that is peppered with what could be called micro-bardos, quite subtle bardo states in-between moments of thought, emotion and sensation. In essence, our entire experience is of bardos. As Tsele Natsok Rangdrol, a Tibetan meditation master of the 17th Century, writes:

In general, all sentient beings dwell exclusively within bardo states, from the initial ground of confusion until realizing the final enlightenment. All the phenomena of ground and path can therefore be simply labelled *bardo.* Still, ordinary people regard the bardo as being neither more nor less than the terrible state of intermediate existence.[44]

Because the bardos are often associated with this intermediate existence between death and rebirth, they can be mistakenly understood as some "place" you go on the way from here (this life) to there (the next life). This is not at all the case. The bardos are aspects or levels of mind. In the Nyingma tradition we talk about two fundamental aspects or states of mind. As Tulku Thondup Rinpoche makes clear:

> … it is useful to recognize that our mind has two aspects: ordinary mind and enlightened mind. Ordinary mind, also known in Mahayana teachings as deluded mind, is conceptual, dualistic, and emotional. Enlightened mind—also known as the awakened state or Buddha-nature—is the true and pure nature of the mind. For most of us, the dualistic concepts, unhealthy emotions, and obsessive sensations (particularly strong clinging and craving) of our ordinary mind cover the enlightened aspect of our mind. These thoughts are like coverings that obstruct us from realizing and manifesting our true nature—like clouds covering the sun.[45]

The ordinary, dualistic mind is called "sem" in Tibetan whereas the boundless, primordially perfect awareness, or true nature of mind, is known as *rigpa.* Rigpa is essentially the Buddha Nature, the essence of enlightenment that is the true nature of all sentient beings. Chokyi Nyima Rinpoche explains these two very different mind states in this way:

> One state is called *sem* and the other *rigpa. Sem* refers to the state of conceptual thinking, involving fixation on some 'thing.' It is a mistaken

---

[44] Tsele Natsok Rangdrol, *The Mirror of Mindfulness*, Rangjung Yeshe Publications, 1987, page 16.
[45] Tulku Thondup, *The Heart of Unconditional Love*, Shambhala, 2015, p. 17.

way of perceiving. Rigpa means free from fixation. It refers to a state of natural wakefulness that is without dualistic thinking. It is extremely important to be clear right now about the difference between these two states of mind.[46]

The bardos are the transitional mind states in-between the activity of the ordinary, dualistic mind or sem; so in-between one thought and another, one emotion and another, one feeling and another, one moment of perception and another. In other words, bardos are the spaces between the delusional activity of compulsive monkey mind. They are momentary breaks in the painful illusion of samsara. They are gateways to the recognition of rigpa. The most profound break in the habitual activity of the monkey mind comes in the Bardo of Dying at the time of our death. This bardo is the gap between this life and the next one. Understanding rebirth is therefore essential to seizing the opportunity that the Bardo of Dying provides.

What is Rebirth?

When viewed from a certain (suspicious) perspective some of the Buddhist teachings can look like mere superstition or even blind, dogmatic faith. In Tibetan Buddhism, among the hardest aspects of the teachings for beginners to come to terms with are the teachings on death, in particular the teachings on the after-death bardo states. As already noted, all of the bardo states are considered powerful opportunities for recognizing the true nature of mind and for ultimate enlightenment, but the Bardo of Luminosity that is revealed at the time of death is seen as the greatest opportunity. This is because in death the dualistic mind or ego completely falls away and all that is left is the true nature of mind that is non-dual with all. A practitioner trained in recognizing that ultimate nature through meditation and Guru Yoga merely

---

[46] Chokyi Nyima Rinpoche, The *Bardo Guidebook*, Rangjung Yeshe Publications, 1991, page 129.

has to ease into it when it arises in the process of dying, and thus will achieve total enlightenment (more on this in Chapters Five and Seven).

We can all directly experience and affirm the truth of the gap between each breath, the gap between sleep and waking and, in meditation, the gap between thoughts. We cannot do this with the bardos in-between death and rebirth, at least not while we are living. For this reason, the bardos between death and rebirth are the most difficult to accept as this requires a leap of faith, a step into belief rather than trust based on direct experience.

Do we need to believe in rebirth to achieve liberation?

Rebirth is a central tenet of Buddhism that many newcomers to Buddhist practice struggle to accept. It shouldn't be imagined, however, that discomfort with the notion of rebirth is a distinctly modern or Western experience. Soon after the Buddha's passing disagreements emerged in the Buddhist community about what the Buddha had really meant when he spoke about rebirth. In fact, these disagreements are among the main reasons there emerged different Buddhist schools of thought. The various Buddhist traditions have always disagreed on what aspect (if any) of a person is reborn, how long after death rebirth occurs and whether or not there is a bardo state. For example, Navayana Buddhists, the largest form of Buddhism in India comprising more than six million adherents, reject rebirth completely. Many Theravadan Buddhists reject the existence of the bardo states, despite them being mentioned in the sutras. That being said, most forms of Buddhism accept some version of the rebirth doctrine. The point is – do we really need to believe in rebirth in order to achieve liberation? The simple answer is no. What we believe or don't believe about rebirth will not hinder our awakening. The only viewpoint or concept that matters to awakening is the philosophy of Shunyata (emptiness), especially as it pertains to non-self (anatta). That aside, whether or not we accept rebirth as a doctrine depends on how we define it and whether or not that definition is logical. His Holiness the Dalai

Lama has suggested about rebirth that if Buddhist beliefs do not correspond to reality, as proven by scientific method, then we should all be willing to discard them. Scientific method is not advanced enough at this point to prove or disprove rebirth. Therefore, until science advances further, we have to rely on logic to determine if we should or shouldn't accept rebirth as likely.

Bardo practice relies on the existence of the bardo states, obviously, and on rebirth. It may be easier to accept the truth of the Bardos of Dying and Becoming if we have a clearer understanding of the Buddhist definitions of death and rebirth. Therefore, what follows are definitions of death and rebirth that are in complete alignment with the early sutras, much of the Mahayana teachings and Dzogchen but do, admittedly, contradict some popularly held viewpoints and beliefs. As the ultimate truth of things is beyond words and concepts these philosophical contradictions are to be expected. What is most important is that we find a viewpoint that enables and supports us to practice so that we can have direct experiences of the truth rather than relying on the words of others. It is also crucial that we not deny, reject or criticize the viewpoints anyone else adopts, no matter how outlandish or illogical they seem to us. The heart cannot remain open when we are judgmental of others. Our hearts and minds become rigid when we cling too tightly to our own ideas and beliefs. There is no joy in bias or prejudice. Without openness, compassion and joy our practice will get nowhere. It's important we don't ignore or underestimate this fact.

What is death?

The medical definition of clinical death is the cessation of all vital functions of the body including the heartbeat, brain activity and breathing. The Buddhist position is that death occurs when heat, vitality (life functions) and consciousness (or sense of self) leave the body and it becomes inanimate.[47] There are some significant differences in these definitions. The medical model accounts for what

---

[47] *Questions of King Milinda*, translated by T. W. Rhys Davids, (M.I.:296)

the Buddha called "vitality" but doesn't address either heat or consciousness. There is often a lingering heat in the body some time after clinical death, especially with great masters whose heart centers can remain warm for many days after death in a state known as *thukdam*. For an ordinary person this heat or warmth might last hours after respiration, heartbeat and brain activity have all stopped. According to Buddhism, once the heat fully dissipates then what remains of the consciousness fades as well. This means that, for Buddhists, true death happens well after medically-defined or clinical death. For many Buddhists, particularly those practicing in the Tibetan tradition, the consciousness of the deceased retains some connection to its former life and body for up to 49 days after death. These differences in how we understand death impact how we deal with the dying and the dead. Ultimately, the main thing we need to know as bardo practitioners is that death is not a single moment but multiple moments all leading to the disentanglement of our fundamental awareness from the body, from the dualistic mind and from our sense of self.

What is reborn?

Before we decide whether or not we believe in rebirth, we need to understand what rebirth is and what it is not according to Buddhist philosophy. There are other philosophical and religious traditions that conceive of rebirth or reincarnation that hold very different views to the Buddha, all of which he rejected outright. Despite popular opinion, Buddhists do not believe in the idea of reincarnation. Reincarnation implies that there is something permanent that is reincarnated into a body, something immortal that survives beyond death, like a soul. True Buddhists don't subscribe to the idea of a soul or spirit. We also don't subscribe to the idea of transmigration, the idea that something inherent to a person transmigrates from one life and body to the next.[48] Instead, many Buddhists accept the notion of rebirth. Rebirth and

---

[48] *Questions of King Milinda*, translated by T. W. Rhys Davids, (M.I.:296)

reincarnation are not at all the same thing, though in English common usage they are used as interchangeable terms, which leads to a lot of confusion.

The first thing to understand about rebirth in Buddhism is that there is not one single way that rebirth is conceptualized or understood. There are multiple conceptions of rebirth in Buddhism, all arising from different interpretations of the Buddha's original teachings and the insight of enlightened masters. The Buddha did not say much at all about rebirth, leading to these different understandings about it. It is not beneficial to be rigid about which of these understandings is right or which are wrong but rather be open to the idea that there is a spectrum of belief about rebirth and to locate where on the spectrum we are comfortable. We certainly shouldn't discount or disrespect others' beliefs. The highest achievement of Buddhism is total openness, total equanimity. It's beneficial to model that equanimity by being open-minded about others' beliefs. On one end of the spectrum are those Buddhists who believe that rebirth is not a literal truth but a metaphor for the fact that energy cannot die, it merely transforms. At the other end of the spectrum are those Buddhists who believe that a core part of the consciousness transcends death and is reborn to a new life. These are the two extremes of Buddhist notions of rebirth.

Fundamentally, it does not matter what we believe about rebirth because, as I've noted already, the direct realization of the truth is beyond our conceptual understanding. We must practice until we experience the truth of things for ourselves. That being said, having some basic sense of what rebirth is in theoretical terms can help us trust the methods of practice so that we actually apply them.

A Continuum of Mind

To inform this discussion about rebirth I will cite Longchenpa, an irrefutable figure in the Nyingma tradition of Tibetan Buddhism. It is important to understand that Longchenpa's position on rebirth is neither radical nor contested in this tradition. It is the mainstream position within that particular Tibetan lineage of practice and thought. It is also in perfect accordance with the view found in the early sutras. Longchenpa writes:

In its [the true nature's] absence of past and future, rebirth is an empty notion: Who is there to transmigrate? And how to wander? What is karma and how can it mature? Contemplate the reality that is like the clear sky![49]

This quote from Longchenpa is not suggesting that there is no rebirth or karma at all, but is denying the continuity of a self beyond death. It echoes the early Sutra teachings that suggest that there is no transmigration and that it is only a certain *potentiality* or *tendency* that is passed from life to life, not a person or self. *The Questions of King Malinda*, part of the early Pali cannon (Sutrayana) from around 150CE, makes it very clear that there is no transmigration.[50] Here again we see the profound similarity between the Nyingma philosophical view and the early sutras. In both, the potentiality or tendency that continues through death is understood as a *continuum of mind* that has no beginning and no end but does have a strong momentum or volition.

This continuum of mind has two aspects. The first is the ultimate source of everything and is pristine, primordial awareness, completely non-dual and empty. This is variously called the *ground of being*, the *ground of all* or *Dharmakaya*. Then there is a dualistic aspect that is both the ground or basis of liberation and enlightenment (nirvana) as well as the basis or ground

---

[49] Longchenpa, *Natural Perfection: Longchenpa's Radical Dzogchen*, translated by Keith Dowman, Wisdom Publications, 2012, no page numbers, Kindle Edition.

[50] *Questions of King Milinda*, III.5.5. See here: https://accesstoinsight.org/tipitaka/kn/miln/miln.3x.kell.html#miln-3-5-05

for delusional thought and dualistic experience (samsara). These two are sometimes described as gold (primordial awareness) and tarnish (ground of duality). The tarnish is the result of conditions and not inherent to the gold. It is this second dualistic aspect of the ground that carries forward the potentials, tendencies and habits (or karma). This ground of duality or samsaric delusion, the "tarnish" on the gold, is called the *alaya-vijnana*, which is commonly translated, quite poorly I think, as "storehouse consciousness". Storehouse consciousness gives the sense of a continuing or everlasting being or entity. This is not what it is at all. It is more like an environment, spectrum or "field" in which certain things or manifestations are more likely than others. Of course, the Buddha never spoke of such a thing as alaya-vijnana. It was developed by later Buddhist philosophical schools, such as the Yogachara of the first or second century CE, who conceived of it as a kind of field or environment that carries the very basic quality of the mind from one life to the next. Alaya-vijnana is considered to carry or hold just the most subtle "perfume" of our mental habits, which then acts as the seed for a mind with similar mental habits to form. Think of it as being the subtlest flavor of the dualistic mind.

As Longchenpa explains, 'In essence, the ground of all ordinary experience serves as a repository for habitual patterns.'[51] Note that the ground is not a repository for the self, the person, it is merely an aspect of the continuum that carries habits, tendencies and patterns. It is the echo or ripple effect of the things we do that are carried forward not who we are; quite simply because there is no "who". The sense of being a separate person is a delusion. Primordial awareness (the gold as it were) has no characteristics of a dualistic self at all. In other words it is empty, and yet it is profoundly

---

[51] Longchen Rabjam, *A Treasure Trove of Scriptural Transmission: A Commentary on The Precious Treasury of the Basic Space of Phenomena (Choying Dzod)*, translated by Richard Barron, Padma Publishing, 2001, p.279.

cognizant. This fundamental awareness is timeless, lucid and the ground or source of everything. It is our ultimate nature and transcends birth and death. Having been born, the body, the dualistic mind and the self must all inevitably die.

The analogy of the ripple effect shows clearly what continues and what does not. Think of a stone thrown in a pond. When the stone hits the water it produces many ripples that move out in a specific pattern. The stone sinks to the bottom and settles there, completely still. The stone is us, our mind and our sense of self. The impact with the water is our thoughts and actions. The ripples are what continues after we are gone – a mere echo of our thoughts and behaviours.

There is a practical exercise that helps us to better understand rebirth. We take up a candle and a match. First, we light the match. We then hold the wick of the unlit candle above but not touching the match flame, making sure that the unlit wick does not touch the flame. We then watch closely. The wick of the unlit candle will begin to smoke and will soon ignite in flame. In this exercise, the heat is standing in as the continuum of mind. Heat is the potentiality of there being a flame at all, but only leads to a flame if there is fuel and oxygen etc. Heat is also the base cause of the fire. To deepen our understanding we can ask ourselves: Did the flame jump from the match to the candle? Is the candle flame the same as the match flame? Or is it a different flame altogether? Spoiler alert – the candle flame was ignited by heat from the match, not by the match flame itself. There are two flames not one. They are in different places and burn from different fuels (one a match, one a paraffin wick) and yet they are causally connected and share almost precisely the same qualities. The flames are not the same flame, yet they both have a similar color, shape and brightness. Furthermore, they are deeply interdependent, in that the heat of one flame is the primary cause of the other. Heat and light are also the primary characteristics of both flames.

On this level these two flames are not the same but also not completely independent.

In *The Questions of King Milinda*, the Buddhist monk Nàgasena (150 BCE) says that both mind and matter (body) are reborn together, but that it is not the person or self that is reborn.[52] It is merely the qualities and tendencies that arise from the continuum of mind again and again due to momentum. Even so, because of the profound causal link between the two beings, they cannot be said to be wholly separate. In response to the question 'He who is reborn, Nàgasena, is he the same person or another?' the monk replies 'Neither the same nor another' and provides the following illustration:

> In the case of a pot of milk that turns first to curds, then to butter, then to ghee; it would not be right to say that the ghee, butter and curds were the same as the milk but they have come from that, so neither would it be right to say that they are something else.[53]

In line with these early Sutra teachings and the Nyingma tradition, my own basic position on rebirth is that nothing that could be described as a person or self survives beyond death. That being said, something does persist beyond death. It is a kind of continuum that is the basis of each life, of all life. This continuum has five deep tendencies:

1. the tendency for a dualistic mind to arise from the ground of pristine and primordial awareness;
2. the tendency for that mind to be similar to the minds that preceded it in terms of its qualities and habits;
3. the tendency for minds of a particular type to "co-emerge" with bodies of a particular type.

---

[52] Bhikkhu Pesala, *The Debate of King Milinda*, Buddha Dharma Education Association, 2001, p. 46.

[53] Bhikkhu Pesala, *The Debate of King Milinda*, Buddha Dharma Education Association, 2001, p. 43.

4. The tendency for that dualistic mind and body to dissolve back into the ground of pristine and primordial awareness from which it came leaving only an echo or ripple that moves forward as the basis of another mind and life.

5. The tendency or momentum for this process of rebirth to continue until it is interrupted or stopped by enlightenment.

This means that when I die nothing about me will continue, except for the basic tendencies of my dualistic mind. Those tendencies will arise as a new mind as part of a new being (human or animal). That new mind will have very similar qualities and tendencies to the mind that preceded it. If the previous mind was dualistic and deluded, the new mind will be also. If that mind's tendencies were altruism and kindness, then the new mind will be altruistic and kind. If its qualities were meanness and hatred then the new mind will be mean and hateful. In other words, our current mind is the causal condition for future minds of our "descendent" beings. Clearly, this means there is nothing immortal about us. Our current self is utterly impermanent and will perish at death.

Nevertheless, as the dualistic mind has the habit of arising within the continuum, a new mind is a certainty. Sit in meditation and watch how the dualistic mind arises anew from moment to moment, seemingly out of nothing. What we consider to be our permanent mind, that we believe has spanned the duration of our lives, is actually millions of brief moments of mind that were born from the ground of awareness, dissolved back into it again (or died) and were then replaced by new moments of mind almost precisely the same as the previous ones. Likewise the self, it is merely an identification with what arises in the mind moment to moment as though it were substantial, continuous and lasting. This means that death is a bit of a non-event – the dualistic mind will continue rising, dying and being reborn as part of a beginning-less and endless continuum. It merely changes identities and labels but remains much the same, unless we change it through practice. If we don't practice the future mind will be very similar to the past mind because the fundamental ground or "storehouse consciousness" carries forward the basic flavor of the previous mind.

According to the laws of physics, energy is neither created nor destroyed, it merely transforms. In other words there is no birth and no death, only transformation or change. In the bardo teachings the energy that is unborn and never dies is described as the Mother Luminosity; the luminosity that is the ultimate nature of all things, the ground of all. The Mother Luminosity and primordial awareness are one and the same thing. According to Buddhism, energy and phenomena or things cannot completely change their basic nature as they transform. Things always change from like into like. A lemon seed does not become an apple tree that produces cherries. What this means in terms of rebirth is that the quality of our mind, especially at the time of death, determines the quality of the future mind, the future being or life, that arises after our death. If that dualistic mind has the habit of recognizing itself (thoughts, feelings and sensations) as a separate and permanent entity, a self or person, then the future mind will make the same terrible mistake and nothing but loss and grief will follow.

If this all seems a bit depressing and scary, it is. This is what we call samsara, cyclic existence, which is undiluted delusion and dissatisfaction if not pure misery. But take heart, the ground (or Mother Luminosity) from which the dualistic mind and the self arises does not die. It cannot die because it was never born. It is without beginning and without end. It is not a thing and yet is definitely not nothing. It is not us and yet we are indeed that. Fundamental, pristine awareness is the source and ground of all. It is that which we seek to return to at the time of death, the timeless and luminous non-dual awareness that is the source of everything. This is why we sit in meditation, and why we do the other bardo practices.

The Mind at the Time of Death

As the mind arises anew each moment, and as the quality and habits of the mind are the cause for future minds, the habits of our mind at the time of death are paramount. Our mind at the time of death is just a moment of mind, it does not carry with it the mark of everything we have done or thought in our lives. According to the early sutras there is no magical storehouse of karma or merit produced in this or any other life in that moment of mind (more on this in Chapter Six). It's simply that the moment of mind is the sum total of its previous habits and behaviors and no more than that. This means it is completely changeable. The quote from Longchenpa shared earlier makes this very clear. What our mind and heart are in that single moment of death is everything. There is great freedom in this. If at the time of death our mind and heart are full of compassion and devotion (yearning for the ultimate) then, if we are not liberated in the bardo, the future heart-mind and the future being will have those qualities.

This doesn't mean that we can think, feel or do whatever we want throughout our lives and then reform and repent on our deathbed. The dualistic mind is the sum total of its ongoing habits. Whatever we have done, and everything we have done, is actually all that it is. It is nothing else if not our ongoing habits. Although in each moment the dualistic mind is completely new it is almost precisely the same as the previous moment of mind. The dualistic mind has the karma or habit, which is simply a very strong momentum, to continue exactly as it is. The mind will stay the same, deluded and full of negativity, until we change it through practice. Therefore, we need to root out all negative thoughts and feelings and their resultant actions right now. Otherwise those habits will continue to resurface until our last breath, and will flare up even more strongly when the constraints of the body fall away at death.

That being said, even if we do commit non-virtue right up until the last moments of our lives, there is still hope at the time of death. We can radically transform our minds in those final moments. Bhikkhu Analayo explains that the last moments of one's life are of particular importance for:

> … influencing and even determining the conditions of the next life through the adoption and upholding of right view at that time.[54]

Analayo goes on to say that 'even a murderer has in principle the potential of transforming himself [or herself] and reaching full awakening within the same lifetime'.[55] The fact that there are so many opportunities to turn the ship of our karma around shouldn't cause us to relax and forget about trying to live ethically. Far from it, it should motivate us to take advantage of those opportunities right now. Why live with a mind overflowing with poison when we don't have to, when we could live with a mind brimming with the joy and contentment of virtue? It is nothing more than an act of extreme self-harm to not turn our minds to Dharma and not turn our lives toward kindness.

For our heart/mind to be pure devotion or compassion at the time of death—and be able to recognize the ultimate nature when it dawns—all harmful thoughts, feelings and habits must be removed or at least weakened long beforehand. Padmasambhava links the meditative practice of recognizing the true nature of mind and rooting out negative thoughts and feelings in the following pith instruction:

> Do like this if you want to practice the true Dharma! Keep your master's oral instructions in mind. Don't conceptualize your experience, as it just makes you attached or angry. Day and night, look into your mind. If your stream of mind contains any nonvirtue, renounce it from the core of your heart.[56]

---

[54] Bhikkhu Analayo, *Rebirth in Early Buddhism and Current Research*, Wisdom Publications, 2018, no page, Kindle edition.

[55] Ibid.

[56] Padmasambhava, *Advice from the Lotus-Born: A Collection of Padmasambhava's Advice to the Dakini Yeshe Tsogyal and Other Close Disciples*, Marcia Binder Schmidt (editor), Rangjung Yeshe Publications, 2013, p.29.

As the time of death could be our very next breath, there is no time to waste. This is why ethics is so profoundly important, whether we are Sutrayana, Mahayana, Vajrayana or Dzogchen practitioners. Aside from our wish never to harm any sentient being, our current and all future lives literally depend on how loving and compassionate we are right now.

It is helpful to think about rebirth not as a new version of ourselves, but as the birth of an entirely new being whose life, and quality of life, completely depends on us. So, think of these future beings as being like our descendants, our children. Thinking this way helps us develop loving-kindness and compassion. We don't want our children to suffer and be unhappy. We want our children to be happy. Therefore, we must practice dharma in this life, in fact right now, and live as ethically as we can so that the quality of the mind that gives birth to the next being is open, loving and perfectly content. This will mean that when the new mind forms, giving rise to a new being, the quality of that new mind will be equally open, loving and content. All future generations depend on us to do this. Thinking in this way we can see that nothing is more important than opening our heart with joy, kindness, love, compassion and devotion. Permeating our entire being with those profound qualities through the methods of meditation and contemplation will lead to the recognition of our true nature. There is nothing in Dharma that surpasses this.

Why Should We Learn about the Bardos?

There are four main reasons we should learn about the bardos. Firstly, we should learn about the bardos because it will open our hearts. This is the purpose of all Dharma study and practice. How does it open our hearts? Because it reveals for us the truth of impermanence, the truth of Shunyata and the truth of our nature, which is Bodhicitta – the awakened mind of love and compassion. Secondly, we should learn about the bardos because they are our reality. There is no point staying in the dark about the true nature of things. Thirdly, we are all going to die. Death is the one experience we are all certain to share. Given that fact, an understanding of the bardos is knowledge that we will undoubtedly benefit from. As Kyabje Dilgo Khyentse Rinpoche once taught:

> Even if death were to fall upon you today like lightning, you must be ready to die without sadness and regret, without any residue of clinging for what is left behind. Remaining in the recognition of the absolute view, you should leave this life like an eagle soaring up into the blue sky.[57]

Fourth and finally, each of the bardos is an opportunity for the Buddhist practitioner to recognize absolute reality and the true nature of mind and thus find ultimate freedom. We cannot miss this opportunity. As Gyatrul Rinpoche makes clear:

> It is so good to learn about the six bardos, to think about the bardos and train in what to do in them. If it were me, I would do bardo practice rather than Yeshe Lama [the highest Dzogchen practices]. I don't think you will get any benefit from thinking that your bardo teacher is not a lama or is not Tibetan or whatever. If you want to overcome the terrors of the bardo, I don't think you can be hung up on that. What is important is what you are learning and practicing.[58]

As is clear by now, the greatest opportunity for liberation and awakening is in the Bardo of Dying, in which all of the constraints of the body and dualistic mind fall away and the ultimate nature or rigpa is revealed naturally. We can make the most of this opportunity with almost no striving at the time of death if we make some effort now, while we're alive. If we meditate consistently from this moment on we will enter the bardos

---

[57] Dilgo Khyentse Rinpoche quoted in *In the Presence of Masters: Wisdom from 30 Contemporary Tibetan Buddhist Teachers*, Shambhala Publications, 2004, p. 229.

[58] Venerable Gyatrul Rinpoche, "On Bardo Practice, June 13, 2014", (unpublished work, January 01 2022), typescript.

with profound confidence and no regrets. Mingyur Rinpoche, author of *In Love with the World: A Monk's Journey through the Bardos of Living and Dying*, puts it this way:

> When we commit ourselves to living consciously, we apply effort and diligence to diminishing our confusion. At the end of our lives, this same confusion dissolves without effort. In the same way that the normal processes of the body cease to function, the movements of the mind subside as well. This includes our sensory perceptions, but also the subtle beliefs and concepts that shape our experience and define our identity. When all these cycles of body and mind stop functioning, all that's left is awareness itself, the unconditioned open space of pure knowing ...[59]

To be prepared for that moment in which recognizing our true nature is much easier, indeed natural, we can live more consciously and take advantage of the other bardos that occur in our day to day lives to train in recognition of the natural state, the true or ultimate nature of mind. There are glimpses of our true nature between each and every thought. That is literally tens of thousands of opportunities to recognize rigpa every day. We cannot waste these opportunities. As Jetsunma Tenzin Palmo has taught:

> If we don't recognize the nature of our mind while we are alive, we will not recognize it at the time of death. We would see this wide, vast and open luminosity and pull back, and fall into unconsciousness, and then we wake up in the bardo. But if we are accustomed to seeing even this less vast [luminosity], but still of the same nature, the nature of the mind, of the clear light nature, then we will recognize it when it comes to us in all its fullness. So, this is why it is very important that we practice now,

---

[59] Yongey Mingyur Rinpoche with Helen Tworkov, *In Love With the World: A Monk's Journey Through the Bardos of Living and Dying*, Random House Publishing Group, 2021, no page. Kindle Edition.

so that we can recognize what we can, NOW, so that at the time of death we can merge with the actual thing and realize it.[60]

Because an understanding of the bardos can lead to total liberation in this lifetime, even if only at the end of this current life, these bardo teachings are considered to be among the most precious teachings in Vajrayana or Tibetan Buddhism. As Gyatrul Rinpoche explains:

> We are all in the bardos all the time. We are in the bardo of this life, we visit the bardo of dreaming every night, the bardo of death can be upon us at any second ... Therefore bardo practice is so important! Everything is our bardo, and it is through these bardos that we perpetuate our delusion; likewise it is through these bardos that finally we will become liberated. If we know how to navigate the bardos, then we will have some hope for liberation rather than confusion.[61]

It goes without saying that because these bardo teachings open the door to liberation in one lifetime, we should take them seriously and put some effort into understanding them. If ever there is a time to overcome our commitment phobia, it is with these teachings. To close this section on why we should learn about the bardos here is a quote from Jetsun Khandro Rinpoche:

> The real intent behind any Dharma practice is to train the mind for the moment of death, so that the moment of death can arise with confidence and without regret; regret in the sense of non-awareness, or ignorance.[62]

---

[60] Jetsunma Tenzin Palmo [Facebook post] 30 December 2021. Available at: https://www.facebook.com/jetsunmatenzinpalmo (Accessed: 30 December 2021)

[61] Venerable Gyatrul Rinpoche, "On Bardo Practice, June 13, 2014", (unpublished work, January 01 2022), typescript.

[62] Jetsun Khandro Rinpoche, *This Precious Life: Tibetan Buddhist Teachings on the Path to Enlightenment*, Shambhala Publications, 2005, p. 58.

The Importance of Applying the Teachings

Like all Buddhist wisdom, the bardo teachings must be put into practice as well as understood intellectually. Knowing the theory is good, but it will not lead to recognition of the ultimate nature. Tulku Urgyen Rinpoche makes this clear when he writes:

> Bardo teachings may sound very fascinating and colorful, but the vital point is one's individual practice right now. Why have medicine when sick, if one doesn't use it? Without training, our studies become mere intellectual understanding ... In fact, there is no way around actual training.[63]

In other words, we must reflect on the teachings and put them into practice. When the teachings are not applied they are like a seed that is never planted and watered. It never germinates and nothing grows. Chokyi Nyima Rinpoche concurs when he writes:

> ... simply studying the teachings is not enough to cut our doubts and gain complete clarity. We must think them over. That is called "reflecting upon" or "contemplating" the teachings. Still, only studying the teachings and thinking about them is not sufficient. At that point our understanding is merely theoretical. In order to experience the truth of the teachings we need to rely on a third point: actual meditation practice.[64]

There is no way of awakening to our true nature that does not rely on our own efforts. We have to learn, reflect and apply the teachings to our lives ourselves. No-one else can learn for us. No-one else can contemplate the teachings for us. No-one else can do our practice. We will not magically

---

[63] 'Introductory Discourse' in Tsele Natsok Rangdrol's *Mirror of Mindfulness*, Rangjung Yeshe Publications, 1987, p. 8.

[64] Chokyi Nyima Rinpoche, The *Bardo Guidebook*, Rangjung Yeshe Publications, 1991, p. 22.

transform. We must undertake the transformation ourselves. It's totally up to our own motivation, our own enthusiasm for the practice, our own diligence. As Dilgo Khyentse Rinpoche taught in *The Heart of Compassion: The Thirty-seven Verses on the Practice of a Bodhisattva*:

> The Buddha is not going to project you to Buddhahood, as if throwing a stone. He is not going to purify you, as if washing a dirty cloth, nor is he going to cure you of ignorance, like a doctor administering medicine to a passive patient. Having attained full enlightenment himself, he is showing you the path, and it is up to you to follow it or not. It is up to you now to practice these teachings and experience their results.[65]

As we experience bardo states every day and as each one of us will inevitably face death there's no time like the present to get started, especially given the fact that the bardo practices can grant our wish to be free of suffering once and for all. Let's not forget that we have multitudes of opportunities to do this—to recognize our true nature and be liberated from the delusion of the samsaric mind—each and every day. Gyatrul Rinpoche drives this point home when he says:

> Everybody is in the bardo already, everybody is facing the bardo of death. We need to know where we are and where we are going. Finally, it is time to open our eyes to that. So please, everybody practice![66]

This sentiment is beautifully echoed by Chagdud Tulku Rinpoche (1930–2002) in the following concise summary of bardo practice:

> Time is very precious. Do not wait until you are dying to understand your spiritual nature. If you do it now, you will discover resources of

---

[65] Dilgo Khyentse Rinpoche, *The Heart of Compassion: The Thirty-seven Verses on the Practice of a Bodhisattva*, Shambhala, 2007, p. 204.

[66] Venerable Gyatrul Rinpoche, "On Bardo Practice, June 13, 2014", (unpublished work, January 01 2022), typescript.

kindness and compassion you didn't know you had. It is from this mind of intrinsic wisdom and compassion that you can truly benefit others ... Moment by moment, we should look at life as if it were a dream unfolding ... In this relaxed, more open state of being, we have the opportunity to gain the infallible means of dying well, which is recognition of our absolute nature.[67]

Because of this urgent need to apply the teachings rather than accumulate conceptual knowledge, I'm going to focus on how to do that for the remainder of this book: how to apply our understanding of the bardos in everyday life. I will do this in the most accessible and user-friendly way as possible. The Dharma is of no value to anyone if it is impossible to adapt it to modern life and genuinely apply it. Therefore, I will outline the simple practices we can do to recognize our true nature while alive and, if all else fails, how to do so at the time of death. The final words for this chapter come from Tulku Thondup Rinpoche:

> ... without wasting any time, you must try to gain at least some spiritual knowledge, experience, and strength of opening, peace, joy, compassion, devotion, positive perception, and wisdom. These are the only source for the creation of meritorious karma and inner wisdom, which will improve this life and equip you to face the next bardos and your future lives.[68]

---

[67] Chagdud Tulku Rinpoche quoted in *Tricycle: The Buddhist Review*, Volume 12, Issues 2-4, 2002, p.21.

[68] Tulku Thondup, *Enlightened Journey: Buddhist Practice as Daily Life*, Edited by Harold Talbott, Shambhala Publications, 1995, p. 55.

CHAPTER FIVE

WHAT EXACTLY IS THE OPPORTUNITY IN THE BARDOS?

Total liberation in this very lifetime is in the palm of your hand.

The reason the bardos are an opportunity is precisely because they are, as already noted, *intervals*. They are a *hiatus* or *gap*. What are they a gap or break in? What are they a hiatus or pause of? They are a gap between moments of mind and between this life and the next, with the greatest interval and therefore the greatest opportunity arising after death. As Mingyur Rinpoche explains:

> If our bodies expire while our minds rest in recognition of emptiness, then we are forever liberated. We have nothing more to learn. In luminous emptiness – the deathless realm – recognition and acceptance are one. We cannot attain unborn deathless reality until we accept death.[69]

The bardos are a break in dualistic mind, the ordinary, compulsive, thinking mind. They are a hiatus in the workings of the self, because the dualistic, thinking mind and the self are almost one and the same, almost. The self is

---

[69] Yongey Mingyur Rinpoche with Helen Tworkov, *In Love With the World: A Monk's Journey Through the Bardos of Living and Dying*, Random House Publishing Group, 2021, no page. Kindle Edition.

actually just a sense of being separate from others, of existing independently, along with an identification with thoughts, emotions and sensations as though they constituted a person, a lasting, separate entity. As I've written elsewhere:

> All thoughts and emotions, fleeting and baseless, are mere empty echoes, triggered by external events or the memory of external events, which themselves are impermanent and devoid of substance. Our thoughts and emotions are described as our "inner life" and yet they have nothing to do with our true inner life. We are not who we think we are and we are not what we think about ourselves. Not only do our thoughts and emotions shed no light on our true inner nature, they are what obscures it. Tragically, we are so focused on our thoughts and emotions that we think they are the sum total of who we are. We identify with thoughts and emotions and misconstrue them for a self. We do not experience that which thoughts and emotions obscures, we are totally clueless about our true nature, our innate pristine awareness. To experience who we truly are all we need do is shift our focus away from thoughts and emotions, and away from the delusion of self they perpetuate. This shift of focus is so profoundly simple, yet it is something so very few ever achieve, mostly because they never even try. Once we have achieved this shift in focus, through simple meditation, and we are settled in our true nature, then we will experience thoughts and emotions not as obscurations but as the natural radiance of pristine awareness.[70]

A bardo, then, is whatever is between moments of dualistic mind, between moments of thinking, feeling and sensing, or between the compulsive shenanigans of the self. There are many words for what is found in the gap: the ultimate or absolute nature, the natural state, Tathagatagarbha, Sugatagarbha or the Buddha Nature. These are all words for what remains

---

[70] Jamyang Tenphel & Pema Duddul, 'Empty Echoes', *Resting in Stillness*, Jalu Publications, 2020, p. 138.

beneath or beyond mentation, beyond thoughts, feelings and sensations and our self-identification with those thoughts, feelings and sensations. What remains beyond dualistic mind is a primordial essence or pristine awareness that is never defiled. All these words point to that perfect essence, or Buddha Nature.

Shunyata or Emptiness

We cannot grasp the concept of Buddha Nature until we grasp the concept of Shunyata or "emptiness". Emptiness is both a much misunderstood and a much over-used term. In English 'emptiness' is a word often used to describe an unfortunate human condition typified by disturbing feelings of emotional numbness and purposelessness. Any dictionary shows as synonyms for emptiness the words barrenness, blankness, and worthlessness. In Buddhism, the word emptiness has nothing to do with emotional dysfunction or worthlessness. Given these negative connotations perhaps emptiness is not the best word to use in this sense but as there is now a long tradition of its use it seems we might be stuck with it. In this book, however, I will mostly use the original Sanskrit term, Shunyata, as it doesn't have any negative connotations.

Despite a plethora of written commentaries and oral teachings on Shunyata even long-term Buddhists often misuse or misunderstand the term. Many believe that it means that nothing really exists. On the other hand people throw it around as though it is a magical incantation that refutes or equalizes everything: everything is emptiness, everything is emptiness. Both of these attitudes are not in line with the Dharma as Shakyamuni Buddha taught it more than two thousand years ago. The truth of Shunyata is not that nothing exists, but that nothing exists in the way we think it does. Put simply, the word Shunyata is an umbrella term that points to some characteristics of reality, phenomena and our world that are, though usually hidden to our dualistic minds, rather wonderful.

On the simplest level Shunyata means that all phenomena—including our personalities, thoughts and feelings—are *impermanent* and changeable. Shunyata implies dynamism and flux. The term Shunyata also points to the fact that all phenomena only exist in *mutual interdependence* with all other phenomena and therefore are never wholly self-sufficient. In this sense it implies profound interconnectedness. Shunyata also means that phenomena are devoid (empty) of an irreducible identity or essence. Things, including ourselves, only *seem* to have inherent existence because of misperception. Based on that misperception we apply labels or names to things that, in effect, give the impression that they are separate, permanent, and independent. This is what we Buddhists call ignorance or delusion; the belief in separately existing, permanent things, especially a separate, permanent and independently existing "self". This is the biggest delusion. The belief in a separately existing, permanent, independent and innate identity or self leads to the separation of self and other, and that inevitably leads to attachment or attraction and aversion or dislike. From there we get all the unhelpful emotions, like fear, anger and hatred. Conversely, understanding Shunyata leads to a sense of freedom, connection, joy and limitless potential.

Our contemplations of Shunyata do not have to be overly mystical. They can be rather practical. One aspect of Shunyata is the idea that things are not how we perceive them to be. They are not lasting, solid and separate but fluid, ever-changing and interconnected. This is easily illustrated when considering objects that appear to us via our senses. Take as an example a tree. Our sense perceptions tell us that the tree is separate from us and all other things, is an independently existing entity and is solid and lasting. We can do away with the idea that the tree is a lasting entity easily. We know all trees die. We've all seen a dead tree. We have evidence of the impermanence of trees. In this moment the tree we are considering is alive, but we know it won't remain that way forever.

The next thing we do away with is the idea that the tree is independently existing. This we can do by recognizing that the tree depends on a wide range of processes and other phenomena to exist – it needs water, oxygen and carbon to survive and is in fact composed of those elements. Its branches reach out into the sky and absorb oxygen and sunlight to sustain itself. Its roots spread out into the soil to absorb nutrients and water. The tree is not composed of *treeness*. It is composed of carbon, water and minerals. If you take out any of those things, there is no tree. Without carbon there is no tree. Without water and minerals there is no tree. If there were no sun there would be no tree. If there were no earth there would be no tree. If the earth had no atmosphere, there would be no tree. The tree is interconnected with and dependent on all other things.

Indeed, if we try to find the essence of the tree, its treeness, we find nothing. Is the treeness in its leaves or branches? Or in its trunk or roots? Looking even deeper, is the treeness, the essence of the tree, the atoms that form it, or the electrons, neutrons and protons that form the atoms? The more we break the tree down into its parts to find its essence, its substantial existence, the more we see that it doesn't have one. The closer and deeper we look, the more we see space or emptiness rather than solid matter. Furthermore, the fact that atoms, neutrons and protons are both particles and waves completely destroys the notion of the tree's solidity. Nothing in the universe is truly solid. It is all pulsing energy. Most of what we perceive as physical objects is actually space and energy, not matter, and even the matter itself is also a particle wave or energy.

What we perceive as a tree is just something our mind has labelled 'tree'. Beyond our mind's processes what we call a tree doesn't exist (there is something there, but it's not that). The great Tibetan visionary and mystic Dudjom Lingpa referred to this misperception or misapprehension of sense information as being like water freezing to ice.[71] Our perception distorts

---

[71] Dudjom Lingpa quoted in B. Alan Wallace, *Mind in the Balance: Meditation in Science, Buddhism, and Christianity*, Columbia University Press, 2014, p. 180.

reality from fluid and interconnected to solid and separate. The direct experience of emptiness through contemplation and meditation is not one of separation, isolation and solidity. It is an experience of oneness, openness and spontaneity. It is also an experience of vast spaciousness and limitless compassion, which is our ultimate nature, our Buddha Nature.

Buddha Nature

As we saw in Chapter Four when we were discussing rebirth, energy is neither created nor destroyed, it merely transforms. According to Buddhism (and the laws of physics) energy and phenomena or things cannot completely change their basic nature as they transform. Things always change from like into like. This is not to say that the transformation is insignificant. Coal cannot become gold, but it can become a diamond. That is an extraordinary transformation, but in their fundamental characteristics coal and diamonds are the same. Coal is a carbon with impurities, such as nitrogen and sulphur. Diamonds are a very pure form of carbon. Likewise, an ordinary deluded being and a Buddha are the same in their fundamental nature. Our Buddha Nature is to our ordinary selves what diamonds are to coal. The transformation from samsaric or deluded being to Buddha is not a change in fundamental nature, but a change in purity. In this sense purity is not about morality or virtue but about awareness, and the capacity to embrace whatever happens, whatever arises in the mind or in our experience, with total equanimity and love. Nyoshul Khen Rinpoche, a great Dzogchen master and scholar of the ancient Nyingma lineage, describes our Buddha Nature in this way:

> Buddha-nature is pure, undefiled, unelaborated, unconditioned, transcending all concepts. It is not an object of dualistic thought and intellectual knowledge. It is, however, open to gnosis, intuition, the nondual apperception of intrinsic awareness itself, prior to or upstream of consciousness. Adventitious obscurations temporarily veil and, like

clouds, obscure this pristine, sky-like, luminous fundamental nature or mind essence—also known as Tathagatagarbha, Buddha-nature.[72]

This means that, as noted in the first lines of this book, in our nature, we are no different to the Buddha. Our true or ultimate nature is already perfect exactly as it is. This is made clear in the Diamond Sutra:

Buddhas and disciples are not enlightened by a set method of teachings, but by an internally intuitive process which is spontaneous and is part of their own inner nature.[73]

This inner nature is one with everything in the universe. In other words, all things of the mind and the world are of the same nature – the clear light, the empty perfection, which are other ways of saying the Buddha Nature. As Tsele Natsok Rangdrol explains:

This original and natural state, the great primordial purity, is itself the original ground [of all]. The aspect of its essence is labelled 'primordial purity,' the aspect of its nature is given the name 'spontaneous presence' and the aspect of its appearing as the manifestation or expression of these two, inseparable, is called 'all-pervasive compassion.' In short, these three are taught to be one single identity with different aspects.[74]

There is no amount of intellectual study or philosophical debate that will lead us to a true and deep recognition of our primordial purity. The dualistic mind cannot understand the Buddha Nature let alone experience it. As Tilopa famously taught:

---

[72] Nyoshul Khen Rinpoche, *Natural Great Perfection: Dzogchen Teachings And Vajra Songs*, Snow Lion Publications, 1995, p. 79.

[73] *Diamond Sutra*, Chapter 7.

[74] Tsele Natsok Rangdrol, *Circle of the Sun*, translated by Erik Pema Kunsang (1990), Rangjung Yeshe Publications, pp. 5-6.

Obsessive use of meditative disciplines or perennial study of scripture and philosophy will never bring forth this wonderful realization, this truth which is natural to awareness, because the mind that desperately desires to reach another realm or level of experience inadvertently ignores the basic light that constitutes all experience.[75]

This does not mean that we should not meditate or study at all, it means that we should use a simple, relaxed meditation technique and do just enough study that we understand the fundamentals. Furthermore, we should approach our practice and study without striving, without wishing to be anywhere other than where we are right now or be anyone other than who we already are. The goal is not to go somewhere else or be someone else. The goal is to awaken to the perfection of this very moment, to the already-present Buddha-mind that is our naked awareness. The fundamental point that Tilopa is making is that we cannot use conceptual thinking to recognize our true nature. It can only be done through relaxed meditation, which empowers the "internally intuitive process" mentioned in the Diamond Sutra. In meditation, by attending to the bardos between each moment, we can directly experience our enlightened nature. As Garchen Rinpoche, a monk and master of the Drikung Kagyu tradition, explains:

Do not worry about enlightenment; the Buddha is within your mind already, ready to be seen. But because we cannot turn inward and are constantly distracted, we fail to recognize the Buddha. When past thoughts have ceased and future thoughts not yet arisen, in this *space between* fixations, you can glimpse the nature of mind abiding like space; this is the Buddha. If you remain within this nature continuously, you are enlightened. Whenever you stop grasping, there is no cause of samsara. Whenever you begin to grasp, you have again created the cause of

---

[75] Lee Hixon, *Mother of the Buddhas: Meditation on the Prajnaparamita Sutra*, Quest Books, 1993, p. 248

samsara. The Buddha is actually not somewhere far away. The Buddha is always ready to be seen. If you do not give up the fixation to a self, but try to escape from samsara by secluding your body, you will still not be liberated. If you give up the fixation to a self, while continuing to live in the world, you will be liberated.[76]

Meditation is the tool we use to glimpse our true nature in the spaces or gaps (bardos) between thoughts. Meditation brings us into the present, enabling us to more readily glimpse reality as it is. *Self-Liberation through Seeing with Naked Awareness* makes this clear:

> In the present moment, when (your mind) remains in its own condition without constructing anything,
>
> Awareness at that moment in itself is quite ordinary.
>
> And when you look into yourself in this way nakedly (without any discursive thoughts),
>
> Since there is only this pure observing, there will be found a lucid clarity without anyone being there who is the observer;
>
> Only a naked manifest awareness is present.[77]

Meditation is also the principal tool for abandoning fixation to our deluded sense of separate, permanent and independently existing self. Meditation enables us to experience what is already there, already perfect as it is. It does not refine or produce anything. Our Buddha Nature needs no refinement or development. Nothing we do could make it better, brighter or more perfect. It is totally complete and perfect already. Likewise, nothing we do could

---

[76] Garchen Rinpoche, "Teaching Transcripts" (unpublished work, January 01 2022), typescript.

[77] Padmasambhava, *Self-Liberation through Seeing with Naked Awareness*, translated by John Myrdhin Reynolds, 2000, Snow Lion, p. 12.

diminish it, limit it, damage it or stain it. Nothing that happens to us affects it. No mistakes we might make matter to the Buddha Nature. No knowledge or skills we acquire enhance it in any way. The Buddha Nature needs no enhancement or embellishment and certainly does not need purification. No good deeds we perform make it more pristine. This truth is dramatically illustrated by Dudjom Lingpa when he writes:

> If one person who had dedicated his [or her] whole life to constructing temples and stupas and to protecting the lives of others and another who had devoted his [or her] entire life to being a butcher, taking the lives of others, were both to identify the ground-awareness, the great freedom from extremes, and persistently apply themselves to practicing that, there would not be even the slightest difference in their attainment of enlightenment.[78]

This does not mean that ethics do not matter. Ethics always matters. Not only does ethics matter, but ethical conduct is the heart of Buddhism. Harming others is never acceptable. What Dudjom Lingpa is saying is that, no matter what we have done in the past, if we turn our minds to Dharma today—renouncing harmful actions from this moment onwards and committing ourselves to recognizing our true nature—then there is still the possibility of enlightenment. Our ultimate nature cannot be ruined or destroyed. There is always a chance for enlightenment. That being said, because our dualistic mind constantly works against this truth—by feeding us the delusion that we and other beings are small, isolated and imperfect—we need to remind ourselves of our true nature through contemplation and then experience it directly through meditation.

In the early sutras (the sutras that are common across all forms of Buddhism) our Lord Buddha Shakyamuni is recorded as saying

---

[78] *The Vajra Essence: Dudjom Lingpa's Visions of the Great Perfection Volume 3,* translated by B. Alan Wallace, Wisdom Publications, p. 235.

"Luminous, monks, is the mind"[79], which was the opening statement to a teaching about the importance of recognizing the luminous nature of mind to progress on the Buddhist path. It is this luminous nature of mind that is the Buddha Nature, which is Shunyata (emptiness) in union with compassion. When Shabkar, in the quote shared earlier in this book, referred to 'the luminous emptiness that is the true nature of mind', he was talking about Buddha Nature.[80] Shechen Gyaltsap Rinpoche describes the Buddha Nature in this way:

> Buddha-nature is immaculate. It is profound, serene, unfabricated suchness, an uncompounded expanse of luminosity; nonarising, unceasing, primordial peace, spontaneously present nirvana.[81]

Even though the mind has this luminous, perfect and immaculate nature, the Buddha Nature teachings are always given in the context of there also being an obscuring dualistic mind (*sem* in Tibetan) that needs to be addressed. The Tibetan tradition is rich with teachings on developing the necessary qualities and meditative skill to overcome this dualistic mind to allow the luminosity of the Buddha Nature to shine through. Although we cannot use conceptual thinking to recognize our true nature, there are ways to support our meditation practice using our everyday thinking mind to develop confidence in that enlightened nature. One of these techniques is to remind ourselves that all beings, from the smallest insect to the most revered saint, are exactly equal in their nature. We are all the same. Our essential nature is the same nature as the exquisite Buddhas. It is helpful to use an aphorism to remind ourselves of this, and to have that aphorism placed prominently in the place

---

[79] *Pabhassara Sutra*, Anguttara Nikāya 49-52.

[80] *The Life of Shabkar: The Autobiography of a Tibetan Yogin*, p. 175.

[81] Shechen Rabjam, *The Great Medicine: Steps in Meditation on the Enlightened Mind*, Boston: Shambhala, 2007, p. 4.

where we practice as well as other places like our bedside and desk. The aphorism I use is:

All beings, in their fundamental nature, are exactly the same as the Buddha, pure and perfect, as am I.

The purpose of this reminder, that in our nature we are no different to the Buddhas, is to give us confidence that we already "have" Buddha Nature. Without this confidence in our true nature it is difficult to rest the mind. As Khenpo Tsultrim Gyamtso Rinpoche notes:

> The purpose of teaching the Tathagatagarbha is to give the meditator confidence that he [or she] already has Buddha Nature. Without such confidence it is very difficult to fully rest the mind free from all conceptual contrivance, because there is always a subtle tendency to try to remove or achieve something.[82]

Without this confidence we cannot drop all our conceptual hang ups and fabrications. We cannot let go of all the dualistic thinking, feeling and sensing we are constantly absorbed with; our habitual stressing about and worrying over the past and future. There is always a tendency to try to fix something, block or suppress something, "purify" something or achieve or gain something. Without confidence in our true nature, we never really relax, never really rest, we are never completely free of the dualistic mind. Perhaps this is why the great Dzogchen master Longchenpa teaches us that confidence is the root of accomplishment in the Dharma:

> There are six indications that you have gained deep indwelling confidence:
>
> You experience the after-death state as naturally peaceful, as though you were being led by an excellent guide.

---

[82] Khenpo Tsultrim Gyamtso Rinpoche, *Progressive Stages of Meditation on Emptiness*, translated and arranged by Shenpen Hookham, Prajna Editions, 2001, p. 79.

You are naturally purified of obscurations, like a gem that gives off a natural luster.

Your meditative experiences well forth naturally, like bubbles rising from fermented grain in the brewing of beer.

You experience supreme bliss intensifying naturally, as if you had drunk strong liquor.

Your experience of mind itself is natural, like a bee's attraction to the nectar of a flower.

You experience blessings coming to you of their own accord, like the natural maturing of a fine crop.

When you have such experiences, you are a great yogin.[83]

What this means is that confidence in our true nature not only makes awakening possible it also removes all obscurations, that is, it purifies karma and all negative tendencies. It also enables the blessings of the Buddha and our teachers to rain down on us without any effort on our part. In the Tibetan tradition realization is not possible without these blessings. This kind of confidence is called Vajra confidence, which should not be confused with confidence in our mundane self, in our worldly skills or knowledge. It is confidence in the cognizant yet empty nature at the heart of all beings. It is certainty that everything arises from primordial purity.

Given how important confidence in our true nature is to our awakening we should remind ourselves each day of this truth – the truth of the equality and perfection of all beings including ourselves. We can take the striving out of the reminder itself by relying on symbols and signs. This is quite simple but highly effective. Write a note to yourself that says "In my nature

---

[83] Longchen Rabjam, *The Precious Treasury of Pith Instructions*, trans. Richard Barron, Padma Publishing, 2006, pp. 110-111.

I am no different to the Buddha, as are all beings." Place this note or sign somewhere you will see it each morning as you wake and each night as you go to sleep. Place copies of this note in other places, like in your office or on your refrigerator door. We can also choose a symbol that reminds us of this reality, for example we could choose flowers. Whenever we see flowers we remember that we and all beings are no different to the Buddha in our essence. We could choose the sky. Whenever we see the sky we remember that we and all beings are no different to the Buddha in our essence. These kind of reminders become effortless, they are just there as we move around our home or go out in the world. This way we remove all striving from our wish to fully and truly recognize the Buddha Nature of all beings including ourselves.

In the *Pabhassara Sutra* the Buddha gave a teaching to a small group of monks about the luminous nature of the mind and how direct perception of the mind's natural luminosity (or Buddha Nature) is a prerequisite for awakening or enlightenment.[84] The Buddha Nature is the true nature of our mind and of all things. Developing confidence in this opens the doorway to realization. Therefore, try to remind yourself of this truth as often as possible and maintain a daily meditation practice (which is the way to directly realize or experience that nature). Dudjom Lingpa taught that recognizing the Buddha Nature is the entire path:

> What is the spiritual path? It is to hold to your own ground within your own nature. What is realization? It is exact knowledge of your own nature's abiding essence. What is liberation? It is enlightenment in your own nature.[85]

---

[84] Anguttara Nikāya 49-52.

[85] Dudjom Lingpa, *Buddhahood Without Meditation: A Visionary Account Known as Refining One's Perception*, translated by Richard Barron, Padma Publishing, 2002, p. 113.

Non-Dual Awareness

The path of recognizing Buddha Nature is the path of settling the mind into its fundamental non-dual state of unadorned awareness. We've already discussed the word we use in the Nyingma tradition of Vajrayana for what is found in the gap, in the bardo, which is *rigpa*. As we've seen already, rigpa is commonly translated as pristine or primordial awareness. My preferred translation is *non-dual awareness*. Non-dual awareness is the direct experience of Buddha Nature. From the Nyingma perspective total enlightenment is defined as nothing more or less than resting without distraction in the ultimate nature, resting permanently in the pristine, primordial awareness that is rigpa. His Holiness the Dalai Lama explains that:

> Our fundamental nature, this essence of rigpa which is utterly natural, is already present and not something that needs to be newly developed. It is simply the nature of the consciousness we already have, and so as long as there is consciousness, its nature will be that of unimpeded all-penetrating rigpa.[86]

So let's just take a moment to reflect on that, as this is a momentous and exciting truth – that in the gap between the shenanigans of monkey mind there is already enlightenment, the ultimate nature. It is already there. It does not need to be created, cultivated or refined. It is right there, right now, closer than our own hearts as my partner Jamyang Tenphel often says. Non-dual awareness is ever present as the true nature of the mind. All we need do is recognize it, feel it, and remain with it. Buddha Nature—or enlightened mind or the ultimate nature or rigpa—is an intrinsic part of us that we can't see because it is just too close. Profoundly close. The traditional metaphor for this situation is that recognizing our true nature is like seeing our own eyes. Our eyes see everything except themselves. This is an important metaphor,

---

[86] His Holiness the Dalai Lama, *Dzogchen: The Heart Essence of the Great Perfection*, Snow Lion Publications, 2000, p.111.

because it indicates that our intrinsic and pristine awareness must look at itself for the recognition to occur, for us to awaken to our perfect nature. We cannot recognize rigpa from within the trap of the self. We cannot recognize rigpa with the dualistic mind. We must turn our intrinsic awareness on itself. This is what we call meditation. This is also why love, compassion, kindness and joy are seen as the true signs of accomplishment, proof of deep practice, because they are the outflowing of our having recognized our true nature.

The bardos are moments in which the ultimate nature, the Buddha Nature, naturally manifests, without effort, without meditation in fact. The bardo teachings give us the ability to recognize that nature as those interval moments unfold. This is what makes these teachings essential. The duration for which the Buddha Nature is revealed in these moments is incredibly brief in all the bardos except the Bardo of Dying. The finger-snap speed with which most of the bardos are revealed and then obscured again by the dualistic mind is an obstacle to recognizing what is happening, to seeing the true nature of mind. It just passes by like a flash. A further problem is that even though rigpa is revealed in these brief moments, we do not recognize it as we have not fully experienced the true nature of our minds before. Thus the opportunity to awaken to our Buddha potential passes as quickly as it comes. In the Bardo of Dying the duration for which the true nature is revealed is longer, rather than micro-seconds it is perhaps minutes. This makes the Bardo of Dying a supreme opportunity. The great Kagyu lineage-holder Jamgon Kongtrul Rinpoche explains this in detail when he writes:

The intermediate state between death and rebirth is an excellent time to recognize *tathagatagarbha*. While we are alive, it takes some effort to experience our true nature, but during the bardo state between death and rebirth we experience it naturally. The only question is whether we recognize it. It is not something we need to search for; in fact, Buddha essence is so close that we fail to recognize it. If we have trained ourselves in daily life, then there is a greater chance that we will become liberated at the moment of death, when Buddha essence naturally manifests. That is why the bardo state presents an extraordinary method of practice.[87]

We can increase our chances of recognizing the true nature of mind (rigpa) in the after-death bardos by training in that recognition now. It is in our best interest to understand what we are experiencing in the bardos of our present life, dreams and meditation and to increase the duration of them. We can understand what we are experiencing in these moments through the bardo teachings themselves. This is quite simple – it just requires receiving the teaching and reflecting on it. This is what this book does. We can increase the duration of the bardos, even the Bardo of Dying, with the simple practice of meditation. That is ultimately all we need, just a consistent meditation practice. The other bardo practices, such as Dream Yoga and Phowa are back-ups and extra support.

Phowa – The Transference of Consciousness

The bardo teachings often include discussion of what is called 'the practice of transference' or *Phowa* in Tibetan. The standard method that most tantric Buddhists use to make the most of the opportunity for liberation in the bardos is the practice of Phowa in the Bardo of Dying. Phowa is said to enable the transference of consciousness (or the mindstream) at the time of death. Phowa relies on visualizations of tantric deities and of the tantric conception of the energetic structure of our bodies. This structure includes energy (chi), called "lung" in Tibetan, channels (meridians), chakras and essences. The transference is effected by visualizing one's consciousness ejecting out of the crown chakra at the top of the skull, which is effected through forceful breathing and mantras. But transference to where? Generally, the practitioner

---

[87] See: 'Jamgon Kongtrul Rinpoche's Bardo Teachings', *Tricycle: The Buddhist Review*: https://tricycle.org/magazine/bardo-teachings/

transfers their mindstream to the pure land of Buddha Amitabha, known as *Dewachen* (Great Bliss). Although sometimes understood as a kind of heaven, the pure lands are mindstates rather than places or realms. As Kyabje Dudjom Rinpoche taught:

> If you want to establish the Buddhist teachings, establish them in your own mind. You will find Buddha within your own mind. If you are looking for a Pure Land, purify your own mind's perceptions. You will find the perfectly pure Buddha-field within yourself.[88]

In the state of Dewachen there is no suffering and no obstacles to practice and so the practitioner can achieve total enlightenment there, and from there choose to be reborn in a form and place that will benefit beings. As Lama Tharchin Rinpoche explains:

> The practice of phowa at the moment of death is the cause for a practitioner to be reborn into a pureland where there is the opportunity to complete the dharma path. If someone has not completed the two stages of the path, then phowa can carry them to liberation.[89]

According to Lama Tharchin Rinpoche there are a number of different types of Phowa. The first is the result of having the ability to rest permanently in the natural state (Dzogpachenpo). In this type of Phowa 'there is no need to wait for death in order to be liberated since the practitioner is already enlightened'.[90] The second type of Phowa is the 'realization of the inseparability of the creation and perfection states. With this realization, you can be liberated

---

[88] Dudjom Rinpoche, quoted in Khenpo Tsewang Dongyal, *Light of Fearless Indestructible Wisdom: The Life and Legacy* of His Holiness Dudjom Rinpoche, 2008, Shambhala Publications, p.191.

[89] Lama Tharchin Rinpoche, quoted in 'Two Levels of Practice, Four Types of Phowa, Dudjom Tersar Ngondro Program, Vajrayana Foundation, 2017, no page numbers: https://dudjomtersarngondro.com/2017/05/12/two-levels-of-practice-four-types-of-phowa/

[90] Ibid.

in the bardo'.[91] This is another way of saying that the practitioner or person has achieved some recognition of the true nature of mind and will be able to recognize that nature when it arises in the Bardo of Luminosity and achieve liberation. This second type of Phowa includes those who have accomplished Guru Yoga. If we have unshakeable, heart-felt devotion—such deep devotion that one's sense of self completely dissolves—then none of the projections of the bardos, none of the visions or appearances, will occur. As soon as we call on the guru the ground luminosity rises. This happens almost instantly. This is quite simply because the self is not there to project anything. There is no dualistic mind. It is only the dualistic mind that creates the experiences of the bardos. An accomplished Guru Yoga practitioner has merged completely with the guru, which means they have become one with the ground luminosity. This is the swiftest and safest journey through the bardos of all. Even if we have not fully accomplished Guru Yoga, if we are able to muster heart-felt devotion at the time of death we will still be able to avoid all of the pitfalls of the bardos. The third type of Phowa is the transference of consciousness into a pureland at the moment of death that we have already discussed. Lama Tharchin Rinpoche elucidates this form of Phowa when he teaches:

> With the phowa of the transference, three reference points are used. The first is the pureland of Amitabha called Dewachen, the second is our own consciousness as the traveler, and the third is the central channel as the path. Normally when you die, you exit through any of the nine doors leading to various types of rebirth into the lower realms. The exit through the central channel is the entrance into a pureland. Phowa seals the other doors which lead to rebirth in samsara. To accomplish the phowa practice, you must complete a seven-day retreat to receive the signs.[92]

---

[91] Ibid.

[92] Ibid.

As you can see by Lama Tharchin Rinpoche's description, the Phowa practice is part of the tantric system and relies on beliefs that are not necessarily part of the worldview or experience of non-Himalayan practitioners. As with all tantric practices, accomplishment relies on devotion for the meditational deities at the center of the practice.[93] For many of those born and raised in Buddhist cultures, this devotion is ingrained. For those born outside of Buddhist cultures, developing devotion for these deities requires layering a whole complex of beliefs and conceptual ideas on top of their existing belief system. This is at best difficult, often ineffective and at worst impossible. It is also unnecessary.

Ultimately the true nature of these deities, these conceptual constructs, is Shunyata. The ultimate view of meditational deities (*yidams* in Tibetan) is that they are conceptualizations of otherwise inconceivable wisdom activity arising from the perfection of emptiness. They are visualizations standing in place of what we cannot comprehend with our ordinary, thinking mind. As it says in Padmasambhava's *Self-Liberation through Seeing with Naked Awareness*, the deities '*represent* the inherent luminous clarity of intrinsic awareness'.[94] The word "represent" is really crucial here. Deities represent something and they are secondary to that which they represent – perfect co-emergent wisdom and compassion or Shunyata. As Dudjom Rinpoche has taught:

> Without realization of profound emptiness, the view that samsara and enlightenment are no other than your own perception, your reliance on any wisdom deity, grasping it as solid and real, will only cause you to become rudra.[95]

---

[93] See Mingyur Rinpoche, 'Guru Yoga and Yidam Practice' in Marcia Binder Schmidt (2004) *Dzogchen Essentials: The Path that Clarifies Confusion*, Rangjung Yeshe Publications, pp. 139 – 141.

[94] Padmasambhava, *Self-Liberation through Seeing with Naked Awareness*, translated by John Myrdhin Reynolds, Snow Lion, 2000, p. 9. Emphasis added.

[95] Dudjom Rinpoche, *Wisdom Nectar: Dudjom Rinpoche's Heart Advice*, Snow Lion, 2005, p. 87.

This means that if we reify the meditational deities we will become rudras, which is a kind of demon whose principle fault is the belief in itself as inherently real. Reification means to think of something that is insubstantial or abstract as substantial or concrete, to think of an illusion or projection as real. If something as fundamental to our existence as our own sense of self is insubstantial, illusory and lacking inherent existence then how can anything else be inherently real?

In other words, belief in the deities as inherently real will prevent us from recognizing that our own sense of self, the heart of the dualistic mind, is utterly false. Without that recognition there is no enlightenment. Dudjom Lingpa (1835 – 1904), the founder of the lineage I hold most dear, made this very clear when he wrote:

> Some will hold that the deities and pure realms exist in their own right, and so even though they engage in sadhana practice they will not awaken to Buddhahood.[96]

Just to drive this point home, Tsongkhapa (1357–1419), the revered founder of the Gelugpa tradition, made it clear that deity yoga will not be effective until we have come close to realizing the empty nature of self and all phenomena.[97] Realization of emptiness, and the realization of non-self in particular, is an exceedingly rare accomplishment. It takes a lifetime of meditation. According to Tsongkhapa this means that almost all of those practicing deity yoga today will not accomplish it in their lifetimes. They will not find enlightenment through that practice. This is yet another reason to turn to bardo practice and Guru Yoga, which lead to realization of non-self (anatta) quicker than anything else.

The swiftest and most profound way to awaken the inconceivable wisdom activity that the meditational deities represent is to use these yidams as objects

---

[96] Dudjom Lingpa, *Buddhahood Without Meditation: A Visionary Account Known as Refining One's Perception*, translated by Richard Barron, Padma Publishing, 2002, p. 139.

[97] Tsongkhapa, *A Lamp to Illuminate the Five Stages: Teachings on Guhyasamaja Tantra*, translated by Gavin Kilty, Simon and Schuster, 2012, p. 98

of devotion.[98] As already noted, without devotion for the meditational deities, tantra does not work. There is no point chanting Om Mani Padme Hum, the mantra of compassion, if there is no devotion for Avalokiteshvara, the bodhisattva of compassion. There is no point practicing any tantric ritual if devotion is not at the heart of it. For many modern practitioners, particularly Westerners, developing devotion for these untouchable, unseen and ultimately illusory meditational deities first requires adopting a whole new culture (that of the Himalayan region). Even if we do manage to do that, developing true devotion for yidams is especially difficult because we must also never lose sight of the fact that the deities are empty in nature. For everyone, Westerners and Tibetans alike, the ability to generate true devotion for an empty deity is exceedingly rare. We may generate devotion, but it is wasted when we forget the deities' empty nature, or we may remember the deities' empty nature but fail to develop true, heart-felt devotion. If it is possible at all, it takes many years. Years that we do not necessarily have given that many of us in the West enter the Dharma late in life and there is no guarantee we have enough time left to learn to quiet the mind and truly rest and uncover our true nature, which is what is most important.

If we do engage in yidam practice we need to believe that yidams are as real as we believe ourselves to be, without falling into the trap of believing in either ourselves or the yidams as innately real. Neither the yidams nor ourselves are inherently existing. Neither we nor the yidams are solid or permanent. Neither are distinctly individual or separate entities. Both are deeply interconnected with all other things, especially the mind. Both the self and the yidam arise from fundamental awareness. It is also their nature to inevitably dissolve back into that awareness. Yidam practice depends on a perfect balance between devotion and the view of Shunyata. Guru Yoga, on the other hand, is one of the only reliable and effective methods for getting

---

[98] See Mingyur Rinpoche, 'Guru Yoga and Yidam Practice' in Marcia Binder Schmidt (2004) *Dzogchen Essentials: The Path that Clarifies Confusion*, Rangjung Yeshe Publications, pp. 139 – 141.

the balance between devotion and Shunyata right, because it works directly on undoing our sense of ourselves as separately existing entities. Even if we have mistrust of authority figures and fear being abused, it is still much easier to develop devotion for a living teacher because they are much more tangible, much more approachable and, on the relative level at least, seem much more real. Of course, if we feel a natural devotion for yidams, specifically Amitabha, then all well and good, the formal tantric Phowa practice will work for us. The point is there are other methods that are quicker, more "natural" for the modern mindset and might be a better fit for the way our minds are right now.

As an interesting and ironic aside – Guru Yoga practitioners will often experience spontaneous visions of yidams accompanied by feelings of deep devotion. A practitioner friend of mine who had no time for yidam practice, seeing it as superstitious Tibetanism, but who was however a devout disciple of his teacher and practiced Guru Yoga every day, began to spontaneously have visions of and "visitations" from yidams, principally Tara and Vajrayogini. That person now has a new found respect for yidam practice and devotion for all yidams, which are, after all, manifestations of enlightened mind that take form because that is the only way we deluded beings can relate to such profound, non-conceptual wisdom. The reason that these experiences arose for my skeptical friend is because the practice of Guru Yoga leads to all the realizations of yidam or generation and completion stage practice. Devotion is a one stop shop for awakening irrespective of what we believe or don't believe, what practices we are drawn to or are averse to, or what culture or faith tradition we're from. The same can be said for truly selfless compassion and love.

In the end, the bardos transcend all cultures and religions. They are not Tibetan or Asian or Western. They are not Buddhist or Hindu or Christian. They are an aspect of reality. If the bardos are real (and in my experience they are) then any person of any background and any belief system should have the same basic experience in the bardos and have the same opportunities for liberation. The bardos are the same for all of us, the only exception being the Bardo of Becoming, in which visions arise based on the person's belief system. The experiences we have in the after-death bardos are all projections of our dualistic minds which are completely imbued with our cultural and religious beliefs. Thus, when a Buddhist enters the Bardo of Becoming they will experience visions of Buddhas, a Christian on the other hand might experience visions of Christ, angels or saints. The bardo teachings tell us that everyone will experience the bardos in a specific order, but also make it clear that the experiences or visions that individuals have will be different based on their karma, belief system, culture and lived experience. In fact, the essence of bardo practice does not require any kind of belief system. This is why in the Dzogchen tradition the word "phowa" has a different meaning. As Khenpos Pema Sherab and Tsewang Dongyal note:

> The highest form is known as the phowa of the Dharmakaya which is meditation on the great perfection. When you do Dzogchen meditation, there's no need to transfer anything, because there's nothing to transfer, no place to transfer it, nor anyone to do it. That's the highest, and greatest phowa practice.[99]

Dzogchen meditation is, in essence, nothing more than simple silent sitting with a relaxed attitude, an openness to whatever happens, and a focus on awareness itself. This highlights the centrality of meditation rather than complex tantric practices and recognition of the truth based on personal meditational experience rather than belief in conceptual ideas that will fade away when we reach enlightenment anyway. It also highlights the centrality

---

[99] Khenchen Palden Sherab and Khenpo Tsewang Dongyal (2000) *A Modern Commentary on Karma Lingpa's Zhi-Khro: teachings on the peaceful and wrathful deities.* Padma Gochen Ling. Source: Archived (accessed: December 27, 2007).

of the Bardo of Luminosity to all bardo practice. In recognizing the true nature as it dawns in the Bardo of Luminosity after death we achieve total liberation without the need for transference to a pureland. If we do not trust that we will practice diligently in this lifetime to recognize the true nature of mind, to recognize rigpa, then we should have a safety net. Phowa is one such safety net. Guru Yoga is the other. In fact, there is a version of Phowa without visualizations or breathing exercises. Below is a very brief stanza from the Dudjom Tersar *ngondro*[100] or foundational practice, which is a form of Phowa or transference without elaborate visualizations or breathing techniques. Instead, this Phowa relies on devotion and the blessings of the Buddhas and is a form of Guru Yoga that also leads to the accomplishment of transference:

> *I pray to the protector Amitabha, the Buddha of Limitless Light,*
> *By your blessings may I accomplish the profound path of phowa.*[101]

---

[100] Ngondro is a set of practices that are considered essential foundations on the tantric Buddhist path. They are: Refuge, Bodhicitta, Mandala Offering, Vajrasattva, and Guru Yoga. Generally students accumulate one hundred thousand repetitions of each practice. Bardo practice does not require ngondro as an accumulation. It should be noted that ngondro can be approached as a lifelong daily practice rather than a preliminary accumulation.

[101] The full ngondro text can be found here: https://www.lotsawahouse.org/tibetan-masters/ dudjom-rinpoche/dudjom-tersar-ngondro

CHAPTER SIX

CONDUCT, KARMA AND MERIT

Karma is completely dynamic and flexible, not unchanging or deterministic at all.

Though Buddha Nature cannot be defiled or diminished it becomes obscured when we engage in negative or harmful activity and accumulate negative karma. Karma is the habit of the mind. If our mind's habits are negative, then this prevents us from recognizing our Buddha Nature, simply because our focus is on the very imperfect quality of the dualistic mind and we are mired in its negative reactions. Let me just make that a little clearer: although our true nature is pristine and cannot be diminished behaving unethically, especially harming others, prevents us from recognizing that true, pristine nature and thus harmful behavior blocks our awakening.

We are all the heirs of our own karma. If we make our minds a home for anger and hate what do we think will be the result? Firstly, we ourselves will suffer, because anger and hate are unpleasant states, they make us miserable. Secondly, other people will become averse to us and perhaps hate us back. No-one wants to be friends with an angry or hateful person, except perhaps for other hateful and angry people. No-one loves or trusts a hateful person. Thirdly, our anger will lead us to harm others. In the end, we will be surrounded by our own hate and the hate of others. Our world will be constricted, fearful and miserable.

If we make our minds a home for blame and never take responsibility for our own actions what do we think will happen? Firstly, we will always feel powerless because we have abdicated our power to others. To feel powerless is to feel miserable and afraid. Secondly, we will feel more and more slighted until we lose all capacity for self-determination. We will trust no-one and no-one will trust or respect us either because we are too quick to blame and point the finger. Thirdly, our judgement and blame will lead us to harm others. Our world will be constricted, oppressive and miserable.

If we allow our minds to fill with greed, what do we think will happen? Firstly, we will never feel that we have enough, we will always be wanting and never feel satisfied. That is suffering. Secondly, people will see us as shallow, selfish and uncaring and everything we say or do will be interpreted as being motivated by selfishness, even when it isn't. Only those equally greedy and selfish will be able to tolerate us. Thirdly, our greed and desire will lead us to harm others. Our world will be constricted, impoverished and miserable.

If we make our minds a home to kindness and compassion, what do we think will happen? Firstly, we will feel happy because kindness and compassion are pleasant states. Kindness is not suffering. Secondly, those who appreciate kindness and compassion and have capacity for it will be drawn to us. We will be liked, loved and respected. Thirdly, our kindness and compassion will prevent us from harming others. Our world will be open, positive and joyous.

Most importantly, when we cultivate compassion and kindness our minds will have the capacity to benefit others. This capacity is what we call *merit*. Merit is not a *thing* you can hold in your hand, nor is it something supernatural stored in some magical bank account. It is a positive *quality of mind* that manifests as a desire and ability to help others and to practice Dharma. Merit is a capacity that enables us to practice compassion, to practice meditation, and to recognize our true nature. This capacity removes obstacles, quite simply because the obstacles to being compassionate, to meditative ability and to recognizing our true empty nature are almost completely of the mind. Merit, or wholesomeness of mind, removes the ego-clinging, selfishness and ignorance that obscures our true nature and frustrates our spiritual growth. Merit is a quality of mind that is compassionate, generous, patient, disciplined, ethical and focused. A mind with merit does not cling to itself, so it recognizes emptiness and is open and spacious. Merit is also the outer effects of this quality of mind – the positive reactions others have to us because we are compassionate, the respect we are shown because we are ethical and committed to the welfare of all sentient beings, the generosity others show us out of respect for our kindness and our focus on spiritual practice, the support we are given to practice Dharma because we have proven ourselves to be sincere.

In the traditional Buddhist teachings there are two Sanskrit words used for merit: *punya* and *kusala*. Kusala refers to the ethically positive or wholesome quality of the mind or of actions. Punya refers to the resulting effects or experiences we have as a consequence of cultivating an ethical or wholesome mind. Oftentimes we Buddhists focus on the worldly benefits of punya, on trying to cultivate "virtue" purely to receive these material benefits. This is contrary to the heart of Buddhist practice, which is to practice with no expectation for worldly benefit but for the sake of enlightenment only. This is why the Buddha himself said: 'even a skerrick of merit [punya] is no use to me'.[102] The focus should always be on a wholesomeness or openness of mind (kusala) that gives the capacity for deeper practice and deeper kindness.

In most Buddhist traditions the principal methods for "making" merit, for changing the conditions of the mind so that they are more conducive to meditation or practice, is through four main practices:

---

[102] Padhāna Sutta.

1. Creating or commissioning sacred images and stupas;

2. Generosity to Dharma institutions, monastics and and teachers;

3. Elaborate offering rituals which in the Vajrayana tradition are called ganachakra pujas or tsok (ritual offering of food and taboo substances).

4. Adhering to the basic Buddhist precepts (non-harm etc.)

All of the above are underpinned by the Buddhist view of co-emergent emptiness (Shunyata) and compassion. In all Buddhist traditions, from Sutrayana to Mahayana and Dzogchen, the foundation of the above practices is the application of certain attitudes to every aspect of our daily lives. These attitudes are known as the *Six Paramitas*. The paramitas are the primary method for making our minds conducive to practice. In other words, the mind is made conducive for practice by living in a more thoughtful, generous, kind and ethical way. The Six Paramitas are generally translated as generosity, ethics (or discipline), patience, joyful effort (or diligence), meditative concentration (or mindfulness), and wisdom. The first five paramitas are both attitudes we can adopt and enlightened qualities of the heart that are already present beneath the adventitious obstacles of the dualistic mind (our negative emotions, thoughts and feelings). The sixth is our fundamental nature and the awakened state. The application of the paramitas are also underpinned by the Buddhist view of co-emergent emptiness and compassion.

These quite diverse ways of making the mind conducive to practice, generosity, keeping precepts, offering rituals and transformative attitudes, are all equally good. We can engage with all, some or just one. We need to engage with the method or methods that inspire us and that actually work for us. We are the only ones who can determine which method changes our mind and supports us to practice in significant and observable ways. No-one else can determine that for us. As for me, I have found that the application of the paramitas has a swift and observable positive effect.

The paramitas are understood and applied differently depending on the tradition or vehicle in which they are taught. In the Sutra vehicle the paramitas are applied through renouncing their opposites, so the paramita of generosity on a Sutra level is renouncing miserliness. In the Mahayana vehicle we actively develop the paramitas. So on that level we practice applying patience when we are angry. In the tantric vehicle we use visualization and other methods to transform the negative emotion into its opposite, so mindlessness becomes mindfulness (or meditative concentration). The Dzogchen approach to the paramitas is to allow the negative thoughts and emotions to dissolve naturally (self-liberate) by simply looking into their empty nature. When the adventitious thoughts and emotions dissolve their true aspect is revealed. Their true nature is co-emergent wisdom and compassion. Until we have the capacity to look into negative emotions and allow them to self-liberate we must apply the paramitas according to the other vehicles, whichever tradition works for us. The capacity to be able to look into adventitious thoughts and emotions and allow them to self-liberate comes in only one way – through practice, specifically the bardo practices and primarily meditation.

This shows that in every Buddhist tradition and on every level of practice the paramitas are very important, they are just understood and applied differently. Ethics are always central to Buddhist practice. We quite simply are not Buddhists if we don't abide by the fundamental ethical precepts of Buddhism, which includes to do no harm to any living being and to avoid deception, greed, drunkenness and unchecked desire (more on this in Chapter Fifteen).

As with merit, karma is not a mysterious force that operates on some magical level and only in the hereafter. It is instantaneous and completely straightforward and obvious. It is right here and right now. It is worth noting that not all Buddhists believe the same things about karma. There is no single authoritative position on it. For example, Navayana Buddhists, who make up the greater majority of Buddhists in India, do not believe in inherited karma. That is, they do not believe that karma is transferred from our current life to any future one. The founder of Navayana Buddhism, Bhimrao Ramji Ambedkar, writes:

> According to science, a child inherits the characteristics of his parents. In the Hindu doctrine of karma, a child inherits nothing from its parents except the body. The past karma in the Hindu doctrine is the inheritance of the child by the child and for the child. The parents contributes nothing. The child brings everything. Such a doctrine is nothing short of an absurdity ... the Buddha did not believe in such an absurdity.[103]

What Ambedkar is saying is that the notion of karma being inherited from a previous life and being completely deterministic is a Hindu idea rejected by the Buddha. This view of karma is controversial for many Buddhists but it demonstrates the diversity of views around core Buddhist ideas. Most Buddhists, including myself, accept that karma does in fact flow from one life to another. My discussion of rebirth in Chapter Four describes how this works. There is however some significant differences among Buddhist traditions and philosophers about the degree to which karma determines our lives, including our potential for enlightenment in a particular life.

One alternative view of karma is that held by some practitioners of Dzogchen, which posits that the true nature of mind cannot be stained, blocked or diminished by any activity in the here and now let alone in some past life. This view suggests that our karma cannot prevent or forestall our enlightenment, no matter how "bad" it is. According to this understanding of karma our Dharma practice has the power to free us in this very life irrespective of our karma. This is a very affirming view. In some Dzogchen

---

[103] Ambedkar, Bhimrao R. Pritchett, Frances W. (ed.). *The Buddha and his Dhamma.* New York, NY: Columbia University Press, 1984, p. 341.

texts, as with some early sutras, karma is understood as merely the changeable habits of our mind, not as some metaphysical storehouse that completely determines every aspect of our lives. These texts present karma as completely workable and not completely deterministic.

What many Buddhists fail to realize is that this is what the Buddha believed as well. The Buddha did not see karma as deterministic and stated that not everything that happens to us is due to karma. For example, he was clear in the *Samyutta Nikaya* that the cause of physical illness and other negative life events might not be due to karma at all.[104] As Bhikkhu Analayo notes, the Buddha taught that:

> … what one experiences now is the fruition not just of past karma in the sense of one's past deeds, but also factors like bodily disorders, change of climate, or external violence.[105]

In other words, the Buddha never believed that there was only one cause for all the things that happen but rather that there were multiple causes for everything. Karma is only one factor in how our experience unfolds. The Buddha also rejected the notion that all karmic seeds necessarily ripen. He used the metaphor of seeds sown in a field. Every farmer knows that not all seeds germinate because sometimes the conditions are not right. The Buddha acknowledged that the conditions may never be right. Furthermore, no matter what our karma might be it is not fixed. Our lives are not at all completely determined. We can change things. Karma is dynamic. As Traleg Kyabgon Rinpoche notes:

> … two of Buddha's principal assertions on karma are that we are personally responsible for our actions in life and that the consequences

---

[104] Traleg Kyabgon Rinpoche, *Karma: What It Is, What It Isn't, Why It Matters*, Shambhala Publications, 2015, p. 49.

[105] Bhikkhu Analayo, *Rebirth in Early Buddhism and Current Research*, Wisdom Publications, 2018, no page, Kindle edition.

of these actions are not fixed. Even if we were to do evil deeds, we are not necessarily condemned …. We can make reparations at the point of death.[106]

The notion that we can make reparations at the point of death is crucial, and it is why the Bardo of Dying is seen as a supreme opportunity. As Mingyur Rinpoche notes with regard to the opportunity for total liberation at the time of death:

… at the time of dying, this pure awareness happens on its own, and the habits of past conditioning no longer have the force to rush in and obscure it. This happens naturally to everyone. It's as certain to happen as death itself.[107]

We've already discussed the fact that we can radically transform our minds in the final moments of life. Why, then, do so many of us believe that our lives and deaths are predetermined by karma? The view of karma that many Buddhists hold today is actually the Hindu view that seeped into Buddhism during the centuries when Buddhism and Hinduism were practiced side by side in the same homes by the same people. Tibetan Buddhism is a rich result of that cross-pollination, just as Chan is a result of the cross-pollination of Buddhism and Daoism and Zen is the result of cross-pollination between Buddhism and the Shinto faith. The Buddhism we practice in the West is understandably returning to the original form of the teachings and embracing the earlier views of rebirth and karma – which is that karma is mainly about the mind and perception and something more of the here and now than past or future lives.

---

[106] Traleg Kyabgon Rinpoche, *Karma: What It Is, What It Isn't, Why It Matters*, Shambhala Publications, 2015, p. 36.

[107] Yongey Mingyur Rinpoche with Helen Tworkov, *In Love With the World: A Monk's Journey Through the Bardos of Living and Dying*, Random House Publishing Group, 2021, no page. Kindle Edition.

The founder of my own lineage, the visionary and saint Dudjom Lingpa, made it abundantly clear that he adhered to this same view of karma when he asked 'where are the amassed effects of harmful actions? Where is their storehouse located?'[108] To answer this question for ourselves he suggests we: 'Examine the manner in which any harm could be done to the emptiness of mind, outwardly or inwardly, above, below, or in between'.[109] Here Dudjom Lingpa is suggesting that the truth of Shunyata means that each moment of mind, though the result or fruit of the previous moment of mind, is able to change fundamentally and is not determined to stay the same because of past karmic debts. It is what it is but it isn't that in any essential way. This apparently radical Buddhist statement about karma is actually not radical at all in the Dzogchen tradition, nor is it radical in the context of the early sutras. As we've already seen, Longchenpa, the great Dzogchen master and preeminent luminary of the Nyingma school, taught that our fundamental essence or rigpa (non-dual awareness) is free of karma. He writes about the true nature of mind: 'In its absence of karma there is no ripening of pleasure or pain' and asks 'What is karma and how can it mature? Contemplate the reality that is like the clear sky!'[110]

This is not to say that there is no cause and effect, nor that the quality of our minds does not have any bearing on our experience right now, or our experience in the Bardos of Dying and Becoming and thus our experience in any future lives. Dudjom Lingpa and Longchenpa are not saying that karma is inconsequential or that it has no impact on the quality of our lives. It certainly does. What Dudjom Lingpa and Longchenpa are trying to teach us

---

[108] *The Vajra Essence: Dudjom Lingpa's Visions of the Great Perfection Volume 3,* translated by B. Alan Wallace, Wisdom Publications, Kindle Edition, no page number.

[109] *The Vajra Essence: Dudjom Lingpa's Visions of the Great Perfection Volume 3,* translated by B. Alan Wallace, Wisdom Publications, no page number, Kindle Edition.

[110] Longchenpa, *Natural Perfection: Longchenpa's Radical Dzogchen,* translated by Keith Dowman, Wisdom Publications, 2012, no page numbers, Kindle Edition.

is that karma has no impact on our true nature. Our true nature is beyond the vagaries of karma. Buddha Nature cannot be dimmed, tarnished or in any way diminished by karma. This is why it is so deeply important to recognize and abide in that nature. If we don't, then our minds and lives will be destroyed by the adventitious emotions that arise due to our karma and our fixation on worldly concerns.

If our mind is a home for hate, hate will be all we know. If our mind is a home for selfishness and greed, then that will be our inheritance. If our mind is a home for blame and judgement, that too is all we will know, we will always feel victimized. In contrast, if we make our minds a home for kindness and compassion, then our world will be kind and loving. It is very simple. The habits of our mind dictate who we are as well as our experience of the world and others. It also dictates the habits of any future moments of mind, both in this life and the next.

This means we have to stop blaming others, including our past lives, for our negative habitual tendencies. Our anger and hatred, our greed and selfishness, these are ours and ours alone. We have sole ownership of them. We have to stop thinking that everything that happens to us is someone else's fault. We need to recognize that anger and greed are destructive. We need to take responsibility for our life and actions. We have to be honest about the current state of our mind and work hard to change it. We have to live simply, ethically and frugally. We cannot consider ourselves true practitioners if we have not mastered our negative thoughts and behaviors. Certainly, we are not ready for so-called higher practices if we do not understand the need for ethics and the prime importance of overcoming our self-cherishing. Dilgo Khyentse Rinpoche once said:

> How will you tame your ego if you think, "There is no good in virtue; nothing wrong with sin; there is no need to accumulate merit; there is no point in purifying myself. I just have to keep my mouth shut and

look at the sky." Even though your mouth is full of profound words about emptiness, if your mind is filled with grasping at solid reality, with attachment and aversion, you are deceiving yourself...[111]

Here Dilgo Khyentse Rinpoche is referring to the Dzogchen practice of sky-gazing and making it quite clear that we cannot truly practice Dzogchen if we do not tame our ego, if we do not live ethically and kindly, if we still see the world and ourselves as somehow solid, substantial and lasting and if our self-cherishing and the attachment and aversion it causes is unchecked. Remember, the word "merit" here is not referring to some storehouse of positive energy, but to a capability of mind, a mind that is motivated and enthusiastic for practice for the sake of others, and virtue is not some magical substance but simply a wholesomeness of mind, a mind infused with love, compassion and joy, a mind that has emerged as a direct result of our renunciation and our practice.

Clearly then, we must always refrain from acting selfishly and from harming others. Furthermore, where we see hate, selfishness and injustice in the world, we must call it out, but without making it personal and with a gentle voice and a compassionate intention, and with no expectation for a particular outcome. We need to interact with others without judgement and blame and we need to tame our mind with meditation. When we change the quality of our mind the world will change with it. Then not only will the world be a much better, kinder place, but we will be content and relaxed. We will also be able to recognize our true nature. If we do not recognize our true nature, we cannot awaken in enlightenment. So there is a direct correlation between our karma (our mind's habits), our conduct and our ability to awaken.

The fundamental thing to keep in mind about karma is this: Karma is in the mind and only in the mind. It is the mind's habitual tendencies and nothing

---

[111] Dilgo Khyentse Rinpoche, *Pith Instructions: Selected Teachings and Poems*, Shambhala Publications, 2015, no page, Kindle Edition.

more than that. Karma is literally the things we think and the emotions we feel and what they drive us to do. It is how we experience and interpret our world. This is why the most powerful methods for transforming karma are focused on the mind, not on performing outer "virtuous" actions or behaviors, though those are important too. The methods the Buddha taught for transforming karma are clearly spelt out in the early sutras. They are:

- Shamata and vipashana meditation for working with the mind and karma directly;

- A correct understanding of the nature of reality (impermanence, Anatta or "non-self" and Shunyata) so that the meditation leads inevitably to recognition of the natural state;

- Living ethically by keeping the five foundational (refuge) precepts and thus taming our behavior.

The Buddha considered these methods sufficient for the job. He said clearly there was no method or secret teaching he had held back.[112] These were the methods he felt we needed. These and only these. Therefore, these methods should be the bedrock of our practice. Anything else we engage with should be seen as supplemental to this foundation, except for devotion and compassion, which are also essential. Why am I saying that devotion and compassion are essential when the early sutras don't seem to mention them all that much? Because the Buddha's journey to enlightenment was motivated by deep compassion, that is very clear, and all the early disciples who achieved liberation showed boundless devotion for the Buddha. Every single sutra evidences this. I think therefore it's clear that compassion and devotion are fundamental to the Buddhist path.

To close this discussion of conduct, karma and merit, I want to make clear that I am not advocating any particular view on karma, merit or any other

---

[112] See Digha Nikaya 16

Buddhist tenet, merely encouraging an openness to and respect for a diversity of ideas and beliefs. Rather than rely on what others say about these things each of us needs to find the truth through practice, through meditation supported by contemplation of the fundamentals. Dogmatism is one of the surest and quickest ways to stifle compassion and kindness. More to the point, equanimity towards all things, including concepts, theories and beliefs, is the greatest conduct.

I am certainly not suggesting that we should not take care to avoid thinking and acting in ways that harm others nor that our actions do not shape our present and our future. I'm saying quite the opposite – if we allow our minds to become habituated with negativity, anger and hatred, all hope for our liberation is lost. That being said, we should not engage in meritorious deeds for the sake of some future life or to clear out some storehouse of karma in order to make our lives better (this one or any future ones). That is a form of spiritual materialism and it is a distraction from true practice. We should act ethically, kindly and with compassion for no reason other than to benefit others. It should not be about us at all. Besides, whether or not we subscribe to a traditional or radical theory of rebirth or karma will have little impact on our potential for enlightenment.

CHAPTER SEVEN

THE BARDO OF LUMINOSITY

Luminous awareness is the absolute nature of absolutely everything.

Because there is nothing more important than achieving enlightenment for the sake of all sentient beings, our discussion of the bardos of living, meditation and dying will focus on how the Bardo of Luminosity manifests within them.

The Bardo of Luminosity is the bardo through which enlightenment in this very life is possible. This bardo is interesting because it appears throughout our lives and also when we are dying. If you remember the other five bardos from the beginning of this book, they are *living, dreaming, meditation, dying* and *becoming*. The Bardo of Luminosity actually appears vividly in all of these except the Bardo of Becoming, which is the process of rebirth. In the Bardo of Becoming the luminosity manifests as all manner of appearances and visions and is thus quite obscured. If you don't believe in rebirth then we don't have a problem here because we can still talk about the Bardo of Luminosity in the context of living, dreaming, meditation and dying.

So, what is this luminosity? In the bardo teachings the fundamental nature of everything, including our minds, is called the Ground Luminosity or Mother Luminosity. This is what the yogi Shabkar described as 'luminous emptiness'. The Mother Luminosity is the ground or source of both samsara and nirvana, both suffering and liberation from suffering. Mother Luminosity is the true nature of all things, including the mind. It is the natural state, the enlightened essence of all sentient beings. It is the Great Perfection or Dzogpachenpo – the self-perfected natural state. This luminosity pervades our whole experience, although we do not recognize or notice it. It is obscured by dualistic thinking and feeling, or, rather, it is obscured by our focus on and self-identification with thoughts, feelings and physical sensations. For those who have recognized the true nature of mind and are resting in rigpa, this luminosity dawns as an actual experience of light, or rather an experience of vast spaciousness pervaded by light. For those of us still trapped in our self-identification with dualistic mind, this luminosity is masked as mental activity. That is, it is the inherent nature or ground of the thoughts, feelings, emotions and sensations that arise in the dualistic mind. In the moment of death the Ground or Mother Luminosity dawns naturally, unmasked, providing an opportunity for total liberation, but only if the dying person has learned how to recognize it. In our everyday life there are many opportunities for training in that recognition, moments or micro-bardos in which the ground luminosity also dawns naturally. Given that, we'll now discuss the Bardo of Living.

Luminosity in the Natural Bardo of This Life

Before we proceed, I just want to make it clear that this way of talking about the Bardo of Luminosity is not exactly traditional. It's not utterly radical either, just a little bit unusual. It is based on the teachings I've received but mostly on my own experiential understanding. That being said, the bardo teachings are already diverse. There is already more than one way to think about bardos. The bardo teachings themselves note that each individual's experience of the transitional states will be different based on things like their social and cultural conditioning, compulsive habits, karma and, importantly, Dharma practice. As Dzogchen Ponlop Rinpoche notes:

It is important to understand … that not everyone has exactly the same experiences. Although we all undergo these dissolutions [of the sense faculties], each of us experiences the process in a slightly different way.[113]

In this bardo we call life, which is between our last existence and our next one, there are a number of gateways to the Bardo of Luminosity and to Buddha Nature or rigpa. Certain subtler levels of mind or bardo manifest during uncontrolled physical processes such as: fainting, going to sleep, ending a dream, experiencing orgasm, sneezing, being emotionally overcome, being startled or awe-struck and, importantly, moments of deep devotion. In each of these experiences the dualistic mind stutters to a halt for a moment and the mind of clear light, or rigpa, is revealed. The pause or gap is usually mere micro-seconds, but even so, those gaps provide a way to enter the Bardo of Luminosity, to recognize the nature of mind.

As these gateways are opportunities, does that mean we should pursue them? The last two (sneezing and being startled) are out of our control. Fainting is also out of our control and is unpleasant and risky. Obviously there is no "fainting yoga", "sneezing yoga" or "getting the bejesus scared out of us yoga". It's not a good idea to take up fainting or sneezing as a spiritual practice. Can you imagine? As for dreaming, most of us have little or no control over that either. We can certainly get some control over it but it takes a great deal of effort and practice over many years. That one is worth pursuing if we have the time, energy and the inclination. In Vajrayana the practice associated with the Bardo of Dreaming, with using sleep and dreams to recognize the true nature of mind, is called *Dream Yoga*. Tulku Thondup Rinpoche explains the benefits of Dream Yoga when he writes:

You should … try to see and feel this life as a bardo experience, to see and feel that it is unreal, just like a dream fabricated by your mind. This

---

[113] Dzogchen Ponlop, *Mind Beyond Death*, Shambhala Publications, 2008, p.141.

will help you loosen the grip of your grasping and craving for this life. In this way, when the dying and after-death bardo experiences come upon you, you will be able to see them as dreams, and will find them familiar and handle them with ease. For when you recognize dreams as dreams, the impact of nightmares becomes ineffective.[114]

The form of Dream Yoga associated with higher tantric practice comes with some risks, namely ongoing sleep deprivation as it requires the practitioner to not fall deeply asleep. It also involves sometimes complex visualizations that can take a long time to perfect and seem "foreign" to some non-Himalayans. It requires sleep postures that feel unnatural to many and lead to restlessness and more insomnia. This form of Dream Yoga requires formal empowerment and extensive teaching from a qualified Vajra Master, which is only given after extensive preliminaries have been completed. There is, however, a form of Dream Yoga that is much simpler and can be done by everyone, beginners or more experienced practitioners. I will outline this practice later (in the *Practicing Dream Yoga* chapter).

There is also a yoga associated with the subtle mind states provoked by orgasm. This is called *Karma Mudra* or Bliss Yoga. This also takes a great deal of effort and practice over many years. Most of us have too much attachment to pleasure for it to be effective. Bliss Yoga only works for those with deep renunciation, with no desire for or attachment to pleasure, with no attachment to the self. Karma Mudra cannot be practiced while one still identifies with physical sensations. For those of us who are still attracted to pleasure and still closely identify with sensations, this practice can become a trap. It can lead to a reinforcement of the ego, a deepening of our identification with thoughts, feelings and sensations, rather than the dissolution of it. It can also lead to deeper attachment to the physical body and the material world. This is not

---

[114] Tulku Thondup, *Enlightened Journey: Buddhist Practice as Daily Life*, Edited by Harold Talbott, Shambhala Publications, 1995, p. 55.

at all what we want. That being said, it is a powerful practice for those able to do it.

The Karma Mudra practice aims at prolonging orgasm so that the resultant gap when the dualistic mind stutters to a halt, in the wake of the bliss, is much longer, providing an opportunity to shine awareness on itself. The focus of Karma Mudra practice is not the orgasm itself, but the stillness of mind afterwards. It also involves sometimes complex visualizations that can take years to perfect, difficult yogic exercises and physical restraint that can be physically uncomfortable or even painful. Karma Mudra is also somewhat masculinist and heterosexist. It is designed for male practitioners more than female ones and for opposite sex rather than same-sex relationships. It is based on concepts of the body having energy channels and centers (chakras) that are polarized according to biological sex. Theoretically, this practice as traditionally taught is not suitable for same-sex couples. Indeed, Chogyal Namkhai Norbu Rinpoche said this to me personally, whilst not going so far as to say that Karma Mudra was impossible for same-sex couples.[115] At the very least, the practice requires same-sex practitioners to engage in some cognitive calisthenics or re-imagining to make it Lesbian, Gay, Bisexual, Transgender and Intersex friendly.

It is important to note that both Karma Mudra and formal Dream Yoga are only effective with a solid foundation of thousands of hours of meditation. As becoming adept at Dream Yoga and Bliss Yoga can take years, and as our death is certain but the time of it unknown, my preference is for a practice that is easier and swifter than these two and that is the pre-requisite for them anyway. In my humble opinion, simple silent sitting practice (Shamata) is a much more accessible and effective practice for recognizing the nature of mind, which then enables us to recognize Mother Luminosity at the time

---

[115] Personal correspondence (email), 8th June 2005.

of death. Shamata is also a much more accessible and equitable practice for women and LGBTIQ+ people than the so-called higher practices such as Karma Mudra. This brings me neatly to the next bardo, that of meditation.

Luminosity in the Bardo of Meditation

This bardo, oftentimes called the Bardo of Samadhi, is the one we enter when we sit in meditation and the dualistic mind is tamed, settled and quiet. Meditation then is a bardo practice. Not only that, it is perhaps the most important bardo practice. The word "Samadhi" means "meditative absorption". According to Dudjom Rinpoche, Samadhi is the state of union with or absorption in ultimate reality or the natural state – with that luminous emptiness.[116] This bardo is 'the period of time we spend in meditative equipoise'[117]. Dudjom Rinpoche further describes the Bardo of Meditation in this way:

> It is called a bardo because it is not like our ordinary current of deluded thoughts, nor is it like phenomenal perception as experienced in the course of life. It is a period of meditative stability, a state of concentration as fresh and untarnished as the sky. It is like a motionless ocean in which there are no waves.[118]

Meditation is a gateway to the Bardo of Luminosity and to the mind of clear light or rigpa. We do not need elaborate "higher" practices such as Karma Mudra to recognize rigpa. All we need is simple meditation. I have said this hundreds if not thousands of times since I began sharing the Dharma with others a decade and a half ago – meditation teamed with compassion and/or devotion is the surest way to recognize the true nature of mind. As revered meditation master Garchen Rinpoche notes:

---

[116] Dudjom Rinpoche, *Counsels from my Heart*, Shambhala Publications, 2001, p. 63.

[117] Ibid

[118] Dudjom Rinpoche, *Counsels from my Heart*, Shambhala Publications, 2001, p. 63.

If you were to practice mindful awareness with great diligence for just a month, if you were to recognize even the slightest thought and not allow your mind to wander off into delusion for that time, even in such a short time you would witness great changes. Fierce afflictions would not faze you so much anymore, because you would have gained personal experience in observing the illusory play. There is in fact just one remedy necessary – mindful awareness. It is the single sufficient remedy that transforms difficulties inside and out.[119]

Furthermore, meditation is also the only practice shared by all forms of Buddhism, from Sutra and Mahayana to Tantra and Dzogchen. Though it does also require some effort, it does not involve complex visualizations or other taxing postures or restraint. It is also much quicker to accomplish, at least to the initial levels. Dudjom Lingpa is reported to have said that Calm Abiding (Shamata) can be accomplished in a mere three months of consistent and diligent practice (in a retreat setting). This is why we should put in every effort to establish a regular sitting practice. According to Jetsun Khandro Rinpoche, meditation is the essence of the entire Buddhist tradition:

> To understand the core essence of Buddha dharma, the only thing asked of you is to give yourself a break. Give yourself a break from thinking you have to do it, see it, achieve it, change it, or bring it to fruition. Give a break to the deep arrogance that assumes this world wouldn't know how to function without you … All the Buddhist teachings and methods come to this single point: Just sit still.[120]

Meditation is not just the foundation of Buddhist practice, it is the fundamental core of it. In meditation we uncover increasingly subtle mind states leading eventually to rigpa, the true nature of mind, the primordial awareness that is

---

[119] Teaching transcript, April 6, 2011. Translation by Ina Dhargye.

[120] See the full discussion by Jetsun Khandro Rinpoche on YouTube: https://youtu.be/sFAQUgdd828

not different to the Buddha mind. Jamyang Tenphel, drawing on the wisdom of his guru, the great Dzogchen master Togden Amtrin, frames the Bardo of Meditation as a "Bardo of Nowness":

> Time is a construct, it doesn't exist. Try to find the past, the future or the present. Try to find and hold a moment of time. Where *is* a moment of time to be found? It cannot be. There is only "nowness", which also cannot be found. This is the Bardo of Nowness. Rest here.[121]

This "Bardo of Nowness" points directly to emptiness and to the Bardo of Luminosity, to the true nature of mind and the true nature of all. The true nature of mind is boundless, beyond the limiting concepts of self and other, here and there, now and then. It has only one significant quality or characteristic – Bodhicitta. Bodhicitta is non-dual wisdom and limitless compassion. It is the non-dual realization of the vast spacious profundity that is emptiness unified with the realization of the profound interconnectedness of all beings that awakens unconditional love for all. It is the awakened mind, the ultimate nature, enlightenment.

Meditation not only uncovers these subtle mind states revealed in the bardos, it extends the duration of these states when they emerge naturally in daily life. This improves the likelihood of recognizing rigpa when these gateway moments occur, especially when we dream, experience orgasm, are surprised, awe-struck or in a devotional state. Meditation slows down and then stops the activity of the dualistic mind, giving us the much-needed space to recognize our true nature. With that spaciousness of mind, with those extended bardos, we will be able to place our awareness on the gap; which is actually placing our awareness on itself because there is nothing else in the gap.

---

[121] Jamyang Tenphel, *The Awakening Heart: Contemplations on the Buddhist Path*, Timeless Awareness Publications, 2023, no page, Kindle Edition.

For the most part, it is important not to chase experiences such as vivid dreams and intense orgasms. Instead we just do our regular meditation practice and allow deeper experiences to unfold naturally. As for being awestruck by the beauty of nature or completely absorbed in devotion, these are healthy to cultivate, but should always be undertaken in concert with sitting meditation.

When any of these experiences occur in the unfolding of our ordinary life—when we dream, feel awe or orgasm—we just place our awareness on itself in a relaxed way with no expectations. This is a much more "user-friendly" way of using those gateways leading to the Bardo of Luminosity than complicated methods such as Karma Mudra. We simply allow our meditation to naturally transform our everyday experience and awaken us to the moments of non-dual awareness or rigpa that emerge when we dream, when we orgasm, when we fall asleep, when we are awe-struck by the beauty of nature or are absorbed by devotion to our gurus, or even when we sneeze or are startled.

Developing mindful awareness (or mindfulness) in the midst of the tumult of daily life will help us when we enter the bardos after death, as the death process can be just as noisy and distracting as life. Reinforcing the importance of meditation to bardo practice, Naropa, a great Indian meditation master of the 10th century, taught:

> Since the consciousness [in the bardo] has no support, it is difficult to stabilize mindful intention. But if one can maintain mindfulness, traversing the path will be trouble-free. Meditating for one session in that intermediate state may be liberating.[122]

In other words, the best preparation for the Bardo of Dying is meditation. On a simple psychological level, meditation helps us to overcome our disabling

---

[122] Naropa, quoted in By Andrew Holecek, Practical Advice and Spiritual Wisdom from the Tibetan Buddhist Tradition, Shambhala Publications, 2013, p. 21.

emotions, our anger and fear, our obsessions and attachments. Importantly, it also helps us to overcome our fear of death, because meditation releases our clinging to self, our existential terror at the demise of the ego. The dualistic mind is in constant fear of its extinguishment. It creates the delusion of permanence, especially of the self, as a way of self-medicating for that anxiety. No matter how heavily we self-medicate by investing in the idea of permanence, the dualistic mind will still perish, along with all other things, including our bodies. The only true medicine is Dharma. It is the only thing that eases suffering and leads to joy, precisely because it extinguishes the dualistic mind and the sense of a separate self. This brings us to the painful Bardo of Dying.

CHAPTER EIGHT

LUMINOSITY IN THE BARDO OF DYING

Liberation can be as simple and natural as a child climbing into its parent's lap.

In our discussion about the Bardo of Dying, I will draw on three pith instructions. The first and main source for our discussion is a pith instruction by the great Dzogchen master and highly revered scholar of the Nyingma school, Longchen Rabjampa (1308–1364), known affectionately as Longchenpa. This brief teaching, known as *Crucial Advice: A Complete Set of Instructions for the Bardos*[123], focuses on the death process. Nevertheless, Longchenpa's pith instructions illuminate how we can seize the opportunity of the bardos in our everyday life. The second source for our discussion is a pith instruction called *The Refined Essence of Oral Instructions*[124], in which Padmasambhava, who established Buddhism in Tibet 1200 years or so ago, gives bardo teachings to his closest disciple, Khandro Yeshe Tsogyal. *The Refined Essence of Oral Instructions* is a terma (treasure teaching) discovered by the terton (treasure revealer) Dorje Lingpa (1346 – 1405). This teaching focuses on the importance of recognizing the true nature of mind while we

---

[123] Translated by Adam Pearcey (2010). See full text here: https://www.lotsawahouse.org/tibetan-masters/longchen-rabjam/complete-set-instructions.

[124] See the full pith instruction in Kunsang, Erik Pema, 'Refined Essence of Oral Instructions', in *Dakini Teachings: A Collection of Padmasambhava's Advice to the Dakini Yeshe Tsogyal*, Rangjung Yeshe Publications, 1999.

are alive in order to achieving total liberation in the bardos. We will also be discussing even briefer pith instructions from Holiness Dudjom Rinpoche, who managed to encapsulate the essence of the bardo teachings on dying in just six lines.

Gratitude

Crucial Advice: A Complete Set of Instructions for the Bardos starts in the same way that all Tibetan Buddhist teachings start, which is with an homage to the Lama: 'At the feet of the sacred master, respectfully I pay homage!'[125] It is important not to just run over that first sentence as though it is a mere prelude, a kind of formality or etiquette that doesn't really matter. In fact, it is very important. The homage to the master is not something to just read over without paying heed. It is a statement of gratitude to our teachers who have given us the method to free ourselves from suffering. The metaphor that one of my teachers uses for this sense of gratitude is that of being trapped in a burning house. Imagine if we were trapped in a burning house, blindfolded and bound. Then imagine someone came along and removed the blindfold and cut our bindings and gestured towards the open door so that we could escape. If that were to happen we would be so thankful, thankful from the depths of our being. Our gratitude would be immense. That's the level of gratitude we are encouraged to have toward our teachers. Why? Because the teachers share the Buddhist methods with us. The Buddhist methods (or Dharma) free us from that which makes our lives miserable. Dharma frees us from disturbing emotions and delusion. Dharma can free us from anger, sadness, panic, anxiety, jealousy, lack of self-worth and self-hatred. Buddhist techniques can free us from feeling not good enough, feeling isolated and lonely, all of these things. These are the things that ruin our

---

[125] Longchenpa, *Crucial Advice: A Complete Set of Instructions for the Bardos,* Translated by Adam Pearcey (2010). See full text here: https://www.lotsawahouse.org/tibetan-masters/longchen-rabjam/complete-set-instructions.

lives, the disturbing emotions. Practicing the Buddha Dharma is a way to be fully liberated from all the things that ruin our lives. The Dharma shows us how to strengthen our ability to release what arises in the mind. This is really amazing! Without the teacher, we would not know how to practice. We would not even know the simplest things about Dharma. We might not even know what the word Dharma means.

We receive lots of teachings from all kinds of sources in our lives. Someone has to teach us how to speak and even walk! Someone taught us the alphabet and how to read. Someone taught us numbers and how to count. As we grow, we learn so many things, from somewhat complex things like driving a car to the most basic things such as cleaning our teeth. We are taught everything by someone else. None of these ordinary things we learn, though they enrich our everyday lives, will actually free us from suffering. When we recognize that Dharma will free us, then our gratitude to the person who teaches us Dharma should be equivalent. That being said, it should be a natural or uncontrived gratitude. It is better to be honest about where we are at than to fake things. It is not helpful to fake gratitude, or fake devotion or fake renunciation. We need to be real about who we are. We all understand what showing respect and gratitude looks like. It doesn't have to be fawning and certainly shouldn't be phony. It can be just showing respect in the way that we feel it, even if it's purely intellectual. We might think 'Oh, I recognize this person has a huge amount of skill. I recognize this person is trying to help me'. Simply show the appropriate amount of respect and gratitude that we can, according to our current place in the practice. This teaching by the Buddha himself shows how important gratitude is to the Buddhist path:

The Blessed One said, "Now what is the level of a person of no integrity? A person of no integrity is *ungrateful* and *unthankful*. This ingratitude, this lack of thankfulness, is advocated by rude people. It is entirely on the level of people of no integrity. A person of integrity is grateful and thankful. This gratitude, this thankfulness, is advocated by civil people. It is entirely on the level of people of integrity."[126]

Gratitude and integrity are deeply linked. Integrity is the quality of being genuine and having strong ethical principles. These are essential to spiritual and psychological growth. As well as being necessary to integrity, gratitude helps us develop patience. If we are grateful for how things are, we are not anxious for them to change. If we are grateful for what we have, we do not rush to acquire more. Patience is the antidote to frustration and anger. Without patience, we will be led around by our disturbing emotions, tugged every which way, like a poor yak being led around by a ring in its nose. Scientists have proven the link between gratitude and patience – people with a strong sense of gratitude are more able to delay gratification, to forego a small or temporary benefit in the present moment in favor of a greater or more lasting benefit later.[127] This shows us that gratitude is also an antidote to greed. Greed flowers when we feel that we don't have enough. Gratitude grants a feeling of having enough. More to the point, greed and gratitude cannot coexist in the same mind. The same goes for most of the worst of our disturbing emotions. Among other unhelpful feelings, gratitude extinguishes jealousy, regret and resentment. Furthermore, when we are grateful or thankful we want to "give thanks", which leads to generosity. This simple thing, this cultivation of gratitude, frees us from so many disturbing emotions and grants us the highly beneficial qualities of integrity, patience, contentment and generosity. How amazing!

---

[126] From the Katannu Sutra (AN 2.31-32), translated by Thanissaro Bhikkhu. For full text see: https://www.accesstoinsight.org/tipitaka/an/an02/an02.031.than.html.

[127] See this article for a summary of evidence for the benefits of gratitude: https://positivepsychology.com/neuroscience-of-gratitude/

Zen teacher Norman Fischer writes:

We take our life … we take existence, for granted. We take it as a given, and then we complain that it isn't working out as we wanted it to. But why should we be here in the first place? Why should we exist at all?[128]

In other words, a lack of gratitude is simultaneously a lack of mindfulness, a lack of attention to our lives and taking them for granted. Ingratitude is a state that is disconnected from the present moment, a state mired in hope and fear about the past and future. When we take our lives for granted we do not enjoy them, we do not recognize them for the gifts that they are. This means that gratitude is also a source of joy. The list of benefits gratitude brings is now growing long: abiding in the present, freedom from disturbing emotions, integrity, patience, generosity and now joy.

Unlike in other faith traditions, Buddhism encourages a boundless gratitude, one that is an attitude of mind not dependent on external conditions. Buddhism suggests that gratitude is most beneficial when it is applied to all of life's conditions, the good and the bad, and all living beings, those who delight us as much as those who bedevil us. Gratitude helps us deal with life's inevitable and multiple difficulties. To be grateful for difficulties—such as illness, loss, grief and any worsening of our physical or material conditions—is to face reality, to recognize the impermanent and empty nature of all things, and rejoice in having been awoken from our delusion of permanence. Our delusion of permanence imprisons us and keeps us cut off from the true nature of existence. Gratitude allows us not only to deal with impermanence but to see it for what it is – a truth that, when taken to heart, leads to liberation from all suffering.

---

[128] Norman Fischer quoted in Barbara O'Brien 'Being Grateful: What the Buddha Taught About Gratitude', Learn Religions, 2019, https://www.learnreligions.com/being-grateful-449576.

Given that gratitude for all conditions, seemingly positive or seemingly negative, and all beings, supposed friends as well as supposed enemies, is our aspiration, our ultimate aim, but something we need to cultivate, where should we start? We start in small ways – each night we jot down just five things for which we are grateful and we contemplate them. This is easy but will bring potent benefits. When we are first cultivating gratitude, it is wise to start with the positive things we are grateful for. Then, when we are accustomed to feeling and expressing gratitude, we move on to neutral things and finally those things that we define as difficulties or struggles.

When we Buddhists advise contemplating something, we mean to adopt a meditation posture, allow our minds and bodies to relax and then reflect on or consider it deeply. While reflecting, it is important to take note of how we feel. What is the quality of our emotional experience? How are we feeling physically? What is happening at our heart center? Connecting with the somatic aspect of gratitude will help us to cultivate a gratitude that is heart-felt rather than merely intellectual.

When contemplating gratitude we sit in meditation for as little as five or ten minutes then call to mind the beings, relationships and things in our lives for which we are grateful. We can bring to mind a person in our lives who we truly appreciate. We can visualize this person and contemplate what precisely we appreciate about them. It need not be something that makes us feel good. It can be something the person requires of us that makes us a better person, or it might be that this person highlights our hidden faults. Simply reflect on this for a few moments and take note of how we are feeling, what our bodies are doing.

When contemplating difficulties, such as illness, we can consider what the difficulties have taught us. Has our illness taught us the truth of impermanence? Has it caused us to become more compassionate towards others who are ill? Has it caused us to realize what really matters, what is most important in our lives? Has it taught us how to be kind and caring towards ourselves and others? Simply reflect on these questions for a few moments. You can even reflect on how gratitude itself has transformed us, giving rise to beneficial qualities and extinguishing harmful ones.

If we're finding it difficult to come up with five things to be grateful for, below are a few to include each day that are universal to all of us:

1. *Our existence itself.* Even if our lives are difficult, if we live with chronic illness or pain, if we experience depression or anxiety, if we have experienced much loss or trauma, the very fact of our existence is still something to be grateful for. Why? Because every moment, every breath in and out, is an opportunity to practice the Dharma and find ultimate liberation for both ourselves and all sentient beings.

2. *There is kindness in the world.* Even if we are bombarded with news of war and strife, poverty and hunger, terror and hatred, natural disasters and other calamities, there is still kindness. His Holiness the Dalai Lama often says that the fact that bad things make the news and good things do not is proof that bad things are less usual than good things. There are millions and millions of acts of kindness happening every moment. Kindness is very common. Be thankful for that. Be thankful that there is goodness in the world.

3. *We have teachers.* When we are born we do not know how to speak. As we grow we learn to speak from our parents and others around us. Then someone teaches us the alphabet and how to write. In fact, we wouldn't even know how to clean our teeth or brush our hair without being taught. Every single thing is learnt from others. There is not a single idea or bit of knowledge in our minds that we did not acquire from someone else. Nothing we know is wholly our own. We should have an immense gratitude for that. And this is just ordinary knowledge or information, we should be even more grateful for those who have taught us Dharma, for it is only the Dharma that will free us from suffering.

As for myself, I am extremely grateful for what my Dharma teachers have gifted me. I have nothing to give to others except what my teachers gave me. This is not modesty. This is merely fact. Anything I may know about Dharma has come from my teachers and has nothing to do with me. We all learn the path from someone, so every benefit we experience on the path comes from those who taught us. These benefits or positive qualities we acquire on the path are not our personal accomplishments. Every understanding that dawns in our minds comes from our teachers and has nothing to do with our personalities or identities. Every moment of calm or clarity, every moment of insight or joy, these are all gifts from those who have taught us Dharma. Therefore, we should be extremely grateful to our spiritual teachers.

Our gratitude does not always need to be expressed outwardly, but doing so is good for us. Regularly expressing gratitude to our teachers leads to humility, which extinguishes arrogance and pride. Ingratitude allows arrogance to thrive and poison us. So, when someone teaches us Dharma or gives us Dharma advice—even in an informal setting like a chat over coffee or a text message—it's important to thank them. There is no need for elaborate public declarations or extravagant gifts. In fact these things are strongly discouraged in Buddhism. A simple, heart-felt thank you is all that is required.

Our list of the benefits that gratitude grants is now quite unwieldy: abiding in the present, freedom from disturbing emotions such as anger, arrogance and greed, understanding of impermanence and emptiness, having contentment, integrity, patience, generosity, joy and humility. Last but not at all least, the most wonderful thing about gratitude is this – a truly impartial gratitude leads to equanimity, which is the foundation of awakening or realization. What is equanimity? Gil Fronsdal (2004) writes that equanimity is:

Neither a thought nor an emotion, it is rather the steady conscious realization of reality's transience. It is the ground for wisdom and freedom and the protector of compassion and love. While some may think of equanimity as dry neutrality or cool aloofness, mature equanimity produces a radiance and warmth of being. The Buddha described a mind filled with equanimity as 'abundant, exalted, immeasurable, without hostility and without ill-will'.[129]

In other words, total equanimity is a quality of Buddhas. Now we can see that without gratitude our path to awakening is uncertain, and certainly replete with obstacles; our every step dogged by disturbing emotions and our minds harried by greed, frustration and anger. Without gratitude we can become so poisoned by arrogance that we become spiritual monsters and even poison others.

The good news is that gratitude is very easy to cultivate. We simply make our gratitude lists, each and every day, and contemplate the items on the list until we actually *feel* grateful. We also remember to say thank you to everyone who shows us any kindness or consideration, including all those who teach and guide us. Without our Dharma teachers we would have nothing to offer others, no way to liberate ourselves from suffering and no way to help liberate all the other beings in this world who need our help. There is no greater kindness than that shown to us by our spiritual teachers, and nothing we should be more grateful for.

Some people think, when they read the first lines of homage in Buddhist texts, 'Oh, this is a Tibetan thing', or 'This is an Asian thing'. Actually, gratitude is not Tibetan or Asian. Gratitude is extremely important irrespective of culture. As we've seen, gratitude is an antidote to greed, or craving, because it gives a sense of having enough. Gratitude is an antidote to anger because it provides patience. If we're grateful for our experience, we don't get angry at others and we feel happy to wait for our experience to evolve naturally. Gratitude brings joy, because when we feel grateful, we feel

---

[129] See: https://www.insightmeditationcenter.org/books-articles/equanimity/

we have enough and actually we feel that our life is abundant. Gratitude is an antidote to almost every disturbing emotion or mind state. It is very, very potently powerful. This is why it's important not to dismiss the homage to the master. The homage to the master is actually a source of joy for ourselves. We are short-changing ourselves if we don't engage with the meaning behind the words.

In this age of distrust of authority, in which some of those with authority in the spiritual space have abused that authority, many of us are understandably cautious and suspicious of authority figures such as gurus and of handing over our spiritual autonomy to another being. Unfortunately this suspicion, if un-tempered by true knowledge and open-heartedness, cuts us off from a unique and potent spiritual path. In the first sentence of his *Crucial Advice*, Longchenpa alludes to this path, the potent practice of Guru Yoga. As I explained in the previous chapters of this book, Guru Yoga is not some kind of celebrity guru fandom. It is about getting to know our own true nature.

In practice-focused lineages like the Drukpa Kagyu and the Nyingma, Guru Yoga is perceived as the most important of all spiritual practices. The Ninth Khamtrul Rinpoche, the current head of the Khampagar lineage, one of the main Drukpa Kagyu lineages, puts it this way:

The Khamtrul lineage of practice emphasizes the Five Special Teachings of the Drukpa Kagyu:

1. The view is Mahamudra
2. The meditation is the Six Practices of Naropa
3. The conduct is the Six Cycles of Equal Taste
4. The fruition is the Seven Supreme Interdependences
5. The fifth one is the dearest of all – the profound path of Guru Yoga[130]

---

[130] From *The Life and Legacy of the 9th Pal Gyalwa DhoKhampa, Shedrup Nyima*, Khampagar Monastery Publisher, 2013.

Some of the practices referred to in this list might not be familiar to us. All we need to know is that of all the highly-revered spiritual practices of this highly-esteemed practice lineage it is Guru Yoga, technically a preliminary practice, that is considered 'the dearest of all'. Furthermore, the great master Kangyur Rinpoche taught that:

> Guru Yoga is the quintessential method of completing the two accumulations by taking as the path the two kayas of the result. For this reason, the Victorious One has said that to be mindful of the teacher for an instant is better than worshiping the Buddhas and Bodhisattvas for many kalpas [eons], and better than meditating on hundreds of generation-stage practices.[131]

It is quite clear that of all the practices in the tantric system, Guru Yoga is the most effective. It is saddening therefore that, in the West, Guru Yoga has largely been misunderstood, which has led to a lot of trouble and drama. Guru Yoga has been approached in the West as simply following the guru around and doing whatever they say, a kind of sycophancy. Sadly, some so-called gurus have taken advantage of this misunderstanding. This is not what Guru Yoga is at all. If a teacher is controlling or abusive, then that person has broken their commitment (samaya) to their students and doesn't deserve the student's loyalty. They deserve the student's compassion, but not their loyalty. As Jetsunma Tenzin Palmo explains:

> If a teacher really acts inappropriately or requests inappropriate behavior on the part of the student, then the student has the right, also as a human being, to say, "No, I'm very sorry, I don't accept that," or, "Well, okay, explain why you're doing this." And if the teacher will not explain, or their explanation doesn't ring true, then I think it's perfectly

---

[131] Commentary by Kangyur Rinpoche on Jigme Lingpa's *Treasury of Precious Qualities: Book One*, Shambhala Publications, 2010, P. 208.

appropriate to say with all due respect, "Well, I'm sorry, I am going to find someone else." Because quite frankly, many teachers, even though they might be very charismatic and even have some genuine experience and realization, might also have a big shadow which they're not facing and which their culture doesn't encourage them to face. And in dealing with that shadow, we have to use our common sense. If the relationship creates a lot of inner distress and trauma, then this is spiritually not in the least bit helpful. So without creating a lot of publicity or difficulty one can just simply say, "Thank you very much for all your teachings", and leave.[132]

The purpose of Guru Yoga is to discover our own true nature, to come to and rest in the natural state of perfection (Dzogpachenpo). Guru Yoga is a meditative practice undertaken on the cushion first and then brought into daily life. It has nothing to do with following the orders of a teacher; unless those orders are about meditation or other spiritual practices. It certainly has nothing to do with following a teacher from place to place, always trying to be near them, or to get their attention. As Dudjom Sangye Pema Shepa Rinpoche once taught:

When we think of the closeness or distance between ourselves and our gurus, it should not be understood in terms of a spatial difference marked by travelling to physically encounter the teacher. It is not about that at all. The closeness of the connection is based on sorrowful disillusionment with samsara, trust, and deep inner confidence in the guru. There will be an experience of closeness or distance according to your inner conviction.[133]

---

[132] 'Relating To The Guru', Shambhala Publications, https://www.shambhala.com/snowlion_articles/relating-to-the-guru/

[133] Dudjom Sangye Pema Shepa Rinpoche, Dudjom International Foundation website: https://www.dudjominternationalfoundation.com/

Jamyang Tenphel describes the true meditative purpose of Guru Yoga as:

> To merge subject and object (the essence of the dualistic state) into the ultimate state beyond duality, the state of the Great Perfection. The practitioner is the subject. The Guru is the object of the practice. By dissolving a visualization of the guru into our hearts again and again with great devotion and reverence, the separation between subject and object dissolves and oneness with Buddha Nature, our true nature, occurs. This is the heart of the practice that leads to the state of liberation. This is why, if done with unshakeable devotion, Guru Yoga is the swiftest of all methods.[134]

To be clear, the guru in the Guru Yoga must be a fully accomplished being. If not fully accomplished, then fully trained and qualified with a deeply compassionate heart. They must also have been empowered to teach by their own teachers. This does not mean that everyone with the title Lama is suitable to use as the focus of our Guru Yoga practice. Far from it. In the Karma Kagyu tradition, for example, anyone who has completed a three year retreat is given the title Lama. Having completed a three year retreat does not mean one is realized or enlightened. Likewise, ordinary monks and nuns, though worthy of our respect due to their commitment to the Dharma and sacrifice for the sake of sentient beings, are not suitable to be the focus of our Guru Yoga merely because they are ordained. There needs to be realization as well. The same is true for those wearing the white robes, the tantrikas or ngakpas and ngakmas. We must choose the focus of our Guru Yoga, the one who will be the presence of enlightened mind in our lives, extremely carefully.

There are different levels of teacher. If you've been around the Dharma for even a short time this becomes obvious. Someone like me—who is

---

[134] Jamyang Tenphel, *The Awakening Heart: Contemplations on the Buddhist Path*, Timeless Awareness Publications, 2023, no page, Kindle Edition.

basically just a simple Buddhist disciple who has been given permission to teach some subjects but is not a Vajra Master, not empowered as a guru— just shares the Dharma to the level that they can. Someone like me cannot be a guru and should not be the object of the kind of homage that opens Longchenpa's *Crucial Advice*. That kind of homage is for those who are fully awakened, for the Buddha, and those who have followed after the Buddha and have achieved realization or enlightenment, such as Padmasambhava and Yeshe Tsogyal, such as Marpa, Milarepa and Machig Labdron, such as lineage masters like Kyabje Dudjom Rinpoche, Kyabje Dilgo Khyentse Rinpoche, Kyabje Sakya Trizin Ngawang Kunga or His Holiness the Dalai Lama who have proven their awakening.

I want to spend a little more time explaining why Guru Yoga is important in the context of the bardo teachings. This may seem controversial or counter-intuitive but, in this age of distrust, in which there are so many misbehaving so-called gurus, Guru Yoga is even more important. Rather than abandoning Guru Yoga we should actually embrace it more deeply and practice it earnestly. Why? Because Guru Yoga is the one practice guaranteed to grant us recognition of our true nature and realization. Ironically, Guru Yoga is the practice that most reliably and swiftly delivers true spiritual autonomy. No other practice leads to freedom from all forms of slavery – enslavement to negative habitual tendencies, enslavement to inhibition and enslavement to the expectations of others. No other practice leads so swiftly to full awakening. As Jamyang Tenphel notes:

> You might think, "Why is Guru Yoga important at all? Why bother with it?" It's important because by gaining some level of accomplishment in it, however small and brief, you gain certainty about your true nature. You know via direct, personal experience that you definitely have Buddha Nature. Then, because you are confident in your Buddha Nature, you also feel confident you can achieve realization in this lifetime. By

accomplishing some measure of Guru Yoga you will develop confidence that your practice isn't just repetitive lip service that may be going nowhere, but that it really can help you realize your true nature and Bodhicitta.[135]

Guru Yoga frees us from the tyranny of the dualistic mind and enslavement to our delusions and disturbing emotions. There is an ancient Tibetan saying often shared by Jetsunma Tenzin Palmo, 'With meditation one *might* achieve realization, with devotion one will *certainly* achieve it.' I've already stated that meditation is a highly effective method for recognizing the true nature. Here we have the idea that devotion is even more effective than that. Kyabje Dudjom Rinpoche explains this when he teaches:

> It is said that if disciples who keep the commitments give themselves wholeheartedly, with devotion, to an authentic Diamond Master, they will obtain the supreme and common accomplishments *even if they have no other methods* … When unmistaken devotion takes birth in us, obstacles on the path will be dispelled and we will make progress, obtaining all the supreme and ordinary accomplishments *without depending on anything else*. This is what we mean by the profound path of Guru Yoga (emphasis added).[136]

In this excerpt, Dudjom Rinpoche is talking about devotion in the context of Guru Yoga. He makes it quite clear that no other method is required. Those practicing Guru Yoga do not need to rely on anything else, no other practices or methods. He also states that through Guru Yoga we will obtain 'all the supreme and ordinary accomplishments'. These accomplishments (or siddhis) are too many to list, but the most important of all is Bodhicitta, the

---

[135] Jamyang Tenphel, *The Awakening Heart: Contemplations on the Buddhist Path*, Timeless Awareness Publications, 2023, no page, Kindle Edition.

[136] Dudjom Rinpoche, *A Torch Lighting the Way to Freedom*, Shambhala Publications, 2016, P. 260.

mind of unbound compassion co-emergent with the realization of emptiness. The accomplishments granted by so-called higher tantric practices do not surpass this. Indeed, Kyabje Dilgo Khyentse Rinpoche has noted:

> There may be very high practices, like *trekcho* and *thogal* in the Dzogpa Chenpo, but for us to practice these at this point would be like giving solid food to a very young baby. He would not be able to assimilate the food, and it would just cause him harm. If we were to try now to practice those advanced teachings, they would just be wasted. Through the blessings that come from genuine endeavor in the practice of this Guru Yoga, on the other hand, the realization of Dzogpa Chenpo will arise by itself from the depths of our being like morning sun, and the meaning of the practice of trekcho and thogal will dawn within us.[137]

By this quote we can see how profoundly important and beneficial Guru Yoga is. Trekcho and Togyal (thogal) are the highest practices in the Dzogchen "system", which itself is considered the highest approach or method in Tibetan Buddhism. In this quote Dilgo Khyentse Rinpoche is making it quite clear that the path of devotion is equivalent to the path of Dzogchen, but with one difference – it can be safely practiced by everyone no matter what their spiritual background or level of experience. Nineteenth century master Patrul Rinpoche wrote that:

> ... all the tantras teach the practice of Guru Yoga, and say that it is superior to all the practices of the generation and perfection phases.[138]

Indeed, one of these Vajrayana tantras states this very baldly:

> Better than meditating on a hundred deities

---

[137] Dilgo Khyentse Rinpoche, *The Wish-Fulfilling Jewel*, Shambhala Publishing, 1999, pp. 92-93.

[138] Patrul Rinpoche, *Words of My Perfect Teacher*, translated by the Padmakara Translation group, Yale University Press Edition, 2011, p. 310.

For ten million kalpas

Is to think of one's teacher for a single instant.[139]

Here we see Patrul Rinpoche, and the tantras themselves, making it quite clear that all the visualization and mantra practices of the tantric system are surpassed by the simple practice of Guru Yoga and devotion. No matter what empowerments we might have, what elaborate "higher" practices we might be doing, none of them are as powerful or transformative as simple devotion. This attitude is typical of the Nyingma tradition and is universally held by all true masters. Nyoshul Khenpo Rinpoche explains this further:

> ... there is a way of recognizing the nature of mind solely through devotion. There are cases of practitioners who simply through their heartfelt devotion attained realization, even though their teacher had already passed away or was nowhere near them physically. Because of their prayers and devotion, the nature of mind was introduced. The classic example is that of Jigme Lingpa and his consuming devotion for Longchen Rabjam.[140]

We can see from Nyoshul Khen Rinpoche's comment above that devotion (mögü) is crucial to natural awakening, which has as its essential foundations not complex tantric practices but simple silent sitting meditation and Guru Yoga. In fact it is now abundantly clear that devotion or Guru Yoga is a path in itself. Jamyang Tenphel puts it this way:

> With devotion we dissolve the self, which leads to the realization of emptiness. It also opens the heart, which awakens compassion and loving kindness. In devotion the twin realizations of wisdom and compassion

---

[139] Quoted in Patrul Rinpoche, *Words of My Perfect Teacher*, translated by the Padmakara Translation group, Yale University Press Edition, 2011, p. 310.

[140] Nyoshul Khenpo Rinpoche quoted in Marcia Binder Schmidt (ed.) *Dzogchen Essentials: The Path that Clarifies Confusion*, Rangjung Yeshe Publications, 2004, p. 136.

are accomplished simultaneously and naturally. This leads to complete liberation.[141]

If we are truly conscious of how short our lives are, how little time we might actually have left, how important it is that we recognize the true nature of mind before we enter the Bardo of Dying, then we absolutely would focus solely on Guru Yoga, which as a practice always includes Shamata. If we are not focusing on Guru Yoga then we have to ask ourselves why. Do we think we will live forever? Do we think we still have plenty of time, even though tomorrow may never come for us? Do we cherish our so-called spiritual autonomy, or our ordinary life, more than we cherish awakening? Are we hypnotized by the cornucopia of tantric deities and practices to the point that it has become just another form of materialism? Are we just too proud to truly cherish the source of the teachings, the source of every bit of our Dharma knowledge? Or are we afraid of Guru Yoga because we do not truly understand it, because it has been misrepresented in the West? Whatever the reason, we need to overcome our reluctance to embrace Guru Yoga as the most reliable method for awakening. The consequences of not doing so are dire.

One of the reasons Guru Yoga is so important is because it is an act of surrender to co-emergent wisdom and compassion. Ultimately, the enlightened guru is wisdom and compassion personified. That's it. There's no person there. So that first statement of homage from Longchenpa we read at the beginning of this section is simply saying, "I surrender and open myself to wisdom and compassion. I allow myself to be a conduit for unbiased love." It's really simple. But in the West it is much misunderstood, this idea of the master and of Guru Yoga.

---

[141] Jamyang Tenphel, *The Awakening Heart: Contemplations on the Buddhist Path*, Timeless Awareness Publications, 2023, no page, Kindle Edition.

Despite being very simple Guru Yoga has swift and deeply profound benefits. This is why Kyabje Dudjom Rinpoche suggests that we:

> ... embrace Guru Yoga as the vital essence of practice, and practice diligently. If you do not, your meditation will grow slowly, and even if it grows a little, obstacles will arise and genuine realization will not manifest in your mindstream. Therefore, earnestly pray with uncontrived devotion. After some time the realization of wisdom mind will be transmitted to your mindstream, and an extraordinary realization that cannot be expressed by words will definitely arise from within yourself.[142]

Here Dudjom Rinpoche clearly links practice accomplishment with Guru Yoga. Without Guru Yoga, our meditation will not stabilize or deepen. The phrase 'earnestly pray with uncontrived devotion' is key. Devotion cannot be faked. This is not a 'fake it till you make it' situation. There is no point pretending to have devotion when you do not. Perhaps this is why so many practitioners end up just being groupies to Lamas, because they have no true devotion so they act it out instead, they put on a show of subservience. Devotion is not a pantomime and it is not subservience. In my humble opinion having no devotion is better than having fake devotion. Indeed, the third Jamgon Kongtrul Rinpoche concurred when he said:

> If one tries to forcefully build up an artificial feeling of devotion and trust, the blessing and the inspiration will be only imaginary and artificial, and so will the fruit (result).[143]

This suggests that if our devotion is fabricated or faked, just a show or performance that has no real depth, then there will be no result, no awakening. If we do not have natural or strong devotion there is a remedy. The remedy is not to perform the act of a servile or fawning groupie. The remedy is to do

---

[142] Dudjom Rinpoche, *Wisdom Nectar: Dudjom Rinpoche's Heart Advice*, Snow Lion, 2005, p. 43.

[143] Quoted in *Kagyu Life International*, Vol.3, 1995.

the Guru Yoga practice itself, the meditative practice in which we visualize the guru and then dissolve them into ourselves.

If we have not yet met our guru, or don't have a relationship with a living teacher we trust, or we are shy about entering the teacher-student relationship because of having experienced abuse or betrayal at the hand of authority figures or even our parents, there is still a way for us to practice this profound method. We can practice Guru Yoga with a teacher from the past, such as Padmasambhava (Guru Rinpoche), Khandro Yeshe Tsogyal or the Buddha himself. In fact, the greater majority of the formal Guru Yoga practices in the Nyingma tradition are focused on Guru Rinpoche. If a living master was necessary then all of those practices would be ineffective. We can choose any true master, male, female or otherwise gendered, who we feel inspired by or feel some respect or devotion to. To develop respect and devotion we simply read their life stories (called *namthar* in Tibetan) and study the written teachings they have left behind. We can have a picture of them in our meditation space, or on our altar. In this way, a strong connection between us and them that transcends time and space and life and death can be formed. Remember from Chapter Three, where I quoted the great Drukpa Kagyu master Togden Shakya Shri who said quite clearly that if we have devotion and faith toward the master, 'there is not even a hair tip's difference if the master is alive or not'.[144]

My teacher and friend Ngakpa Karma Lhundup Rinpoche once advised: 'Merge your awareness with your Lama and realize that the teacher and you have always been together right from the beginning. There is no such thing as meeting or parting. Let yourself be who you are'.[145] Khenpo Tsewang

---

[144] *Togden Shakya Shri: The Life and Liberation of a Tibetan Yogin*, by Kathog Situ Chokyi Gyatso, translated by Elio Guarisco, Shang Shung Publications, 2011, p. 159.

[145] Quoted in *Resting in Stillness*, by Martin Jamyang Tenphel and Pema Düddul, Jalü Publications, 2020, p. 102.

Dongyal Rinpoche makes this point about his own master, Kyabje Dudjom Rinpoche, when he writes:

> Many of us had the good fortune to encounter the precious living body of His Holiness Dudjom Rinpoche. Those of us who did not have this opportunity are still connected to his Dharmakaya mind, and have unlimited access to his wisdom, love and power. Thus, if you have a connection to his Dharmakaya mind, it is the same as meeting him in person.[146]

To a master such as Dudjom Rinpoche, an authentic source of true refuge, death is nothing. Alive or dead, the Dharmakaya mind of such masters is beyond time, beyond form and ever present. To receive the wisdom and blessings of such beings all we need do is subdue our ego-cherishing with gratitude and reverence and, most importantly, open our hearts. Then the master will be right here with us, defying death and time, bathing us in the radiance of their limitless love, compassion and wisdom. Kyabje Dudjom Rinpoche himself wrote:

> This fresh fundamental nature of self-manifest awareness
>
> That faults and stains have never tainted
>
> Is the original lord, Dharmakaya Lama.
>
> He dwells together with you, never separate,
>
> Yet dualistic grasping's power prevents you from recognizing this abiding nature.[147]

It is clear then that Guru Yoga is learning to be authentic to our true nature. It is not about slavishly following another. That being said, Guru Yoga

---

[146] Khenpo Tsewang Dongyal Rinpoche, *Inborn Realization: A Commentary on His Holiness Dudjom Rinpoche's Mountain Retreat Instructions*, Dharma Samudra, 2016, p. 1.

[147] Dudjom Rinpoche, *Wisdom Nectar: Dudjom Rinpoche's Heart Advice*, Snow Lion, 2005, p. 113.

does require a level of surrender, namely the surrender of our clinging to a supposedly separate, inherently existing self. We also need to surrender our egotistical belief that we know better than anyone else what is beneficial and what is not. Learning to connect with our true nature from the root guru, the teacher for whom we have devotion, even if he or she has passed away, is far more powerful than learning from any other living teacher because of the mind-to-mind transmission, which is more accurately a heart-to-heart transmission that depends completely on open-hearted surrender. As Jamyang Tenphel and I have written elsewhere:

> This kind of learning is experiential and goes straight to the heart, whereas learning from the words of another teacher remains largely a conceptual understanding and does not penetrate deeply. Thus, even if our teacher has passed away or lived a very long time ago, we should not give up on fostering a connection with them as devotion to them will always be the swiftest route to deep, heart-felt understanding and realization.[148]

Dudjom Rinpoche states that the end result of Guru Yoga is an 'extraordinary realization', otherwise known as the mind of enlightenment or Bodhicitta. Therefore, the truly essential spiritual practices are simple meditation and Guru Yoga. These are the two practices that will help us to recognize the nature of mind, and thus prepare us to easily recognize the Mother Luminosity at the time of death. As Sera Khandro, a great yogini of the Dudjom lineage, has taught:

> If you do not pray with devotion to the wish-fulfilling master the requisite and desired accomplishments will not come, so diligently cultivate a mind filled with devotion.

---

[148] Martin Jamyang Tenphel and Pema Düddul *Resting in Stillness*, Timeless Awareness Publications, 2020, page 102.

If you do not give rise to the four powers of devotion toward the master, the Buddha of the three times, the blessings of the wisdom mind transmission will not enter you, so diligently give rise to devotion.[149]

Khenpo Tsewang Dongyal Rinpoche describes devotion as 'the constant call of your own enlightened mind'.[150] It is essential that we answer that call. To do that we have to recognize that devotion and Guru Yoga are not about an external exhibition of subservience but about an inner yearning for wisdom, about becoming one with the ultimate nature of all. I will close this section with a succinct quote from Dudjom Sangye Pema Shepa Rinpoche:

Merely by praying to and meditating upon the master, you too will awaken as Buddha. On the basis of faith and fervent devotion, it will happen.[151]

---

[149] See 'A Song of Amazement Inspired by Practice Experience', translated by Christina Monson (2015), https://www.lotsawahouse.org/tibetan-masters/sera-khandro/song-of-amazement.

[150] Khenpo Tsewang Dongyal Rinpoche, *Inborn Realization: A Commentary on His Holiness Dudjom Rinpoche's Mountain Retreat Instructions*, Dharma Samudra, 2016, p. 130.

[151] Dudjom Sangye Pema Shepa Rinpoche, Dudjom International Foundation website: https://www.dudjominternationalfoundation.com/hh-dudjom-rinpoche-iii-sangye-pema-shepa/whispers/

CHAPTER NINE

IMPERMANENCE

Impermanence is also luminous, as beautiful as a jewel.

The next stanza from Longchenpa's *Crucial Advice* says:

Although you have gained this life of freedom and advantage, it will not last. So keep in mind these instructions for the moment of death.[152]

This is a bald statement about the ephemeral nature of existence. We will all die. It is a great tragedy, but it is an unavoidable truth. Everything is impermanent – the external world, our bodies, our minds. Each thought rises like a wave, peaks and then dissolves of its own accord. Every emotion we have rises, peaks, collapses and then disappears completely. The same is true for every feeling and sensation we have, even every relationship we have. Everything goes away. It all just disappears. Everything is completely and undeniably impermanent. This is really important. Namgay Dawa Rinpoche says that impermanence is the heart of the Buddha Dharma, that if we do not awaken to impermanence we will continue to chase worldly things and thus remain mired in suffering. First we must recognize impermanence intellectually, then we need to really feel it. That first stanza of the *Crucial Advice* is pointing particularly to the impermanence of the body and of the

---

[152] Longchenpa, *Crucial Advice: A Complete Set of Instructions for the Bardos,* Translated by Adam Pearcey (2010). See full text here: https://www.lotsawahouse.org/tibetan-masters/longchen-rabjam/complete-set-instructions

dualistic mind. Death is unavoidable. There is no point pretending that it doesn't happen. As the great sage Nagarjuna famously said:

Life flickers in the flurries of a thousand ills,

More fragile than a bubble in a stream.

In sleep, each breath departs and is again drawn in;

How wondrous that we wake up living still![153]

The truth of impermanence is ubiquitous. It is so ever-present that we don't see it. In that sense it is a bit like our own nose. Everywhere we look, we see, hear and touch only impermanent things. Sadly, we mistakenly think these things are permanent, but there is nothing permanent or lasting, nothing at all. Some longer term cycles—like the cycle of day and night or the seasons—give the illusion of permanence but these are also temporary. Even stars and suns come to an end, go dark. Eventually our own sun will dim and then there will be no more cycle of dawn and dusk. Why be attached to material things that are so ephemeral? It is completely illogical to invest time, energy and emotion into things that will not last and cannot provide enduring happiness. Furthermore, every single thing we own we will lose. Things deteriorate, cease to function, break or are lost. The impermanence of physical things makes our attachment to them illogical and delusional.

Likewise, our thoughts and emotions are impermanent. Thoughts and emotions are like mirages; unreal things that exist for mere moments before they fade away. It is this mirage of thoughts and feelings that we identify with and call our "self", our personality or identity. Why invest energy and emotion into this "self" that is little better than a passing hallucination? Why put so much stock in thoughts and feelings that are so fleeting? To do so is

---

[153] Quoted in Patrul Rinpoche, *Words of My Perfect Teacher: A Complete Translation of a Classic Introduction to Tibetan Buddhism*, AltaMira Press, 1998, p. 41.

illogical and delusional. Grasping onto thoughts and feelings as though they are real and lasting leads to intense suffering.

Also, as this stanza of Longchenpa's states so starkly, all who are born inevitably die. This is an inescapable truth. Everyone we know, everyone we love, will one day die. We too will die. Though our own death is certain, the time of our passing is unknown. It could be in a decade or a year. It could be in an hour or in mere minutes. There is no way of knowing. One of the biggest obstacles to practice is the misguided belief in an inevitable tomorrow. We put off practice thinking we will do it sometime in the future. That future is a fantasy that may never come. There may be no tomorrow for us. If we realized the truth of impermanence, we would dedicate our lives to the practice of Dharma right now and not defer it for a moment. The most common reason for someone not practicing enough or not practicing diligently is that they have not realized the truth of impermanence. As noted earlier, this realization of impermanence cannot be a mere intellectual understanding. It must be felt. It must take root in the heart.

Some may think that impermanence is the cause of all suffering. This is untrue. Our delusion that impermanent thigs are permanent and our resultant attachment to them is the cause of all suffering. Indeed, impermanence makes realization possible, as deluded mind states are also temporary and therefore can be swept away. Belief in a permanent self, or in lasting emotions, leads many to feel that they cannot change. This traps them as they are, separated from the wonder of awakening by their own delusions of self-permanence.

Impermanence is not a negative. Indeed, it can help us to see and appreciate beauty. We appreciate rainbows all the more because they are so temporary. Without the change made possible by the impermanence of all things there would be no butterflies, no flowers and no sun showers. Most importantly, without realizing the truth of impermanence and the renunciation it inspires there is no enlightenment. Therefore, take time to deeply contemplate impermanence and take the truth of it to heart. The following words from Patrul Rinpoche (1808–1887) make for an effective daily contemplation to help us realize the truth of impermanence:

Whatever is born is impermanent and is bound to die.

Whatever is stored up is impermanent and is bound to run out.

Whatever comes together is impermanent and is bound to come apart.

Whatever is built is impermanent and is bound to collapse.

Whatever rises up is impermanent and is bound to fall down.

So also, friendship and enmity, fortune and sorrow, good and evil, all the thoughts that run through your mind – everything is always changing.[154]

When we truly feel the truth of impermanence we develop a revulsion for all worldly things: hope for gain and fear of loss; hope for pleasure and fear of pain, hope for good reputation and fear of bad reputation, hope for praise and fear of blame. When we rid ourselves of these worldly concerns, our minds turn then to the only thing that eases suffering, the Buddha Dharma, which leads us to the only thing that does not die, because it was never born – the true nature, which is the ultimate nature of our minds. Given that everything is impermanent and we may enter the Bardo of Dying at any time, we need to regularly contemplate the bardo teachings and keep them in mind.

True Nature Of Mind

This next stanza of Longchenpa's *Crucial Advice* is really quite important:

Now, during this intermediate period of the bardo of this life,

---

[154] Patrul Rinpoche, *The Words of My Perfect Teacher: A Complete Translation of a Classic Introduction to Tibetan Buddhism*, AltaMira Press, 1998, p.46.

Decide, with complete certainty, that the wisdom of your own awareness is Dharmakaya.[155]

This stanza is pointing to everything I've been saying so far, that the bardos are gaps in dualistic mind that reveal the true nature of mind, the Dharmakaya. Dharmakaya is simply another word for Buddha Nature, true nature of mind, ultimate or absolute nature. The word 'Dharmakaya' is also used to refer to the subtlest manifestation of an enlightened being. 'Kaya' means body. The Dharmakaya or Dharma body means, essentially, a body of luminous space. That's not how the word is being used here. What is being referred to here is that our own awareness is non-dual with the Buddha Nature. Ordinary awareness *is* the Buddha Nature. It isn't anything mysterious or far away or fancy.

To recognize the unity of our own awareness with the Dharmakaya we simply have to refine or cultivate our ability to rest undistractedly in our own ordinary awareness exactly as it is right now. Our ordinary awareness— that which is aware of you reading right now—is the Dharmakaya, which is one with everything. Our own ordinary awareness is the absolute nature of all. That's what that word Dharmakaya is referring to. It is referring to the absolute nature of all, the absolute and pristine and perfect nature of all, just to be really emphatic. Longchenpa is saying that we must become certain in this truth. How do we do that? Through meditation focused on uncovering the true nature of mind. This is a form of meditation that emphasizes relaxing into our natural state as it is right now (see Chapter Twelve). Guru Yoga will also give us this certainty. Longchenpa continues:

And sustaining the ongoing experience of its self-radiance, the meditation which is naturally clear,

Everything will only enhance naturally arising wisdom!

---

[155] Longchenpa, *Crucial Advice: A Complete Set of Instructions for the Bardos,* Translated by Adam Pearcey (2010). See full text here: https://www.lotsawahouse.org/tibetan-masters/longchen-rabjam/complete-set-instructions

What Longchenpa is referring to in the first line of this stanza is the form of meditation that is focused on recognizing the true nature of mind, recognizing rigpa. Longchenpa is saying that in order to become certain that one's own awareness is non-dual with the absolute or ultimate or perfect nature of all (Dharmakaya) we need to meditate and recognize the nature of mind and then rest in that state, rest in rigpa. 'Sustaining the ongoing experience of its self-radiance' is another way of saying to rest in rigpa. And then luminosity will dawn. The phrase "naturally clear" is implying that luminosity.

The second line in the stanza says that once we recognize and rest in rigpa everything will only enhance naturally arising wisdom. This is a profound statement, which means that when we are resting in that state, when we are resting in the true nature of mind, whatever arises in the mind, any thought, any feeling or emotion, any sensation and any external objects or events we perceive, simply enhances our natural awareness.

This is an important point – a fully enlightened being still has thoughts, emotions, etc. They rise, like wisps of smoke and then vanish almost instantly, as if blown away by a gentle breeze, they self-liberate. Nothing has to be done with them, because there's no fuel in them. There's no attachment to them. So Longchenpa is saying that everything that arises, everything we experience, will just enhance our awareness. Everything that one experiences will just illuminate one's enlightenment.

Death: Dissolution Of Senses And Mind

During the Bardo of Dying our sense perceptions drop away and there are illusory experiences that feel as though we are rising, falling or shaking. There may also be an experience of haziness. As Longchenpa describes:

During the bardo of dying, when the four elements dissolve,

There will be the illusory experiences of rising and falling, shaking, and haziness.

And the dissolution of earth, water, fire, wind and space.

The sense faculties too will cease to function.

The first few lines of this stanza suggest that the bardo state in-between this life and the next can be somewhat distressing and distracting, especially if there is pain. This is why, in the quote shared earlier, Naropa suggested that mindfulness or meditation is essential to successfully traversing the Bardo of Dying. We don't need to worry too much about these symptoms, the shakiness etc. The most important thing, which Longchenpa goes on to say later, is to just recognize that whatever occurs as we're dying is a manifestation of the mind. It is all just a manifestation of the mind. It's nothing to worry about. It's nothing to be afraid of. It is also nothing to hang on to. Not everyone will experience all of the confusing, distressing or distracting experiences described in the bardo teachings, so it is important not to focus on them too much but rather focus on the remedy for everything that might eventuate as we die, which is to develop our meditational capacity.

When Longchenpa tells us that as we die the elements dissolve and 'the sense faculties cease to function' he is referring to the progressive dissolution of the dualistic mind that is tied to the cessation of bodily functions. In the Tibetan Buddhist worldview the physical body is composed of the basic elements (earth, water, fire, air/wind and space). Each of the senses are tied to particular elements. Traditionally it is said that as the elements dissolve, the associated sense perception dissolves along with them.

As the body's functions cease, sense faculties cease as well and this leads to the various layers of the dualistic mind, the sense consciousness, falling away also. As Ngakchang Rinpoche describes with beautiful succinctness:

With physical death the psycho-physical elements dissolve into each other and disappear into primal emptiness. Earth dissolves into water. Water dissolves into fire. Fire dissolves into air. Air dissolves into space and space dissolves into itself. Then we enter into the chönyid bardo [Bardo of Luminosity] in which the son & mother clear lights are united.[156]

The table below shows the relationship between the senses and the elements according to Buddhism.

Table 2: Relationship between the Sense Organs and the Elements

Sense Organ	Sense Object	Sense Consciousness	Element
eye	visual objects	visual consciousness	Earth
ear	sound waves	auditory consciousness	Space
nose	odors	olfactory consciousness	Air
tongue	tastes	gustatory consciousness	Water
body	tangible objects	tactile consciousness	Fire

It is not too important to learn this way of viewing things in detail, but it is helpful to understand what we will directly experience as we die, especially which functions will drop in which order. This gives us milestones that tell us where we are in the process so that we will know when the opportunity for total liberation will arise so that we can seize that opportunity with all our being.

In Vajrayana Buddhism there are always four aspects or levels to everything: the outer, inner, secret and most secret. In terms of the bardo teachings, the outer level often has to do with the body. The inner level often has to do with the mind or thought forms. The secret level has to do with the true nature of mind, or rigpa, and the most secret level is the level of the ultimate or absolute nature of everything – the Mother Luminosity. These aspects or levels are also applied to our personal experiences at the time of death.

According to the Tibetan view, the weakening of our life-force (prana) as we begin to die causes the earth element to dissolve into the water element,

---

[156] See *The Nine Bardos of the Aro gTér: https://aroencyclopaedia.org/shared/text/n/nine_bardos_ar_eng.php*

like rock salt in a stream.[157] The outer sign of that occurrence is weakness or the loss of physical strength. The inner or cognitive sign is that the mind becomes dull and perhaps melancholic. At this point, the manifestation of luminosity is still obscured by dualistic mind but manages to shine through in a masked form. This is referred to as the secret sign. As the earth element dissolves into water the secret sign is the manifestation of a vague sense of mirage.

As the prana or energies supporting our life continue to weaken or dissipate, the water element dissolves into the fire element, like dew evaporating under the sun. An outer sign of this is that the mouth goes dry. The main inner sign is a sense of haziness. There can also be some anxiety. The secret sign of luminosity, still obscured by dualistic mind, is that our experience becomes misty, like smoke or steam that glimmers a little.

After that, the life-force dissipates even more and the fire element dissolves into the wind element, like a candle being blown out. The main outer or physical sign of this is a sensation of cold and the heat of the body dissipating. The inner signs are that the mind seems to flicker, alternating between clarity and opacity. The perceptual ability is failing. The secret sign of this is the appearance of red lights that are described as being like fireflies. Remember, this perception of fireflies is our innate luminosity managing to appear through the obscuration of the dualistic mind.

Then the wind element dissolves into awareness or mind itself, like a breeze dissipating in open space. The main outer or bodily sign of this is difficulty breathing. The inner sign is bewilderment, and possibly life-like visions, perhaps of past experiences and people we are close to, perhaps of frightening things (such as monsters or demons), perhaps of wonderful

---

[157] For a more traditional description of the dissolution of the energies, elements, sense perceptions and consciousness see Tsele Natsok Rangdrol, *Mirror of Mindfulness*, Rangjung Yeshe Publications, 1987.

things such as angels (dakas and dakinis). The visions that appear depend on the habits and quality of one's mind. The more kind and compassionate the mind, the more benign or beautiful the visions. It is important to remember that these visions are produced by the dualistic mind. They are not visitations from an afterlife. The secret sign that manifests here is described as being like a flaming torch. The dualistic mind is losing its power and so our innate luminosity is really beginning to shine through, albeit in this masked way.

At this point the sense-faculties of the eyes, ears, nose, tongue, and body have been degenerating and dissolving one at a time in a specific order (see Table Two). The ability to perceive shapes, sounds and odors or to taste or feel textures is lost. With the final loss of the sense of touch the dualistic mind, consciousness, loses its last anchor – sense perception, the source of stimulation that keeps it going and perpetuates the sense of being an entity in a body isolated from everything else. With no anchors and no sense stimulation the dualistic mind or consciousness itself dissolves into space. In other words, our samsaric delusion is unravelling, stuttering towards its inevitable halt. This is when the external breathing stops. In the Western world this is the point that marks the beginning of clinical death. To the outside observer the skin loses color and pales and there's only slight warmth remaining at the heart. Up until this point, and perhaps a little beyond, there is still a possibility that the dying person can be revived.

In *The Refined Essence of Oral Instructions*, Padmasambhava describes these stages of dissolution as follows:

By earth dissolving in water, the body becomes heavy and cannot support itself. By water dissolving in fire, the mouth and nose dry up. By fire dissolving in wind, body heat disappears. By wind dissolving in consciousness, one cannot but exhale with a rattle and inhale with a gasp.

At that time, the feelings of being pressed down by a huge mountain, being trapped within darkness, or being dropped into the expanse of space occur. All these experiences are accompanied by thunderous and ringing sounds. The whole sky will be vividly bright like an unfurled brocade.

Moreover, the natural forms of your mind, the peaceful, wrathful, semi-wrathful deities, and the ones with various heads fill the sky, within a dome of rainbow lights.[158]

All of these experiences may occur, but what occurs depends on our cultural conditioning and beliefs, so we may experience something quite different. Whatever arises, it is crucial that, as these experiences unfold, we not be swept up in them. We must observe without becoming absorbed in them, without being overwhelmed and without reacting in an overblown way. Tulku Thondop Rinpoche puts it like this:

How should these dissolution stages be dealt with by common people? First, you must realize that you are in the process of dying. You should try to take the experiences of dissolution as peacefully as possible. You should try to remember that all the bardo appearances and experiences are the fabrications of your own mind, like dreams. You should not be attached to them, get irritated by them, or be afraid of them. With peace and naturalness, you should watch or be one with the true nature of your own mind, calmly and clearly, instead of running after and grasping at thoughts and experiences.[159]

---

[158] See the full pith instruction in Kunsang, Erik Pema, 'Refined Essence of Oral Instructions', in *Dakini Teachings: A Collection of Padmasambhava's Advice to the Dakini Yeshe Tsogyal*, Rangjung Yeshe Publications, 1999.

[159] Tulku Thondup, *Enlightened Journey: Buddhist Practice as Daily Life*, Edited by Harold Talbott, Shambhala Publications, 1995, p. 58.

Now, as the dissolutions come to an end, we are reaching the exciting bit. The opportunity for total liberation that the dying process offers is approaching. According to the bardo tradition, soon after the breathing stops what remains of the dualistic mind, the subtle clinging to a sense of self and the attendant attachment and aversion that clinging generates, unravels swiftly. Once the subtle remainder of dualistic mind and its clinging thoughts are collapsing there are three stark, pared back experiences that occur. These are referred to as the redness, whiteness and blackness, or the red appearance, white appearance and black appearance. The bardo teachings indicate that these experiences can unfold in one of two ways. Blackness always occurs last but the redness and whiteness can occur either first or second. As Tsele Natsok Rangdrol states, 'It is not definite at this time which of the two, the whiteness or the redness, will manifest first'.[160] The traditional tantric explanation for why the red vision shows first is that the person dying has stronger male energy, meaning the weaker female energy or red vision dissolves first. Likewise, someone who experiences the white vision first has stronger female energy. For me, this tantric explanation is a little simplistic, we are all blends of both male and female and gender is completely empty of inherent existence. Arya Tara, a Buddha from another time and world, reputedly said about herself:

Here there is no man nor woman – no self, no person, no dualistic mind. The labels 'male' and 'female' have no essence; the foolish worldly ones are thoroughly mistaken.[161]

Furthermore, in the *Vimalakirti Sutra* the Buddha is recorded as pronouncing:

In all things, there is neither male nor female.[162]

---

[160] Tsele Natsok Rangdrol, *Mirror of Mindfulness*, Rangjung Yeshe Publications, 1987, page 31.

[161] A similar version of this teaching is quoted in 'The History And Importance Of Tara', *Namchak website*: https://www.namchak.org/community/blog/the-history-and-importance-of-tara/

[162] Vimalakirti Sutra, Verses 61 -63. See the full sutra here: https://www2.hf.uio.no/polyglotta/index.php?page=fulltext&vid=37&view=fulltext

This is an all-encompassing statement. The Buddha is not allowing any exceptions. How then can there be male and female energies? Male and female essences? How can there be a sacred feminine or a sacred masculine? Given this, we need to realize that the tantric conceptualization of the subtle or energetic body is just that, a conceptualization. Indeed, even the tantric system acknowledges that biological sex and gender have nothing to do with whether or not we have predominately "male" or "female energy". It is more likely that the quality of the mind is what really matters here, whether or not our minds have more attachment (red vision) or aversion (white vision).

The bardo teachings however do often deploy this notion of gendered energies so we will entertain it for a moment to get a sense of how these things are traditionally understood. The white appearance or vision is believed to be the manifestation of the energetic inheritance we receive from our fathers (the White Bodhicitta) and the red vision is believed to be the manifestation of the energetic inheritance we receive from our mothers (Red Bodhicitta). The white appearance or vision is said to be like moonlight, space filled with a white light. Beyond the white vision, there is no return, the physical body and the person cannot be revived. Perhaps this is why there are so many stories of people who were clinically dead being revived and reporting that they experienced a white light. The red vision is said to be like the sky at dusk, space filled with red light.

Traditionally speaking, the white inheritance from our fathers manifests in our life and minds as aversion (or anger) and the red inheritance from our mothers manifests as attachment (or desire). As these visions manifest and dissipate those negative inheritances dissolve. Their dissolution gives rise to the blackness, which is the energetic manifestation of ignorance, our delusion that we exist as separate and permanent beings. In a way the blackness is the manifestation of our most subtle sense of self. The blackness is described as like being enveloped in a shroud, a heavy darkness. With the fading of the black vision, that ignorance or delusion dissolves also. This means that the subtle sense of self is completely fading away. Remember at the beginning of this book we defined the self as merely a sense of being separate from others, of existing independently, along with an identification with thoughts and feelings as though they constituted a person. This delusion is now unravelling.

In-between the blackness and the dawning of the Mother Luminosity, our opportunity for ultimate liberation, some of us will faint in terror at being separated from life and our sense of self. This is the subtle self freaking out at the realization of its impermanence and inevitable demise. Others, however, will not faint at this point. Those who have achieved some stability in meditation or have recognized the true nature of mind will remain calm and lucid. The word "faint" is used because the deluded mind can still come back or re-awaken as the result of karma. Karma in its most subtle form is simply the habit of the dualistic mind to emerge anew in each moment; just as one thought forms after a previous one despite there being no substantial link between them. Thoughts are not truly linked or joined in that way. Rather than thinking of thoughts as links in a chain it is better to think of them as bubbles rising from the same stream. There is just the habit of thinking (the stream), so one thought follows another. Likewise, there is the habit of the self existing, so the self and the subtle dualistic mind will re-emerge. The dualistic mind can also be understood as a bubble rising from the stream that is the self's habit of existence. This habit of existence is the seed of rebirth. It is a subtle, almost primal, form of consciousness.

Before the full form of the dualistic mind re-emerges, there is an opportunity to break the karmic bubble machine. With the passing of the black appearance there is a true bardo, a profound gap, an island of stillness between the stream of movement that is samsaric existence. This gap gives rise to what is called the Bardo of Luminosity, the dawning of the ground of all. This is the Mother Luminosity, our one true mother. When those who fainted into unconsciousness regain some basic level of consciousness they will be met with a fleeting moment in which the empty luminosity, the naked nature of mind, appears. Sadly it will pass unrecognized. Those accomplished in meditation will experience this luminosity for much longer durations and will recognize it instantly and thus have the chance to merge with it, to reunite with the one true mother and be free of suffering once and for all and attain enlightenment. How extraordinary is this!

The table in Appendix One illustrates the dying process discussed above and shows the order in which the sense faculties cease to function and the experiences we all have as we progress through the bardo between this existence and the next. These experiences are like milestones or road signs, they indicate where we are. The reason for understanding this process and learning about these milestones is so that we know what to do when this is all happening to us. This will be our direct experience as we die. First, we will be unable to see. Then we will lose our hearing and our sense of smell will go. Our ability to taste will go after that. Finally, our ability to feel our body goes, we lose our sense of touch.

What I want to emphasize and draw your attention to in Table 2 is the internal signs. These are the stand out landmarks of our journey through the Bardo of Dying. It is also important to recognize the outer or physical signs that are bolded in the table, those are also clear landmarks. The column labelled "Factor Dissolving" contains information relating to Buddhist philosophy around existence, around what constitutes material things. You don't necessarily need to memorize that stuff to get benefit from the bardo teachings. Certainly it would not be a bad thing to learn about the elements and factors, if you feel inclined to do so. What's really important here is the information that is bolded. These are the things that will give you your bearings in the Bardo of Dying. These are the things that will let you know where you are in the process. It is worth returning to this table again and again so that the milestones or signposts that will help guide us to the Mother Luminosity are fixed in our minds.

CHAPTER TEN

SHUNYATA AND LUMINOSITY

When our bodies have died and our minds fallen away all that remains is luminous awareness – the pristine Dharmakaya.

Let's circle back now, to the moment in the bardos before the three appearances or visions manifest and continue with Longchenpa's advice. He writes:

At that time, remind yourself:

'Now I am dying, but there is no need to fear.'

Examine: 'What is death? Who is dying? Where does dying take place?'

Death is merely the return of borrowed elements.

In the face of rigpa itself, there is no birth or death.

It is hard for us to imagine that when the sense faculties cease to function in the dying process we still have the ability to think. To convince yourself this is possible consider the fact that in deep sleep our sense faculties are suspended, we don't see, hear, smell or taste anything, and yet we still dream. The difference between sleep and dying is that in one we wake into this illusory waking life and in the other we wake into a dream-like bardo beyond death. Longchenpa suggests in the stanza above that once the sense faculties cease we should examine death.

What Longchenpa is suggesting that we do at this point in the dying process is to ascertain the true nature of the death process. We each need to do these contemplations in the moment, but here is a spoiler: the true nature of death is that it is illusory and empty. Just like everything else. In an ideal situation we will be able to do these contemplations and recognize the illusory nature of death in the moment we are dying. Sadly, some people will not have the presence of mind to ask these questions while they're dying. For some of us death will be either too sudden or too painful to be able to do this. But that's okay, because we've got a cheat sheet, we know what the landmarks in the bardo are and we know what to do when the Mother Luminosity dawns.

This is not to say these examinations are not good to do while we're alive, they certainly are. While we are alive we should regularly ask ourselves: What is death? Who is dying? Where does dying take place? This line of enquiry leads us to the Buddhist concept of Shunyata. The fact that all things are deeply interconnected and impermanent. The fact that all things lack an inherent or substantive existence. All things are fluid and dynamic.

Choose any object you like and analyze it to learn the truth of this: a tree, a flower, your own body. If you take time to look for the thing we call tree or flower or body, you will not be able to find a single, separately existing thing. You just won't find it. You'll find that all things break down into parts and the further you break it down the more interconnected everything is. You can't find "treeness" in the roots alone, nor the trunk alone, nor in the bark, branches or leaves. You can't find "youness" in your legs, arms, torso, or even in your head. You are not merely your body parts. But also, you are not your thoughts or feelings either, because something remains when thoughts and emotions subside and the mind is quiet.

If you keep analyzing down to smaller and smaller parts eventually you get to atoms, and then beyond that to space, which means things have no inherent existence in and of themselves. All things depend on all other things to exist. If you take out one part of a thing, it no longer exists as it was, as we thought it did. This is Shunyata. When we recognize Shunyata, when we are able to not merely understand it intellectually but *live in its spacious openness*, then that is the gateway to realization, to accomplishment of the path of Dharma. The stanza from Longchenpa above is telling us to see death in that light. To see that truth. Death is empty and illusory. It isn't something to be fearful of, or to fixate on as being a permanent, real, existing thing. The final line of this stanza—*In the face of rigpa itself, there is no birth or death*— very strongly points to this empty nature of death. Rigpa, the true nature of mind, is unborn and therefore undying. It is beyond time; beyond now and then, beyond past and future. It is beyond subject and object; beyond the self and beyond other, beyond you and beyond me. In rigpa the self, the dualistic mind, does not arise because rigpa is beyond delusion. In essence, in rigpa there cannot be death because there is nothing to die, no self or person fabricated out of multiple compound factors. That is a characteristic of the dualistic mind (sem) only. Beyond the dualistic mind and beyond death there is simply timeless, luminous awareness.

The Three Appearances Or Visions

Although death of the self, on the ultimate level, is a projection of the dualistic mind, on the relative level, which is where we all live and where we are all trapped, it must be experienced and dealt with appropriately. It is a moment in which we can either find ultimate freedom or condemn ourselves to further misery. Because we really don't want to miss the road signs alerting us that the moment of our potential liberation is looming, I'm going to go over the three appearances—the red, white and black visions —again, and in greater detail. In the bardo teachings these three experiences are sometimes referred to as appearance (white vision), expansion (red vision) and attainment (black vision). This relates to tantric ideas that are not essential to understand to safely navigate the Bardo of Dying, though do learn about them if you are inclined to do so.

As you may remember, which vision appears first is different for each of us. Depending on our karma (the habitual tendency of our mind) either the red or white vision will appear first. So what is the white appearance? It's described in the table in Appendix One as clear vacuity or space filled with white light. It is an expanse of white filling our whole field of vision.

We are not seeing this with our eyes, as our eye sense is no longer functioning, we are perceiving it with our minds. It's just the perception of whiteness. We briefly discussed the Buddhist tantric idea about what this is. In Tibetan Buddhism everything is divided up into male and female energies; again, it's quite heterosexist. The tantric explanation of the white appearance is that the male essence is coming to the fore as other things fall away. It is also considered that this is the dissolution of one of the three main poisons – anger. As Jamgon Kongtrul Rinpoche taught:

> In the appearance experience, the outer sign is that everything becomes whitish, and inwardly our consciousness becomes dull. In this stage, aggression and anger dissolve.[163]

It is not important to believe deeply in this gendered conception of the bardo experience. Whether we believe this or not doesn't matter. As for myself, I don't think that's particularly useful to dwell on. Why? Because, as I've already said, male and female are ultimately empty of inherent substance. In the truer sense the white appearance is the radiance or display of the mind. What I think is actually useful to note is that this white appearance is a flag or signpost. It is something we will experience, it's not something to be enamored with, it's not something to be afraid of. It is just something that

---

[163] See: 'Jamgon Kongtrul Rinpoche's Bardo Teachings', *Tricycle: The Buddhist Review*: https://tricycle.org/magazine/bardo-teachings/

marks where we are. The white appearance signals to us that the Mother Luminosity is about to dawn, it is coming after the black vision that will soon rise.

At this point there is still a very subtle mind, a more subtle form of our dualistic mind. There is still a perceiver here. There is still a subtle sense of self that is experiencing these appearances, these visions. The next thing that happens is very clear vacuity or space filled with red light. Now, again, the Tibetan Buddhist way of thinking about this is that this is the female potency or energy or inheritance manifesting. It also is seen as the dissolution of desire or attachment (especially attachment to self). Jamgon Kongtrul Rinpoche describes this experience, known as expanding or increasing, in this way:

> Outwardly, we perceive everything in reddish hues. Our inner awareness could be compared to seeing fireflies at night: we can see flickers of light, but not a constant gleam. At that time, the conflicting emotion of attachment dissolves.[164]

Once more, it doesn't matter what we believe is happening here. The red vision will still arise. This red light is also not something to be afraid of, not something to cling to, not something to pursue. We just treat all these experiences or manifestations the same way we treat everything that occurs in our meditation. It is just stuff that arises that will naturally dissolve of its own accord without us intervening. We don't need to do anything. This all just happens automatically as we die. We just watch, we just observe. No need to intervene at this point. Then, the next manifestation is that of blackness or darkness. As Jamgon Kongtrul Rinpoche taught:

> The third of these experiences is known as attainment. During this time, our outer experience is of darkness, a sort of blackout. Inner awareness, here, is like a candle inside a vase. Because the candle is inside the vase,

---

[164] Ibid

it is able to shine clearly. During this time the conflicting emotion of ignorance is dissolving.[165]

Now, the interesting thing about this experience of blackness is that it can cause people to feel frightened, because it is dark. Many of us associate darkness with oblivion. Oblivion causes some of us to feel terror. If we do feel frightened at this point, then we can swoon into unconsciousness. This will not happen if we are able to remain calm and mindful. There will simply be a momentary pause, much like the gap between thoughts we experience in meditation.

This is the point at which that last vestige of the person, the last part of dualistic mind, falls away. If we were not Buddhists this moment is what we would call final death. But is that it? Is that all there is? The bardo teachings tells us that this isn't the end. After the white, red and black appearances something else dawns. Chokyi Nyima Rinpoche puts it this way:

> The luminous bardo of dharmata occurs after the outer elements, the sense faculties and sense bases as well as the inner gross and subtle thoughts have dissolved. It follows the completion of the three experiences of whiteness, redness and blackness at the end of the painful bardo of dying.[166]

At this point, very clear vacuity or space filled with clear light or luminosity arises. This is the most precious moment. The Mother Luminosity dawns and total and permanent freedom is possible. Everything to do with the dualistic mind, the person we think we are, is gone. And yet, there is an awareness of this spacious luminosity. Chokyi Nyima Rinpoche explains:

> The three experiences of whiteness, redness and blackness are accompanied by the cessations of the three poisons – attachment, anger

---

[165] Ibid

[166] Chokyi Nyima Rinpoche, The *Bardo Guidebook*, Rangjung Yeshe Publications, 1991, page 112.

and delusion. Whiteness is accompanied by the complete cessation of the forty thought states resulting from anger. Redness appears together with the cessation of the thirty-three thought states resulting from attachment. Blackness marks the cessation of the seven thought states resulting from delusion. What remains when all of these thought states have ceased is simply the unconstructed nature of mind called Dharmakaya. In Dzogchen terminology, this is called basic wakefulness and is the naked awareness itself.[167]

To put this in much simpler terms, every last skerrick of the deluded, dualistic mind and its negative emotions is gone. Why is the Mother Luminosity experienced at this point? It appears at this point because the Mother Luminosity is our true nature and the process of dying has cleared away all that obscures it. As Chokyi Nyima Rinpoche makes clear:

It is simply because all sentient beings already possess an enlightened essence, the sugatagarbha. This essence is present and permeates anyone who has mind, just as oil completely permeates any sesame seed.[168]

Let's go over this a little bit more so that we really get it. Given that the Mother Luminosity is always present as our true nature, why don't we recognize it right now? Quite simply, we don't recognize it because we are deluded. Our true nature is obscured by dualistic mind, which is ignorance. Even so, at the end of the dissolution stages, after the whiteness, redness and blackness have appeared, there is this 'momentary lifting of the veil of delusion, leaving all obscurations temporarily yet totally absent'.[169] At this time the ground of wisdom or Mother Luminosity is vividly present. The natural state is revealed

[167] Chokyi Nyima Rinpoche, The *Bardo Guidebook*, Rangjung Yeshe Publications, 1991, page 113.

[168] Chokyi Nyima Rinpoche, The *Bardo Guidebook*, Rangjung Yeshe Publications, 1991, page 116.

[169] Chokyi Nyima Rinpoche, The *Bardo Guidebook*, Rangjung Yeshe Publications, 1991, page 116.

without all the overlays of dualistic thinking, feeling and sensing. The true nature of our mind is naked and clear. Here is the opportunity for total liberation, because here there is no ordinary mind anymore. There is just the Buddha Nature remaining. And it is aware of itself. So, what do we do at this point? Let's return to Longchenpa to find out:

> When space dissolves into pure luminosity,
>
> The six consciousnesses dissolve into the basis of all, the Dharmadhatu,
>
> As awareness parts from the inanimate, there is an experience of pure awareness, devoid of phenomena.
>
> Separated from the ordinary mind, the great primordial purity of dharmakaya dawns.
>
> Through having recognized this here and now in training,
>
> You will be freed directly, in a single instant.[170]

Here again Longchenpa mentions the Dharmakaya, which is another way of saying enlightenment, unbound awareness without a sense of the person or a sense of self. According to Longchenpa, all that is required at this point is not some fancy tantric stuff. All we need do is simply recognize what this is. To "recognize" means to *feel* it, to be one with the true nature of mind.

The metaphor used to describe this is of a child reuniting with its mother. There is still, at this moment, a subtle, gossamer thin separation between rigpa and the ground luminosity. The Mother Luminosity is what is *appearing* here and what is witnessing it is called the Son or Child Luminosity. The Child Luminosity is the experience of rigpa or the Mind of Clear Light in one's present meditation practice. The idea is that we are a child reuniting

---

[170] Longchenpa, *Crucial Advice: A Complete Set of Instructions for the Bardos,* Translated by Adam Pearcey (2010). See full text here: https://www.lotsawahouse.org/tibetan-masters/longchen-rabjam/complete-set-instructions

with our mother. It's so beautiful, nothing to be frightened of. We just embrace Mother Luminosity.

Jetsunma Tenzin Palmo, emphasizing our need to become familiar with the luminous nature of mind while we are alive, puts it this way:

> If a son is used to seeing the mother, then at the time when she's completely revealed at death, the son will race towards the mother; but if the son has never seen the mother then when the mother appears the son will not run towards her. He will pull back, thinking 'Who's this strange being?' In other words, unless we are very familiar with the nature of the mind during our lifetime we will not be able to recognize it at the time of death.[171]

There is all kinds of technical language for this moment of the Child Luminosity meeting the Mother Luminosity: becoming one with the mind of the guru; becoming one with Buddha; becoming one with the true nature. Whatever language is used doesn't actually matter. All we need to know is that our separation ends there. Our isolation ends there. Our suffering ends there. Liberation is ours if we simply recognize what this is, that this is the Mother Luminosity, which is the ground of everything, including our own mind, and embrace it. In that embrace we will be free.

So, this is the moment. It is really important. This is the gateway to total liberation in this lifetime, if one hasn't already achieved it before one dies. I don't think I can make it any clearer how important this moment is in the dying process and in our whole lives. It is the most precious moment we will ever experience.

Given it is such a precious moment we should do everything we can to prepare for it. What is the best way to prepare? I've noted repeatedly that it is simple sitting meditation. As Tsele Natsok Rangdrol taught:

---

[171] New Year's Retreat: A session with Jetsunma Tenzin Palmo (teaching video). See: https://youtu.be/-qgy707_mKw

The supreme method for recognizing the ground luminosity of the first bardo and attaining liberation is to become fully resolved about the mind right now in the bardo of the present life, and then to exclusively concentrate, beyond meditation and distraction, on continuous practice of the ultimate nature of ordinary mind, the unfabricated and natural state of dharmakaya. Knowing how to maintain it, unspoiled by the obstacles of defects or defilements, mental constructs and fabrications, is crucial not only in the first bardo but at all times.[172]

If we have not meditated enough during our lifetime this precious moment will flash by and we will fail to seize the opportunity for liberation. We will be lucky if the opportunity lasts more than a second in duration. Not lucky, actually, it would require practice to be a second long. Otherwise, it will be microseconds. According to the bardo teachings this opportunity will last for as long as we are able to rest in rigpa in our daily meditation. If we can rest in rigpa for seven minutes, that's how long this opportunity will last. As Tsele Natsok Rangdrol writes:

> It is taught that the whiteness, redness, and blackness last no longer than one instant of completed action. When, after that, the dharmakaya luminosity of death, the co-emergent wisdom, dawns, it does not usually last longer than a finger snap for ordinary people who have not practiced. Some can stay for the "duration of a meal." Also, people who have practiced slightly can remain for as long as they once could retain stability in the practice of meditation. That is called a "meditation day." It is taught that one remains in this luminosity for between one and five such days.[173]

If you can rest in rigpa permanently then you can take your time resting in that state before choosing to become one with Dharmadhatu or to be

---

[172] Tsele Natsok Rangdrol, *Mirror of Mindfulness*, Rangjung Yeshe Publications, 1987, p. 55.

[173] Tsele Natsok Rangdrol, *Mirror of Mindfulness*, Rangjung Yeshe Publications, 1987, p. 53.

reborn for the benefit of sentient beings. True meditation masters do take their time. This is what we call *thukdam*. When a master passes away, he or she rests in this spacious awareness. Sometimes they rest in thukdam for days and days. Khandro Semo Lhanzey Wangmo, a Dudjom yogini and the granddaughter of Dudjom Rinpoche, stayed in the state of thukdam for 15 days, which is really extraordinary.[174] During thukdam the body does not decay. The body remains lifelike, and there is a sense of warmth at the heart. If you put your hand on the heart of a master in thukdam, there is warmth there. Often there's no bad smell, there's no awfulness, there's no rigidity. It is actually very inspiring to witness. More recently, the aunt of one of my other Lamas, Ngakpa Karma Lhundup Rinpoche, passed away. She was a nun and more than 80 years old. She was in thukdam for four days[175]. She was quite an inconspicuous practitioner. No-one had any idea that she was a highly accomplished yogini. Usually, the profound practitioners keep their accomplishments secret. When they pass away, it becomes evident.

This ability to rest in pure awareness at the time of death is why meditation is so important; because meditation is the simplest and easiest way to train in recognizing the true nature of mind, the clear light, or ground luminosity. According to Tulku Urgyen Rinpoche:

Being adept in the bardos of meditation and dreaming is sufficient. Nothing more remains to be done. But without reaching some degree of stability in meditation and the ability to recognize dreams, I am sorry to say, one cannot avoid enduring the bardo of dying.[176]

---

[174] See: 'Remembering Khandro Semo Lhanzey-la', https://www.dudjomtersar.org/post/remembering-khandro-semo-lhanzey-la

[175] See: 'Tibetan Nun Enters Rare Meditative State After Passing Away in India', *Tibetan Journal*, May 26 2020, https://www.tibetanjournal.com/tibetan-nun-enters-rare-meditative-state-after-passing-away-in-india/

[176] See Tsele Natsok Rangdrol, *Mirror of Mindfulness*, Rangjung Yeshe Publications, 1987, p. 3.

CHAPTER ELEVEN

LUMINOSITY IN THE BARDO OF BECOMING

Through the power of the guru's compassion, you will definitely be liberated.

Now, as Longchenpa notes in the next stanza of *Crucial Advice: A Complete Set of Instructions for the Bardos,* if you miss that opportunity to merge with Mother Luminosity as it flashes by, then you enter the Bardo of Becoming and rebirth:

> This is how it all arises, but should you fail to recognize it,
>
> The dream-like bardo of becoming will dawn.
>
> At that time, by recalling a pure land,
>
> And taking refuge in the lama and the yidam deity,
>
> Some will find freedom in a pure Buddha paradise,
>
> And some will gain the seven qualities of birth in a higher realm,
>
> And be assured of gaining liberation in the next life.[177]

If you have a bit of practice under your belt, at that point in the Bardo of Becoming you can call out to your Lama, your teacher, or to the Buddha.

---

[177] Longchenpa, *Crucial Advice: A Complete Set of Instructions for the Bardos,* Translated by Adam Pearcey (2010). See full text here: https://www.lotsawahouse.org/tibetan-masters/longchen-rabjam/complete-set-instructions

Because enlightened beings are not bound by time, space or physical matter or bodies, they can intervene for you in the Bardo of Becoming if you miss the opportunity in the Bardo of Luminosity. The truth of the Buddhas' and enlightened masters' ability to transcend time and space is revealed in our meditation practice. If we have practiced diligently with open-hearted devotion this truth is apparent to us.

Dudjom Rinpoche's Bardo Pith Instructions

Now we will discuss a very concise teaching on the bardos by Kyabje Dudjom Rinpoche, Jigdral Yeshe Dorje. Dudjom Rinpoche summarized the bardo teachings in one paragraph, which is quite extraordinary, but of course Dudjom Rinpoche was extraordinary on every level. He writes:

> When the time comes for you to die, mingling awareness and the absolute expanse of luminosity, remain in the state of evenness. This is the very best form of transference. Alternatively, dissolve your mind, in the form of a ball of light, into the teacher's heart. By developing skill in this transference technique, you will be liberated. If you are unable to do that, you should recognize the deluded perceptions experienced in the intermediate state as having no intrinsic reality. Using devotion as the path, simply remember your teachers: through the power of their compassion, you will definitely be liberated in a pure Buddhafield.[178]

Now that's what we're talking about! When the ground luminosity or the Mother Luminosity dawns before our Child Luminosity, our naked or pure awareness, we simply embrace the Mother Luminosity and merge with it. Remember, this embrace, this experience of merging, is described as a child climbing into its mother's lap. It is very intimate and beautiful. In the quote above Dudjom Rinpoche is saying that this is the ultimate way to achieve

---

[178] Dudjom Rinpoche, *A Torch Lighting the Way to Freedom*, Shambhala Publications, 2016, p. 271.

liberation at the time of death. When we die, we simply mingle our awareness with the absolute expanse of luminosity, and then remain in that state of evenness. Just remain there. Of course, time doesn't matter in this. At that point, when the ground luminosity manifests, past, present and future do not exist. This is what we call the fourth time, which is non-time, eternal non-time. Dudjom Rinpoche then says that this is the very best form of transference. By transference he is referring to the practice called Phowa in which one transfers their awareness to a pure Buddha field, a mind state in which there are no obstacles to practice and enlightenment. This union with the Mother Luminosity is far superior to any Phowa practice based on psychic energies and channels or transference to pure lands.

If we haven't practiced enough in our lifetime to recognize and merge with the Dharmakaya or to transfer our awareness to a Buddha field, Rinpoche provides an alternative practice to apply in the next bardo, the Bardo of Becoming or Rebirth. This practice is essentially about applying a specific understanding to our experience in the intermediate states. In the Bardo of Becoming we start to see all kinds of wild displays or visions, some of them scary, some of them beautiful. All kinds of manifestations, all kinds of images and scenes, all kinds of sound, light and movement are thrown up by the dualistic mind.

In a recent world-first a team of neuroscientists recorded the activity of a dying human brain and discovered 'rhythmic brain wave patterns around the time of death that are similar to those occurring during dreaming, memory recall, and meditation'.[179] In other words, the idea that a person's life flashes before their eyes as they die may be true. We Buddhists recognize this as the experiences of the Bardos of Dying and Becoming, in which the mind throws

---

[179] Vicente R, Rizzuto M, Sarica C, et al. 'Enhanced Interplay of Neuronal Coherence and Coupling in the Dying Human Brain'. *Frontiers in Aging Neuroscience*. 2022; 14. Accessed February 22, 2022. https://www.frontiersin.org/article/10.3389/fnagi.2022.813531

up all kinds of images (what we call "appearances") based on its habitual tendencies. As we die, our mind projects images and sounds in line with its dominant habits. In our last moments it is like we are watching a movie that is the essence of who we are. A loving mind experiences love and light and joy. A hateful mind experiences darkness, violence and fear. As Buddhists we believe our future rebirth will have the same quality and characteristics of that movie (those appearances or mind projections) as they are the seed of the future consciousness, the future being. To put this metaphorically, our experience will be either *The Sound of Music* or *Nightmare on Elm Street*. Both our experience in the Bardo of Becoming and our future lives will mirror these projections. This is why it is so important to live a good life, to be kind and loving, to avoid doing harm as much as possible. Apart from not wanting to harm others, we don't want our future life to be a horror movie sequel.

These manifestations or visions, depending on how we react to them, will draw us to the next life. We need to avoid being swept up in all that. If we get swept up in it all we will become disturbed, frightened or even attracted or drawn in to what we are experiencing. All of these reactions (fear, attraction etc.) are obstacles to our liberation and will push us toward an unhappy rebirth. The method for avoiding being swept up by all of these displays of the dualistic mind is to remember: 'This is all just a projection of mind. None of it is truly real. Just relax.'

We can train for this death experience in our daily lives by remembering the bardos when we go to the cinema or are watching television. It is particularly effective when we are watching action films, with all the car chases, explosions and loud noises. As we watch the movie we simply remind ourselves that it is all just a projection. None of it is truly real, even though it is very compelling and we are getting drawn in. Each time a loud noise or sudden movement startles us, or each time a particularly attractive actor or actress causes us to feel desire, we remind ourselves that the reactions we are having are built on nothing, on mere projections. As we are watching our favorite programs on television we can do the same thing, simply remind ourselves: 'This is all just a projection. None of it is truly real. Relax.' This will give us the habit of not getting swept up in our reactions and the wisdom to recognize everything that flashes in front of us as a projection, an illusion cast by the mind.

Dudjom Rinpoche advises that these visions that appear in the Bardo of Becoming or rebirth are our cue for one last opportunity to escape the cycle of suffering existence. As these images, scenes and sounds start to flash before us, we can remember they are mere projections and then visualize our mind as a little ball of light and shoot it into a visualization of our teacher, into the teacher's heart. This visualization is simply a trigger for actually merging with enlightenment. That is ultimately what we're doing by visualizing this. It seems like it couldn't be true, because it is so simple, but by visualizing our Lama we are in effect calling out to them and they will come, because they are enlightened and can. This is why it's so important that our teacher be enlightened. It would be ludicrous to visualize someone who isn't enlightened and shoot the ball of light/mind into their heart. That will achieve nothing. This is why we have to be very careful in choosing a teacher, especially in the Vajrayana tradition. If we're not practicing in this way, in the Vajrayana, then the risks are lower. If we have an enlightened teacher or feel devotion for the Buddha we can visualize them and visualize our mind as a little ball of light that shoots into their heart.

Namgay Dawa Rimpoche, a grandson of Kyabje Dudjom Rinpoche and a Dudjom lineage holder, teaches an even simpler form of this practice. He often says that it is well and good to learn elaborate Phowa practices but at the time of death we might not have time to apply what we've learned, to do the complex visualizations etc. 'What if we are hit by a bus?' he often asks. 'If we are hit by a bus we won't have time to visualize all these red and blue colors. But we will have time to call out to our Guru, to simply say *Lama Khyenno.*' Lama Khyenno means "Guru, remember me" or "Guru, know me". It is a heart-felt request for the teacher's blessings. It also is a way to hold the guru in the heart. On another level, Lama Khyenno is a call for our own heart/mind and the guru's heart/mind to merge as one. Namgay Dawa Rimpoche explains that reciting Lama Khyenno is a simple way of initiating the recognition that our mind, the Lama's mind and the Buddha's mind are all already one. He suggests that we repeat *Lama Khyenno* when we wake each morning and then repeat it throughout the day as we feel moved to do so. As we go to sleep, it can be the last thing we utter – *Lama Khyenno.*

Jamyang Tenphel uses a slightly different version of this. He simply visualizes his guru's name as a glowing word. That is very simple. His guru's name is Togden Amtrin. On Jamyang's practice room wall he has a poster that is a black background with gold writing that says "Amtrin". This is one of Jamyang's preparations for the moment of death. When he passes away, hopefully a long time from now, rather than dissolve his mind into a little ball of light and then shooting that into his teacher's heart, he will visualize the word Amtrin as shining golden light and trust his Lama to take care of him. This is very nice and very simple. If you have deep devotion for a guru, you can do that. If you don't have a living Lama, it doesn't matter. Any enlightened being will do, living or not, so long as the devotion is there. You can also simply visualize the Buddha, and shoot your mind in the form of a little blue light or a little white light into the heart of the Buddha. This is perfectly fine. In fact, this is fantastic! Developing skill in (practicing) this transference technique is very helpful. Do it, it's a good idea.

If for some reason we are unable to do this as we are dying, we should at least recognize the things we perceive in the bardos as having no intrinsic existence or substance. As Dudjom Rinpoche says 'recognize the deluded perceptions experienced in the intermediate state as having no intrinsic reality'. Understand that everything you are experiencing is like a dream, like a movie, none of it is truly real. It has no intrinsic reality, which we will have practiced recognizing whenever we go to the cinema and while watching television etcetera. Everything that we see and hear, all the noise and light, is a projection of our own mind. In *The Refined Essence of Oral Instructions*, Padmasambhava makes this abundantly clear:

> At this point, know this: The feeling of being pressed down is not that of being pressed by a mountain. It is your own elements dissolving. Don't be afraid of that! The feeling of being trapped within darkness is not a darkness. It is your five sense faculties dissolving. The feeling of being dropped into the expanse of space is not being dropped. It is your mind without support because your body and mind have separated and your breathing has stopped. All experiences of rainbow lights are the natural manifestations of your mind. *All the peaceful and wrathful forms are the natural forms of your mind. All sounds are your own sounds. All lights are your own lights.* Have no doubt about that. If you do feel doubt, you will be thrown into samsara. Having resolved this to be self-display, if you rest wide awake in luminous emptiness, then simply in that you will attain the three kayas and become enlightened. (emphasis added).[180]

Illusions like reflections, mirages and rainbows cannot harm us. Likewise, the things we see and hear in the Bardos of Dying and Becoming should be seen for what they are: illusory lightshows with no substance and no power over us. The *Bardo Thodol* (the *Tibetan Book of the Dead*) cautions us not be afraid of the lights, not to fear the sounds, not to be scared by the colors. In essence, we need not be afraid of our mind's own display.

---

[180] See the full pith instruction in Kunsang, Erik Pema, 'Refined Essence of Oral Instructions', in *Dakini Teachings: A Collection of Padmasambhava's Advice to the Dakini Yeshe Tsogyal*, Rangjung Yeshe Publications, 1999.

No matter how bright the lights we might experience, how deafening the sounds we might hear, how vivid the colors, how strange or overwhelming the things we see, we need to remain calm and recognize that all these things are just projections of the mind, the mind's illusory display. At its heart this display is also the ultimate nature itself. As Khenchen Palden Sherab and Khenpo Tsewang Dongyal point out:

> Everything we see is a display of primordial wisdom, the lighting up of the true nature. Why should we be scared or frightened by our own mind? In considering the moment when we are presented with the clear light of our true nature, perhaps we're a bit apprehensive and afraid, but Guru Padmasambhava and the Buddha both teach us to regard birth and death as mere thoughts and dualistic notions.[181]

The last two sentences from Dudjom Rinpoche's pith instruction give us another, even simpler, technique for finding peace at the time of dying: *Using devotion as the path, simply remember your teachers: through the power of their compassion, you will definitely be liberated in a pure Buddhafield.* This is the method of Guru Yoga. According to this tradition, when we think of our teachers with devotion they intervene and through the power of their compassion we will be liberated from this human realm into a Buddha field. This is nothing to sneer at, though it is a step down from being able to embrace the Mother Luminosity. When we embrace the Mother Luminosity, we are completely liberated, with no need for another existence as an ordinary being. When one uses this next technique of devotion in the Bardo of Becoming, one is still reborn, but we are born in an auspicious place, a Buddha field or at least a higher kind of birth. This is a failsafe if we miss the opportunity in the Bardo

---

[181] Khenchen Palden Sherab and Khenpo Tsewang Dongyal (2000) *A Modern Commentary on Karma Lingpa's Zhi-Khro: teachings on the peaceful and wrathful deities.* Padma Gochen Ling. Source: Archived (accessed: December 27, 2007)

of Luminosity, or if we were too distracted or swept up to muster devotion earlier in the dying process.

We simply remember our teachers, again, provided that they are enlightened or realized. Any ordinary Buddhist instructor is not going to cut it. We need to be sure they actually can help us. It is tricky these days, with so many fake teachers and so many people who are very good at pretending to be enlightened. How can we be sure? Usually, other more senior practitioners can help us recognize whether not a teacher has the necessary qualities. There is an element of trust. If we are not able to give that trust, then we can use historical enlightened beings such as the Buddha, Padmasambhava, who firmly established Buddhism in Tibet, and Yeshe Tsogyal, the first Tibetan to become enlightened and one of the first women in recorded history to achieve ultimate enlightenment. Yeshe Tsogyal herself suggests that, for those practicing in the Tibetan tradition, Padmasambhava (the Lotus-Born) is their predestined guru:

> In general terms, and for the people of Tibet in times to come, the Lotus-Born is your predestined teacher.[182]

Of course, as Padmasambhava's closest disciple, Yeshe Tsogyal and he are one and the same. Their minds have merged through the guru/disciple relationship. This means that Yeshe Tsogyal is also our predestined guru. Apart from Padmasambhava and Yeshe Tsogyal, there are many realized beings we can rely on, all of the lineage masters for example. To build a connection with them and develop faith, we simply read about their lives. We can also have pictures of them on our altar or in our room (or both). This is so that we can quickly visualize them when we pass away. We need to prepare.

---

[182] Yeshe Tsogyal quoted in Dudjom Rinpoche, *A Torch Lighting the Way to Freedom*, Shambhala Publications, 2016, p. 239.

I will close this discussion of the Bardo of Becoming with a stanza from a short teaching by Sera Khandro, a great twentieth century female master of the Dudjom lineage, that sums this all up:

When your consciousness journeys

through the long treacheries that lie beyond death,

the best protection is your master, the supreme jewel,

so, pray with devotion and make aspirations to see everything purely.[183]

---

[183] 'Concise Spiritual Advice', translated by Christina Monson (2020). Full text: https://www. lotsawahouse.org/tibetan-masters/sera-khandro/concise-spiritual-advice

CHAPTER TWELVE

PRACTICING THE BARDO TEACHINGS

Bringing purpose and joy to living and dying.

As we've seen, Longchenpa suggests in *Crucial Advice* that we recognize the true nature of mind "here and now in training".[184] I've made it clear that all we need do to prepare for the Bardo of Dying and embrace the opportunity of the Bardo of Luminosity is adopt a regular sitting meditation practice. A powerful support for our meditation is the bardo practice of Dream Yoga. Furthermore, if we want to recognize our true nature swiftly, in this very lifetime, it would also be wise to practice Guru Yoga. I'll now go over each of these bardo practices in detail.

Meditation

Meditation is about the bardo between each thought, feeling and sensation, in which is found rigpa, or pure, non-dual awareness. In other words, meditation awakens us to the Nirmanakaya aspect of our true nature, its movement and activity, its natural compassion, which then gives rise to direct experience of its deeper nature, its vast openness (Dharmakaya). Ultimately, the purpose

---

[184] Longchenpa, *Crucial Advice: A Complete Set of Instructions for the Bardos,* Translated by Adam Pearcey (2010). See full text here: https://www.lotsawahouse.org/tibetan-masters/longchen-rabjam/complete-set-instructions

of meditation is to abide in that vast openness and its radiance, which is compassion and love, otherwise known as our fundamental goodness. As we have already discussed, that fundamental goodness is not something we have to create or refine. It is already present and completely perfect as it is. As Mingyur Rinpoche notes:

> Meditation is about learning to recognize our basic goodness in the immediacy of the present moment, and then nurturing this recognition until it seeps into the very core of our being.[185]

Meditation reveals the way our ordinary thoughts and feelings arise from primordial awareness itself and so are not separate from it but of the same perfect taste. Each thought and emotion is a wave arising from the ocean of primordial perfection or Shunyata. These waves, this movement, in its essence or true form, is none other than compassion.

The *Bardo Thodol* or *Tibetan Book of the Dead*, gives clear instructions on how to recognize the true nature of mind in the form of "three considerations":

> First, recognize that past thoughts are traceless, clear and empty. Second, recognize that future thoughts are unproduced and fresh. Third, recognize that the present moment abides naturally and unconstructed.[186]

To recognize that thoughts are traceless or unproduced is not to merely think that this is how they are. It means to directly experience them that way. This can only be done if we develop our meditation muscles to the point where this recognition becomes natural and effortless. As noted earlier, meditation practice is easier and swifter than other supposedly higher practices, which have meditation as a pre-requisite for them anyway. Through simple

---

[185] source: http://learning.tergar.org/course.../joy-of-living-level-3/

[186] Padmasambhava, *Bardo Thodol* (*The Tibetan Book of the Dead*), Penguin Classics edition, translated by Gyurme Dorje, 2008, p. 41-42.

meditation we can increase the duration of the bardos, even the Bardo of Dying, so that we are able to recognize the true nature of mind and then, at the time of dying, recognize the Mother Luminosity that manifests like a clear dawn. It is hard to believe but quite true that ultimately all we need to ensure our liberation in this lifetime is a *consistent* meditation practice. The emphasis is on consistent. That practice needs to be motivated by altruism. It should also be based on an understanding of the Buddhist fundamentals (anatta, anicca and Shunyata etc.). Preferably, our practice should be fueled by devotion. This should give us some confidence. We only need this simple practice to be able to free ourselves as the Mother Luminosity dawns. This is achievable, if we just sit each and every day. Apart from opening the door to liberation at the time of death, meditation has many other benefits. Tulku Thondup Rinpoche puts it this way:

> Through training in meditation we purify the two obscurations— emotional afflictions (nyon sgrib) and intellectual duality of the mind (shes sgrib)—and we perfect the twofold accumulation (tshogs) – meritorious deeds (bsod nams) and realization of wisdom (ye shes). As the result of such meditations we realize the intrinsic awareness of the mind, the essence of which is openness (or emptiness – stong pa nyid) and the nature of which is clarity (gsal ba) and compassionate power that is ceaseless and all-pervasive.[187]

But what approach to meditation should we have? How exactly do we sit in order to recognize the true nature of mind? There are some basic instructions for meditating in order to bring the bardo teachings to life. Some of these instructions have to do with the time of day we meditate. They are summarized by Jamyang Tenphel below:

---

[187] Quoted in Tulku Pema Rigtsal, *The Great Secret of Mind. Special Instructions on the Nonduality of Dzogchen*, translated by Keith Dowman, Shambhala Publications, 2013, p. xi.

We meditate at dawn as night turns into day to simulate the death process of experiencing the dawning luminosity of Rigpa, the dawning radiance of the clear light.

We meditate at dusk as the day turns to night to simulate the process of dying. Light turning to blackness whilst remaining equanimous without fear.

This is why many great masters choose to die at the auspicious time of dawn. As radiant luminosity arises at dawn so does their total enlightenment dawn. The outer dawning luminosity reflects their inner dawning luminosity of liberation.

Sitting with open spacious awareness at dusk and especially at dawn, just sitting openly and at ease, helps us to recognize Rigpa, the mind of clear light. These are the best times for formless meditation, rather than form-based practices such as prostrations, sadhanas and other prayers.[188]

If dawn and dusk are not ideal times for us to meditate, then we just meditate at a time that works for us. The main thing is that we approach meditation with enthusiasm and joy.

Always Remember Joy[189]

Joy is an incredibly important aspect of all Buddhist practice. It is one of the *Four Immeasurables*, the characteristics of the enlightened mind. Joy is also one of the *Seven Factors of Awakening* – the qualities of mind that, when cultivated

---

[188] Jamyang Tenphel, *The Awakening Heart: Contemplations on the Buddhist Path*, Timeless Awareness Publications, 2023, no page, Kindle Edition. Jamyang Tenphel received these instructions directly from his guru. They come from the Longde cycle of the Dzogchen teachings. For a more thorough discussion see Chogyal Namkhai Norbu Rinpoche's book *Dream Yoga And The Practice Of Natural Light*.

[189] This section is based on an article published in *Tricycle: The Buddhist Review* as 'Awakening to Joy: A Simple Method for Developing Enthusiasm for Practice', January 02, 2022: https://tricycle.org/article/awakening-joy-meditation-practice/

in a balanced way, lead to total enlightenment. Whether we are beginners or more advanced, it is impossible to accomplish any of our Dharma practices without it. Quite simply, without joy there is no enlightenment. Joy is the fuel, the nourishment, which helps our practice grow strong and stable. Jamyang Tenphel often says: 'If we imagine our practice to be like a seedling, joy is the water that helps the seedling to grow. Without joy, the seedling will wither and die.' The Buddha himself encouraged us to value joy highly when he taught:

> Live in joy, in love, even among those who hate. Live in joy, in health, even among the afflicted. Live in joy, in peace, even among the troubled. Look within, be still; free from fear and attachment. Know the sweet joy of the way.[190]

By starting our meditation practice with joy in our hearts, we begin to associate all Dharma activity with joy and we will, in time, begin to look forward to practice. Meditation will become something wonderful we look forward to doing each day, rather than a chore or a bitter medicine we feel we have to swallow. This is called joyful enthusiasm for practice. Luckily for us, there is a simple way to awaken to joy and ignite joyful enthusiasm for Dharma.

The Path of Joy

This profound yet simple practice comes from Jamyang Tenphel. It arose from his Guru Yoga practice and is inspired by the wisdom approach of the late Kyabje Togden Amtrin (1922 – 2005), who was a great, realized yogi of the Drukpa Kagyu school of Tibetan Buddhism and a Dzogchen master. I received instruction on this practice from Jamyang Tenphel over a number of years. The Path of Joy has become a core part of my practice and is a powerful method to deepen in meditation and all other Buddhist practices.

---

[190] From the Dhammapada, quoted in Jack Kornfield, *A Lamp in the Darkness: Illuminating the Path Through Difficult Times*, Sounds True, 2014, no page, digital edition.

The concise pith instruction for this practice is: *Arouse joy and rest in its natural radiance! Not only is this the heart of the path, but indeed it is the heart of Awakening.*[191] It's a great idea to print this out and pin it up where we can see it every day. Let's unpack what this instruction means. Although this practice is rooted in core Buddhist teachings such as the *Seven Factors of Awakening*, it is not about learning lists or getting involved in conceptual thinking or analysis in any way. It is about connecting with an intrinsic quality that is within us already. Our hearts are already naturally joyful. It's just that this natural joy is crowded out by the constant activity and stress of our daily lives and the constant chatter of our over-burdened minds.

The Path of Joy begins with us choosing an object that brings us simple, uncomplicated joy. It can be anything. All that matters is that the thing we choose ignites joy, no matter how subtle. We then gently place our awareness on and calmly observe the object. We simply gently gaze at a flower, a tree, birds, a beautiful piece of art, or even a picture of our guru. It could be gazing relaxedly at a beautiful mountain, a slow-moving river, the ocean, or a wide blue sky. If we are more affected by sound than visuals, we can place our awareness on the sound of wind gently blowing through trees, of water flowing soothingly down a stream, or beautiful birdsong.

We don't choose objects that will excite the mind such as music or TV or smart phones, as we are not looking to make the mind more active or agitated. Jamyang puts it this way: 'We want to simply rest the mind on an object that touches our hearts in a gentle, relaxed and carefree way. By connecting with something external that brings us joy our inner joy is able to shine through.' In other words, the outer joy in natural objects is like a magnet that brings forward the much greater, deeper and more lasting joy that is an expression of our true nature.

---

[191] Jamyang Tenphel, *The Awakening Heart: Contemplations on the Buddhist Path*, Timeless Awareness Publications, 2023, no page, Kindle Edition.

We then sit and observe our object of choice for ten minutes or so, without analyzing or thinking about it. We simply rest our awareness on it without clinging to it or grasping at it with our minds. Just sit and rest the mind at ease on the object in the present moment. Dudjom Rinpoche (1904 – 1987) called this type of practice resting our awareness in "present-nowness".

This is not an analytical exercise, or an intellectual game. It's an exercise in allowing joy to begin to resonate within our being naturally, so that when we sit and meditate, our hearts will be open and receptive to whatever arises. We are not trying to force or fake joy, but rather we are allowing joy to arise effortlessly in its own time and in its own way.

After spending ten minutes doing this, we then sit in Calm Abiding meditation (Shamata) for a further ten minutes. When we first begin with this joy practice, we do ten minutes of joy practice, then ten minutes of Shamata. As we grow accustomed to sitting in meditation and simply observing the breath, we extend the meditation component of the session to 20 minutes, and then 30 minutes and so on. Thus, we do ten minutes of joy then 10, 20 or 30 minutes of mediation. By using this format, all of our Dharma practice becomes infused with joy from the beginning.

Over time, we will find that doing this practice enables joy to arise more swiftly and easily. Then we can slowly reduce the time spent on formally arousing joy with an object and simply rest in joy's natural radiance without contrivance. We then seamlessly enter into Calm Abiding practice with the glow of joy in our hearts, which will naturally deepen our meditation practice, allowing us to rest in stillness and peace. When we rest in stillness and peace compassion also naturally arises.

If we are going through a difficult period, and experiencing things like depression or anxiety, we might feel that joy is hard to come by. If this is the case we can try thinking back to the things that used to bring us joy before our current low period. Spend some time dwelling on the objects or experiences that brought us joy in the past. For me, this is walks in the rainforest. If I am having a rough time feeling joyous in the present I think back to one of my walks in my favorite forest. I allow myself to feel the joy of that past moment in my body. When we think of past joyful experiences we can bring them into the present by placing our awareness on that joy and allowing the sensation of it to naturally grow. This will support us until the temporary troubles pass and we are able to cultivate joy in the present. Generally speaking in the Dharma, we try not to dwell too much on the past, but when our current situation is difficult it is okay to do so as a temporary remedy. Whatever happens, we should be gentle and kind with ourselves. It is counterproductive to be hard on ourselves in any way, as this is the antithesis of the joy practice.

The benefits of joy

Bringing joy into our hearts at the beginning of our Dharma practice opens us up to giving rise to the other Four Immeasurables more easily. For most of us, joy is the easiest of the Four Immeasurables to develop, which is why it makes sense to start with it. Once joy becomes a regular experience in our hearts and a quality of our practice, we then naturally begin to feel loving-kindness, compassion and equanimity (generally in this order).

When coupled with simple meditation this joy practice allows our hearts and minds to become more open, flexible and even. It also makes our meditation deeper and more stable, which eventually leads to the spontaneous arising of love and compassion. This is the ultimate result of the joy practice, it gives rise to the Great Bodhicitta, which is nothing less than the self-perfected natural state (or Dzogpachenpo).

To begin with, this practice may feel like an intellectual, mind-based experience. However, over time this practice will be felt in the heart. As

Jamyang Tenphel notes, 'The positive qualities of compassion and kindness eventually become truly *felt experiences,* which is the whole point of Dharma practice – to awaken our natural capacity for kindness, compassion, joy and equanimity'.[192]

The Path of Joy is a shortcut. Buddhist practice naturally leads to joy, but it can take years before practitioners reach that point. By evoking joy each day before we sit in meditation we are jump-starting the process and getting to the point where practice and joy are inseparable much sooner. As a result, we begin to feel more warmth and kindness towards those we meet, and are more capable of dealing with difficulties with resilience, composure and acceptance. Jamyang puts it this way: 'We will feel less discrimination, prejudice and disturbing emotions like anger and fear. Most importantly, if we do this joy practice each day we will feel our hearts opening up more and more until our capacity for compassion and love is truly boundless'.[193] In other words, joy leads to recognition of our true nature, which is the union of the realization of emptiness (wisdom) with limitless compassion. That is Bodhicitta, the awakened mind, which is our natural state. To close this discussion of joy as a practice here is an excerpt from a teaching by Lama Shenpen Hookham, a Western-born, female teacher of both the Nyingma and Kagyu traditions:

> Spend time doing things or simply remembering moments in your life that touch, move or expand your heart. It may be simple things like watching the cat rolling and stretching in the sun, it may be watching a bird soaring high in the sky, it may be listening to certain pieces of music, or certain scenes from books or films. It may be through smelling washing fresh from off the line, the taste of good food, the sound of

---

[192] Jamyang Tenphel, *The Awakening Heart: Contemplations on the Buddhist Path,* Timeless Awareness Publications, 2023, no page, Kindle Edition.
[193] Ibid.

splashing water, or the feel of cotton or velvet. Be conscious of how the whole experience feels – the joy in the heart and the sense of freedom and space to enjoy yourself. The sense of joy and freedom is coming from the *chitta* – the essence of your being. The experience may only last a few seconds before being covered over by habitual patterns of thought. Nevertheless, you know in your heart that you have glimpsed something of value that you will be able to return to because it is the nature of your being to be able to experience things in that way.[194]

Abiding in the Natural State

What follows are basic tips to meditation practice that should be helpful for both absolute beginners and more advanced meditators.[195] The form of meditation described here is focused on recognizing the true nature of mind. It is common to the Drukpa Kagyu and Nyingma traditions of Tibetan Buddhism. In these practice-focused traditions Shamata (Calm Abiding meditation) and Vipashana (Insight meditation) are often practiced together, as one. However, for the sake of clarity, we'll discuss Shamata and Vipashana separately.

The Natural View

I'd like to start this discussion of the philosophical view that supports our meditation with a quote from Dudjom Rinpoche, Jigdral Yeshe Dorje, one of the greatest masters of the twentieth century:

Although hundreds or thousands of explanations are given,

There is only one thing to be understood:

---

[194] Lama Shenpen Hookham, 'From a teaching on Love and Compassion', *Buddha Within* website, https://buddhawithin.org.uk/2020/04/03/appreciate-simple-pleasures/ (Accessed 1 October 2022).

[195] This section on how to meditate is taken from Jamyang Tenphel and my book *Resting in Stillness*, Timeless Awareness Publications, 2020, pp.47-51.

Know the one thing that liberates everything,

Awareness itself, your true nature.[196]

As the quote above shows, the most important practice in Buddhism from a Nyingma perspective is experiencing the true nature of mind, or recognizing our intrinsic non-dual awareness. This is made abundantly clear in Padmasambhava's *Self-Liberation through Seeing with Naked Awareness*:

Everything that is expounded by the Victorious Ones of the three times

In the eighty-four thousand gateways to the Dharma

Is incomprehensible (unless you understand intrinsic awareness).

Indeed, the Victorious Ones do not teach anything other than the understanding of this.[197]

Though this is a Dzogchen pith instruction it is in complete accord with the Sutrayana teachings. We need only remember the instruction of the Buddha that opened Chapter One—'Look to your own nature which is intrinsically pure'[198]—to understand that the Dzogchen view and the view expounded in the sutras are deeply aligned. This attitude or view is applied in both Shamata and Vipashana. This has always been the approach of the practice lineages, such as the Nyingma and Drukpa Kagyu, as is made clear in *The Refined Essence of Oral Instructions* when Padmasambhava says to his consort and disciple Khandro Yeshe Tsogyal:

...if you attain stability [in the recognition of the true nature of mind], you will be able to assume your natural state in the bardo and become

---

[196] Dudjom Rinpoche, *Wisdom Nectar: Dudjom Rinpoche's Heart Advice*, Snow Lion, 2005, p. 125.

[197] Padmasambhava, *Self-Liberation through Seeing with Naked Awareness*, translated by John Myrdhin Reynolds, 2000, Snow Lion, p. 10.

[198] Dhammapada, verse 379, translated by Anne Bancroft.

enlightened. Therefore, the most vital point is to sustain your practice undistractedly from this very moment.[199]

Stable recognition of the true nature of mind can only be done in the practice of meditation. A qualified master can introduce the true nature to the student with "pointing out instructions" but skill in meditation is necessary for those pointing out instructions to have an impact, for the student to recognize or experience rigpa. Stability in the recognition of the true nature, which is realization itself, is achieved most easily with one simple method – silent sitting. Simple meditation, approached in the way taught by Padmasambhava in *The Refined Essence of Oral Instructions*, and outlined in the next section, leads not only to recognition of rigpa but to the ability to permanently abide in the naturally perfected state.

Meditation is most fruitful when it is supported by what are called *The Three Essentials of Vajrayana*.[200] These are:

1. Renunciation;

2. Compassion or Bodhichitta (a heart that is open and spacious as well as joyful, devoted and loving);

3. Pure perception (seeing ourselves and all others as perfected beings or Buddhas.

I would add to these three a fourth essential: Basic knowledge of the Buddhist fundamentals such as Shunyata (emptiness) and impermanence. We especially need to grasp the empty nature of mind. In fact, meditation without understanding the view of emptiness is not all that beneficial. It is true that we can come to an understanding or experience of

---

[199] See the full pith instruction in Kunsang, Erik Pema, 'Refined Essence of Oral Instructions', in *Dakini Teachings: A Collection of Padmasambhava's Advice to the Dakini Yeshe Tsogyal*, Rangjung Yeshe Publications, 1999.

[200] For more on The Three Essentials of Vajrayana see Khenpo Tsewang Dongyal Rinpoche's teaching 'Renunciation, Bodhichitta and Pure Perception': https://youtu.be/Q369C5DM7hw

emptiness through meditation, but that is less likely to happen if we do not already have a "mental picture" or a sense of the view, if we do not have a conceptual understanding of Shunyata. As Kyabje Dilgo Khyentse Rinpoche points out:

> People always say, 'Meditate! Meditate!' but unless you have established a firm and unmistaken understanding of the view of voidness [Shunyata], what is the point of meditating? Failure to recognize the void nature of mind is the very source of samsara. This void nature, with its inherent compassion, is recognized when the mind, free of the influence of thoughts, awakens to the simple awareness of the present.[201]

Contemplating emptiness regularly will support our meditation practice. Put simply, Shunyata means that all things are interconnected, interdependent, impermanent and are devoid of any lasting, intrinsic self-nature or essence. We don't need to obsess over this idea, we don't need to do huge amounts of intellectual fussing and study, we just need to accept and understand in what ways things are impermanent, in what ways things are interdependent, and in what ways things lack an inherent self-nature.

As for renunciation, Padmasambhava emphasizes the need to abandon worldly things in *The Refined Essence of Oral Instructions* when he says:

> Don't remain in places of ordinary people; practice in seclusion. Give up your clinging to whatever you are most attached to as well as to whomever you have the strongest bond with in this life, and practice. Like that, although your body remains in human form, your mind is equal to the Buddha's.[202]

---

[201] Dilgo Khyentse Rinpoche, *The Heart Treasure of the Enlightened Ones*, Shambhala Publications, 1993, p. 343.

[202] See the full pith instruction in Kunsang, Erik Pema, 'Refined Essence of Oral Instructions', in *Dakini Teachings: A Collection of Padmasambhava's Advice to the Dakini Yeshe Tsogyal*, Rangjung Yeshe Publications, 1999.

Jetsunma Tenzin Palmo notes the importance of renunciation, and suggests that it might be more effective for contemporary Buddhists than elaborate tantric practices, when she says:

> One aim of tantra originally was to help practitioners to overcome the rigid mental and physical constraints of their society through extreme behavior. Imagine the monks slipping out of Nalanda monastery in the dead of night to go to the charnel grounds, passing the night among corpses while drinking alcohol out of skull cups! These were radical practices to break through their fixed boundaries and it surely was a cathartic experience! However, in these days when the whole world is being marketed to drink alcohol, take drugs, enjoy promiscuous sex and eat sirloin steaks, none of that is at all liberating! It is merely normal social behavior. In these current times perhaps a much more radical act would be genuine renunciation.[203]

Adding to this, Kyabje Dudjom Rinpoche makes it very clear that renunciation is essential when he writes:

> Nowadays we all boast that we are Dharma practitioners, but we have not severed our attachment to the things of this life, we have not turned our minds away from cyclic existence, we have not relinquished even the smallest of our desires — for friends and relations, entourage, servants, food and clothes, pleasant conversation, and the like. As a result, any positive activities we undertake are not really effective. Our minds and the Dharma go different ways.[204]

Renunciation means to turn our minds away from anything that blocks or delays our ability to experience the true nature of mind. Buddhists see three

---

[203] Jetsunma Tenzin Palmo [Facebook post] 27 April 2021. Available at: https://www. facebook.com/jetsunmatenzinpalmo (Accessed: 27 April 2021)

[204] Dudjom Rinpoche, *A Torch Lighting the Way to Freedom,* Shambhala Publications, 2016, p. 136.

things as the main problem: attachment, sometimes called desire or craving; aversion, sometimes called anger or hate; and ignorance, which means, basically, not understanding Shunyata or emptiness. Renunciation truly takes root in our heart/minds when we understand Shunyata and impermanence and when our hearts are wide open; another reason why the fundamentals (impermanence, non-self, compassion and Shunyata) are so important. The easiest form of renunciation is outer renunciation, epitomized by the monastic tradition of monks and nuns. The easiest way to undermine attachment and aversion is to abstain from seeking pleasurable things and stop avoiding unpleasant things. The easiest way to cut attachment to things is simply not to have them. Likewise, the easiest way to undermine sexual desire is simply to not engage in it.

If we are not monks or nuns then we have to maintain an inner renunciation, which is an awareness of our wants and fears and a commitment to release them. When a want or desire arises we do not immediately indulge it, if at all, we look at it and understand what it is. In looking at it, it will immediately weaken. In time it will dissolve completely. Likewise our fears or aversions. When fears arise, we look directly at them and watch as they dissolve by themselves. We do not engage with or act on our fears or aversions. In time, our attachments and aversions will weaken and disappear. To "look at" attachments and aversions means to place our awareness on them, gently but unflinchingly. When we do this they are all released in the luminosity of awareness. The problem is not with things themselves, the objects of our desire are not a problem. They are completely neutral. The problem is in our mind. These things we want and fear are completely impermanent. So why desire them? Why be afraid of them? They will vanish in time of their own accord. Renunciation means to see the objects of our fear and desire clearly, as empty and impermanent, and not allow the dualistic mind to enslave us to its irrational attachment and aversion.

Despite what many might think, renunciation does not lead to a limiting or closing down of our lives nor to a shuttering of our experience. It leads to a vast openness and evenness. The most important aspect of the Buddhist view is this openness or loving spaciousness. Sri Singha, who was the main teacher of Padmasambhava, and thus the source of the great practice lineages of Tibet, put it this way:

> There is no difference between Buddhas and sentient beings other than their scope of mind. What is called mind, consciousness, or awareness, is of a single identity. The mind of a sentient being is limited. The mind of a Buddha is all-pervasive. So develop a scope of mind that is like the sky, which has no limit to the east, west, north, or south.[205]

The Natural Posture

When we think about meditation, we think in terms of postures – postures of body, speech and mind. In other words, what we do with our body, what we do with our speech and what we do with our mind. This meditational posture is the same in both Shamata and Vipashana. Contrary to popular opinion about meditation, we should not put excessive effort into controlling how we are sitting. Our posture should not be rigid or taught. Padmasambhava demonstrates this in *The Refined Essence of Oral Instructions*, in which he gives the following comprehensive teaching about meditation:

> Although there are many profound key points of body, rest free and relaxed as you feel comfortable. Everything is included in simply that.

> Although there are many key points of speech such as breath control and mantra recitation, stop speaking and rest like a mute. Everything is included in simply that.

> Although there are many key points of mind such as concentrating,

relaxing, projecting, dissolving, and focusing inward, everything is included in simply letting the mind rest in its natural state, free and easy, without fabrication.[206]

Here Padmasambhava is saying that the best meditation posture for the body is the one that is most comfortable for us, so long as our spine is more or less straight. The best posture for speech is complete silence. He lists a number of tantric methods (breath control and mantra recitation) but says these are not essential, that simple silence is enough. Silence is the best mantra. Padmasambhava then says that the best mental attitude is to simply let the mind be, to allow it to relax into its natural state. Again he lists a number of tantric methods (concentrating, relaxing, projecting, dissolving and focusing inward) that he deems are inessential. What is essential is to leave the mind alone, *free and easy, without fabrication*. Here Padmasambhava sums up the entire path in one paragraph. It's quite extraordinary.

In these stanzas Padmasambhava is saying to his closest student, Yeshe Tsogyal—and through her he's also saying it to us—that we don't need all the complicated tantric stuff. We don't need all these complicated, esoteric things. We just need this simple approach. Echoing Padmasambhava, Dudjom Lingpa puts it this way:

Stay in a pleasant grove with all your requisites at hand;

Your body, leave as it is without fabrication,

Like a corpse;

Your speech, leave as it is without fabrication,

Like a mute's;

---

[206] See the full pith instruction in Kunsang, Erik Pema, 'Refined Essence of Oral Instructions', in *Dakini Teachings: A Collection of Padmasambhava's Advice to the Dakini Yeshe Tsogyal*, Rangjung Yeshe Publications, 1999.

Your mind, leave as it is without fabrication,

Free of conceptual extremes.

That is the very pinnacle of all meditation practice.[207]

When Padmasambhava refers to the natural state, and Dudjom Lingpa talks about being free of conceptual extremes, what do they mean? What is the natural state of the body, of speech, and the natural state of the mind? Consider the natural state of the body – when it is not animated by thought and impulses, it is still. When we are deeply asleep our body is completely still. So the body's natural state is stillness. The natural state of speech, of our voice, is silence. Again, when we are not compelled by thoughts and impulses to speak or gesticulate, we are silent and still. So the natural state of speech is stillness as well. Likewise, when the mind is not agitated by thoughts and impulses, it is still, lucidly aware but still. So the natural state of the mind is also stillness. To let the mind rest in its natural state, free and easy, without fabrication, is to do nothing, to simply rest in stillness. This does not mean to stop thinking altogether. Trying to stop thinking is the opposite of doing nothing. It is intervening and fabricating something. Thinking arises in response to our experience, our perception of the world. If we are alive we will always have thoughts, but they are not our true nature and as we deepen in practice they will be fewer and fewer.

Padmasambhava and Khandro Yeshe Tsogyal were able to rest in this profound stillness. Whether or not we can, that's a whole other question. Can we honestly say we are able to rest free and relaxed, just sit still and be quiet, just leave the mind alone? Thinking, to have thoughts, is not leaving the mind alone. To think is to interfere with the mind, to fabricate things in the mind. We might believe thought just comes naturally, but it does

---

[207] Holly Gayley and Joshua Schapiro, *A Gathering of Brilliant Moons: Practice Advice from the Rime Masters of Tibet*, Wisdom Publications, 2017, p.43.

not. Thought is produced, it is fabricated. The natural state of the mind is stillness. The natural state of the body is stillness. The natural state of speech is stillness. This is our natural state. Everything we do interrupts that natural state. Moving, talking, thinking, these interfere or intervene or cover up or obscure the natural state. Padmasambhava is essentially saying, 'Do nothing', which is a Dzogchen dictum that is often misunderstood. It doesn't mean just laze about. It means don't actively think or ponder, don't talk, don't move. Just rest, relaxed and free. We might think that doing nothing is easy, but it is not. To do nothing requires a regular meditation practice, and meditation is simple but not easy. Just try to sit still and silent for an hour and see how quickly you start to fidget and sigh. The dualistic mind incites movement, triggers all kinds of activity, because in the stillness and silence it is extinguished and it does not wish to be extinguished. When we are not used to sitting in stillness it feels as though we have to apply force to be still, but true rest is not forced. True rest comes from just letting everything go, from a form of renunciation in fact. A renunciation of the impulse to move, think, feel and act.

Even though it seems very difficult to totally still the mind, it can actually be done quite quickly. Stilling the body and the speech, which are easier to quiet, helps to tame and quiet the mind. So we start by simply sitting still in silence. There is a story that Yeshe Tsogyal accomplished this form of practice in just seven months. Now there is a challenge! If Yeshe Tsogyal can achieve this perfect state, resting in the true nature, in just seven months, then surely we can do it in this lifetime. I think that's encouraging. Even though we haven't done hundreds of hours of meditation, haven't done decades of retreat, we can still do it. It won't be as quick as seven months, but that kind of achievement is not lifetimes away. It is achievable. We can do it; because it's really just about stopping. Just stopping and resting. Then the true nature of the mind reveals itself. We don't have to do anything. We just need to rest. So this is, I think, really inspiring.

Now that we are inspired, let's learn the mechanics of meditation. The physical posture we most often use in meditation is:

- Spine more or less straight but not tight or taut
- Eyes open but half-lidded, a relaxed, open gaze gently looking at the space a few feet in front
- Tongue is curled so that its tip touches the roof of the mouth just behind the teeth
- The mouth is relaxed and lips are slightly open
- Hands are laid flat, palms down, on the thighs or knees.

In his much revered *Stages of Meditation*, Kamalashila (740-795) writes:

Then, they should sit in the full lotus posture of Vairochana or the half-lotus posture, on a comfortable cushion. The eyes should not be too widely opened or too tightly closed. Let them focus on the tip of the nose. The body should not be bent forward or backward. Keep it straight and turn the attention inward. The shoulders should rest in their natural position and the head should not lean back, forward or to either side. The nose should be in line with the navel. The teeth and lips should rest in their natural state with the tongue touching the upper palate. Breathe very gently and softly without causing any noise, without laboring, and without unevenness. Inhale and exhale naturally, slowly and, and unnoticeably.[208]

This meditation posture is known as The Seven Point Posture of Vairochana. A little known fact is that this posture is said to achieve, with much less effort and no precursor practices required, what the complicated and taxing physical yogic postures and breath work of tantric Buddhism (such as Tsa Lung and Trulkhor) achieve; that is, the clearing of the chakras, internal

---

[208] Quoted in The Dalai Lama, *Stages of Meditation: The Buddhist Classic on Training the Mind*, Shambhala Publications, 2019, p. 82.

channels or meridians and settling of the bodies energies (lung in Tibetan, Chi in Mandarin). It also does it with none of the risks associated with those other practices. Another little known fact is that practices like Tsa Lung, Tummo and Trulkhor can, if done improperly, lead to devastating problems or "side effects" such as pain, anxiety, constant restlessness and mental illness. Some of these effects may never lift.

In other words, this simple silent sitting practice, if we apply it each and every day in a relaxed, open-hearted way, is much safer and makes the so-called "higher" yogic breathing practices unnecessary. This is why this specific physical posture is preferred, but if it doesn't feel comfortable, we can meditate with eyes shut and the tongue just resting on the floor of the mouth, with lips softly closed. In terms of mental attitude or posture, Padmasambhava gave this simple four part instruction on how to meditate:

Don't dwell on the past.

Don't anticipate the future.

Remain in the present moment.

Leave the mind alone.

Padmasambhava repeats these instructions in *Self-Liberation through Seeing with Naked Awareness*:

You should relinquish all notions of the past and abandon all precedents. You should cut off all plans and expectations with respect to the future. And in the present, you should not grasp (at thoughts that arise) but allow (the mind) to remain in a state like the sky.[209]

---

[209] Padmasambhava, *Self-Liberation through Seeing with Naked Awareness*, translated by John Myrdhin Reynolds, 2000, Snow Lion, p. 18.

I received these meditation instructions a number of times from a number of Lamas. They are the bedrock of all meditation instruction, both Buddhist and non-Buddhist alike. Without letting go of the past and the future we will always be mired in the misery of false hope and irrational fear. Most recently, Ngakpa Karma Lhundup Rinpoche explained them to me in this way:

> Not chasing after past thoughts and experiences, not inviting future expectations and plans, not even remaining in the present which has either positive, negative or neutral thoughts and emotions. Remain in the fourth part which is free from the past, present and future. This is our true primordial state, free from fabricated, uncontrollable thoughts and concepts.[210]

This echoes a famous pith instruction from the omniscient Longchen Rabjampa about the true nature of mind or rigpa:

> It is neither in the past,
>
> Nor in the future.
>
> It does not enter the present,
>
> Remaining where it is,
>
> Do not use mind to look for mind;
>
> Just leave it as it is![211]

All of these are pretty straight-forward instructions. Although these points are often taken from Dzogchen pith instructions they are in complete harmony with the Sutrayana teachings, especially this teaching from the Buddha found in *The Middle Length Discourses* on the importance of focusing on the present moment:

---

[210] Ngakpa Karma Lhundup Rinpoche, personal communication, 16 August 2021.

[211] Longchenpa, *Natural Perfection: Longchenpa's Radical Dzogchen*, translated by Keith Dowman, Wisdom Publications, 2012, no page numbers, Kindle Edition.

You shouldn't chase after the past or place expectations on the future.

What is past is left behind.

The future is as yet unreached.

Whatever quality is present you clearly see right there, right there.

Not taken in, unshaken, that's how you develop the heart.[212]

Note that the goal of resting in the present moment is not only calm, clarity and stillness of mind but to develop the heart, to awaken joy, compassion and loving kindness. Remaining in the present means to not engage in fabrications of the future and the past. To be free of these fabrications is to be free of the dualism of hope and fear. As the Buddha notes in the Dhammapada:

> The person who clings to nothing of the past, present and future—who has no attachment and holds on to nothing—that person, I call a Holy Person.[213]

One of the things that causes us to suffer greatly is our habit of hanging on to past hurts, past suffering. Our continuing focus on these hurts traps us in them, keeps us in a prison in which we relive our past suffering moment by moment. This is a kind of hell. A terrible but completely unnecessary hell. Dwelling on past suffering, the ways we have been hurt or harmed by experiences or by others, prevents us from being free from those experiences. Dwelling on the past blocks any kind of psychological healing let alone liberation. Of course, if we have been abused we need to speak out, we have a right and an emotional need to seek justice, but seeking justice is not dwelling on our past pain, living in our past misery. Justice is being heard, being believed, receiving appropriate care and having those who

---

[212] *The Middle Length Discourses*, Pali cannon, MN 131.

[213] Dhammapada, Chapter 26, verse 421.

harmed us held to account. Furthermore, it is very important to recognize and accept that emotional states triggered by past suffering are completely impermanent. They disappear of their own accord if we don't feed them, if we avoid nourishing them by dwelling on them day by day. In the present moment our minds and hearts are free of all the pain and misery of the past. The past is dead and gone. It is less than dust. In the present moment we are free of everything that has ever harmed us. This is why Padmasambhava taught:

> Do not pursue former suffering. Everything, whether good or bad, is past and gone. Do not anticipate future suffering. No matter what suffering may befall you now, do not give in to it, but develop courage again and again.[214]

This echoes current research in psychology that suggests that those who suffer from prolonged or unrelenting sadness and fear often have an entrenched habit of focusing more on the past than on the present.[215] An unbalanced focus on the past always leads to sadness and anxiety and makes it very difficult to overcome past hurts and trauma.

In terms of the third of Padmasambhava's points from *Self-Liberation through Seeing with Naked Awareness*, which is *Remaining in the present moment*, Jetsunma Tenzin Palmo often points out that if our attention is on our breathing, we are already in the present moment. Nothing else to do. There is no past or future if we are abiding with our breath.

As for *Leaving the mind alone*, this means to just relax, if thoughts come, let them come, and then let them go again. Thoughts will naturally dissipate

---

[214] Padmasambhava quoted in *Dakini Teachings: A Collection of Padmasambhava's Advice to the Dakini Yeshe Tsogyal*, Rangjung Yeshe Publications, 1999, p. 6.

[215] Kamila S, Hasanuzzaman M, Ekbal A, Bhattacharyya P. 'Investigating the Impact of Emotion on Temporal Orientation in a Deep Multitask Setting'. Sci Rep. 2022 Jan 11; 12 (1): p. 493.

if we don't engage with them or get swept up by them. In *The Jewel Treasure of the Dharmadhatu* it says:

Whatever happens, let it happen

Whatever is appearing, let it appear

Whatever arises, let it arise

Whatever is, let it be as it is

Whatever is not, let it not be[216]

We need to remember that thoughts are like waves, they rise, they peak, then they break and dissipate. We don't have to do anything with them, we just let them come and go of their own accord. Jetsunma Tenzin Palmo describes it this way:

Think of the mind like a vast space. Instead of being very focused, like a torchlight … we are like the open sky. And in the open sky, birds fly through, bees fly through, planes fly through, anything flies through but there is no catching it, and it leaves no trace. It just flies through because there is open space. And so, this open awareness is just being present without catching on to anything. Whatever sounds we hear, whatever thoughts we think, whatever feelings come up, they just come up and then they go. And we don't hold them, we don't look at them, we just allow them to manifest and allow them to pass. So it's this very open spaciousness. It's just sitting, in a state of presence, without grasping on to anything, just allowing whatever is, and just to be aware, just to be present. I mean, it's very simple but that doesn't necessarily mean that it's easy.[217]

---

[216] Quoted in Thinley Norbu, *A Cascading Waterfall of Nectar*, Shambhala Publications, 2006, p. 193.

[217] Jetsunma Tenzin Palmo [Facebook post] 20 December 2021. Available at: https://www.

Thought is not a problem. Thought is the natural radiance of the mind, but like the radiance or rays of the sun, a little bit is good but a lot can be bad. We don't want sunburn. So, just allow thoughts to come and go on their own. Don't get entangled in them or swept away by them. Padmasambhava's advice about how to view dualistic thinking is:

> When conceptual thinking occurs while resting in meditation, whatever arises does so out of your own mind. Since mind does not consist of any concrete essence whatsoever, thinking is itself empty of any real entity. Like the analogy of a cloud that appears within space and vanishes again into space, thinking occurs within mind and dissolves again into mind.[218]

These cloud-like thoughts naturally dissolve. It is their nature to do so. We don't need to do anything for them to dissipate. We just rest and let them go away in their own time.

The simple meditation instructions from Padmasambhava listed earlier are echoed in Tilopa's (988–1069 CE) *Six Words of Advice*, composed more than two centuries later:

1. Don't recall
2. Don't imagine
3. Don't think
4. Don't examine
5. Don't control
6. Rest

---

facebook.com/jetsunmatenzinpalmo (Accessed: 20 December 2021).

[218] Padmasambhava, *Advice From the Lotus-Born: A Collection of Padmasambhava's Advice To The Dakini Yeshe Tsogyal And Other Close Disciples*, translated by Erik Pema Kunsang, edited by Marcia Binder Schmidt, Rangjung Yeshe Publications, Kathmandu, 1994, p. 37.

When fleshed out these meditation instructions are:

1. Let go of what has passed.
2. Let go of what may come.
3. Let go of what is happening now.
4. Don't try to analyze or figure out anything that arises in meditation.
5. Don't try to make anything happen in the mind or stop anything from happening.
6. Relax, right now, and rest.

The final of the six—*Relax, right now, and rest*—is the most important, because if we are truly resting we are not recalling, imagining, examining or controlling. It is also the hardest for us to achieve. It takes a lot of practice. When we are truly resting, we notice that the mind is spacious, clear and lucid. These qualities of the mind are reflected in three traditional metaphors used to help meditators recognize the true nature of their minds:

1. A mind that is empty like space
2. A mind that is clear like a mirror
3. A mind that is like waves dissolving back into the ocean.

These can also be described as stillness, clarity (or awareness) and movement (or thought). When we understand that this is what the mind is like, it helps us to let go of the things obscuring the mind's spacious, mirror-like quality; all the pondering and emoting (fabricating) which is not our true nature. To close this section here is a pith instruction from Jetsunma Tenzin Palmo which summarizes this discussion perfectly:

A mind which is open and which allows things to be—which holds lightly to things and allows them to flow, to come into being and leave again—is a happy and peaceful mind.[219]

---

[219] Jetsunma Tenzin Palmo [Facebook post] 27 September 2021. Available at: https://www.facebook.com/jetsunmatenzinpalmo (Accessed: 27 September 2021)

The Natural Object

All meditation needs an object, an object on which to place our awareness and attention. This is where we find some differences between Shamata and Vipashana. In Shamata the object is something external to the mind. In Vipashana the object is normally internal to the mind, such as thoughts, feelings, sensations and, in later stages, awareness itself. In our tradition of Shamata we mostly use the breath as our object. We just gently place our awareness on our breathing. The attention we place on the breath should not be rigid, it's not forced concentration. The attention we place on the breath should be light, like a feather landing on the ground. It's a very soft landing. You will notice that awareness of the breath causes our breathing to naturally slow (which is good). If the breath is not your preferred object, you can use an external object, a crystal, or a nice flower or plant, or an image of the Buddha. If you meditate with your eyes closed, breath is the most practical object, but you can use sound, a pleasant sounding chime or the humming of a Tibetan singing bowl. Sound meditation sessions should be short, otherwise we might find we can't meditate without the sound. We need to be able to mediate in all situations. This is why the breath is a very practical object. The breath is with us wherever we go.

At first, the most important thing with meditation practice is not how much you do, but developing a consistent routine. Meditation should be seen as an essential part of everyday life. Meditation will be deeper if you practice at the same time and in the same place every day. If during your practice you find your mind wandering, just gently bring it back to your breath. Thoughts will come, that's fine, just let them come and let them go.

Insight into the Nature of Mind

As we learned above, in our tradition the view and posture of Vipashana is the same as for Shamata but the object is different. In Vipashana the object is not the in-and-out of breath but the coming and going of thoughts, feelings, sensations and, as we progress and deepen in our practice, the mind or awareness itself. As already noted, in practice-oriented traditions, the practice of Shamata and Vipashana are usually undertaken in tandem. That being said, the benefits of Vipashana are only attained if we have established a foundation with Shamata and our sitting meditation has deepened significantly.

We will return to *The Refined Essence of Oral Instructions* for our discussion of insight meditation. Remember that Padmasambhava pointed out that everything about meditation is included in the instruction to simply let the mind *rest in its natural state, free and easy, without fabrication*. He then goes on to say:

> The mind doesn't remain quietly in that state. If one wonders, 'Is it nothing?' like haze in the heat of the sun, it still shimmers and flashes forth. But if one wonders, 'Is it something?' it has no color or shape to identify it but is utterly empty and completely awake—that is the nature of your mind.[220]

The mind doesn't remain quietly in that state. This is so undeniable. If we have spent any significant amount of time sitting in meditation, we know that this is all too true. We will become distracted. The essence of meditation, and its benefit, is found in returning from the distraction. Eventually we recognize that distraction is part of our meditation. We can use distraction as an educational tool in deepening our ability to stay focused on our meditation object, which is usually our breath. Every time we are distracted, we bring ourselves back to the breath. That repetition creates a habit. It also creates neurons in our brains. Over time we have a deeper and deeper habit of staying gently focused, and we have more and more neurons in our brains to make that gentle focus automatic or natural. And then there's much less movement, much less thought and much less distraction. This is because there is now a

---

[220] See the full pith instruction in Kunsang, Erik Pema, 'Refined Essence of Oral Instructions', in *Dakini Teachings: A Collection of Padmasambhava's Advice to the Dakini Yeshe Tsogyal*, Rangjung Yeshe Publications, 1999.

deeply automatic habit of staying relaxed and gently focused. There is also a lot of neurological change. There is so much brain matter supporting our practice that remaining still becomes natural. After it physically becomes natural to be still, it cognitively becomes natural to be still, then the true nature of mind starts to show.

To treat distraction as a tool in our meditation, whether in Shamata or Vipashana, means that whenever we notice that we've been swept away by thought we just gently bring ourselves back to our object, so that we're just resting our awareness on our breath or object. It's really very simple. Remember those two aspects of mind that we discussed earlier, dualistic mind (sem) and the true nature of mind (rigpa)? There are these two aspects so long as we are in a deluded state. This dualism is our reality. Once we become realized these aspects are non-dual, there is just rigpa, pure spacious awareness. Even so, external stimuli are still happening and so sensations will arise and thoughts will be created. For realized beings thoughts and sensations are the ornaments of the true nature of mind. The awareness and the movement in that spacious awareness (the thoughts and sensations etc.) are completely non-dual. It's a very different kind of thing. The actual components of the mind don't change dramatically, there is still thought and sensation etc., but now these things, this movement, are the ornaments of awareness.

Once we have realized our true nature the thoughts and sensations are always beneficial. They enhance pure awareness. At the moment, in our deluded state, all these thoughts, sensations and feelings completely smother our true nature. Though the components of the mind are the same, the effect is different. That is really interesting, isn't it? It means that nothing needs to change in the mind. This is profound news. Nothing needs to change. We don't need to chase some other mind. We don't need to build, create or make some other mind. We just need to let this mind be what it is, just leave it alone, and its true nature will shine through. That is all we need to do. It is very simple, but it does take some time and consistent effort in meditation.

Returning to the next lines from the *Refined Essence*, they are: *If one wonders, 'Is it nothing?' like haze in the heat of the sun, it still shimmers and flashes forth. But if one wonders, 'Is it something?' it has no color or shape to identify it but is utterly empty and completely awake—that is the nature of your mind*. This section of the pith instruction is referring to Vipashana. First, Padmasambhava gave instruction about Shamata, or Calm Abiding meditation, now with these lines he is discussing the Vipashana technique of querying the nature of thoughts and of the mind itself, or rather awareness itself. This is the order we need to follow – Calm Abiding first and then Insight meditation, even if in the same sitting session.

There are a range of different questions we ask ourselves when we are investigating the mind. Again, these depend on what tradition we are in – Theravada, Mahayana, Vajrayana or Dzogchen. In each of these traditions, the way we approach Vipashana can be somewhat different. In the Theravada tradition there is a lot of body scanning, observing what the body is doing by placing our awareness on any physical sensations that arise. If there is a feeling, we feel it, we don't push it away, we don't judge it, and we don't ignore it. We just feel it. We become aware of what the body does, how it is working, what's going on. This is a very useful mindfulness method for remaining in the now, in the present moment. However, it can lead to hypervigilance about body sensations. This is a particular problem for people with anxiety, who make up 18% of the population, or close to one in five of us. That kind of body-scanning meditation can exacerbate anxiety symptoms so is not for everyone. This is why meditation practice needs to be tailored to the individual, not applied as a cure-all, a one-size fits all kind of thing.

In the Theravadan and the Mahayana traditions there is also a mindfulness practice in which we actively track thought back to its source. As an example, if I find myself thinking about pink poodles I ask myself 'How did that weird pink poodle thought start? Where did it come from?' Then I might recall that I had been thinking about the Gold Coast, a city in my home state which is a lot like Miami, with white sand beaches and lots of high-rise apartment buildings. I then recall that when I was thinking about the Gold Coast I had a visual impression of neon signs. The Gold Coast has a lot of neon signs. As I track the chain of thought backwards I realize that it was that impression of neon signs that made me think about pink poodles – because there is a famous neon sign of a pink poodle that advertises a sixties era Gold Coast motel called The Pink Poodle. To those of us of a certain age who grew up in Queensland in Australia that Pink Poodle motel is a symbol of the essence of the Gold Coast. Now I know where the thought came from. This mindfulness practice is very helpful in showing how our thoughts are stimulated by external things, which includes memories. Memories are external to the true nature of mind. All thoughts therefore can be shown to be not intrinsic to us at all, not who (or rather what) we are in our essential nature.

When we understand how thoughts arise, that they are generated by a process that is completely external, that is not coming from inside us, we are no longer under the impression, the erroneous idea, that our thoughts are natural to us, that they somehow mean something, that they're important to who we are. Thoughts are completely stimulated by the "outside", by sense perception and mental factors such as impressions and memories (which are fabricated recollections of external events and experiences). As I've written elsewhere:

> All thoughts and emotions, fleeting and baseless, are mere empty echoes, triggered by external events or the memory of external events, which themselves are impermanent and devoid of substance. Our thoughts and emotions are described as our "inner life" and yet they have nothing to do with our true inner life. We are not who we think we are and we

are not what we think about ourselves. Not only do our thoughts and emotions shed no light on our true inner nature, they are what obscures it. Tragically, we are so focused on our thoughts and emotions that we think they are the sum total of who we are. We identify with thoughts and emotions and misconstrue them for a self. We do not experience that which thoughts and emotions obscure, we are totally clueless about our true nature, our innate pristine awareness. To experience who we truly are all we need do is shift our focus away from thoughts and emotions, and away from the delusion of self they perpetuate. This shift of focus is so profoundly simple, yet it is something so very few ever achieve, mostly because they never even try. Once we have achieved this shift in focus, through simple meditation, and we are settled in our true nature, then we will experience thoughts and emotions not as obscurations but as the natural radiance of pristine awareness.[221]

When we talk about that which is external to us, the outside world, we are talking about something that we cannot directly experience as we are now. Everything is filtered through our senses and perception which are biased and distorted by their very nature. We cannot see, touch, hear, smell or taste anything as it really is. We cannot connect directly with reality, at least, not while we are in this deluded, non-awakened state. All that we can actually connect with is distorted perception and delusion, what in Buddhism we call samsara (illusory existence). This is what we mistakenly think is our reality or the outside world. Because of this disconnection from reality, everything that is stimulated by that perception is also delusional. All of our thoughts, emotions, impressions and memories etcetera are completely distorted and delusional, real but not true. This is why we must gain insight into the nature of the dualistic mind (sem) and recognize the true or ultimate nature of the

---

[221] Martin Jamyang Tenphel & Pema Düddul, *Resting in Stillness*, Timeless Awareness Publications, 2020, p. 136.

mind (rigpa). If we do not, we will remain mired in this delusional illusion for our entire lives and when we enter the Bardo of Dying we will miss the opportunity for liberation it offers us. So, we need to adopt this practice of insight meditation right now, while we are alive and have the chance. We need to look into the mind, into thought, query what it is, where it comes from, where and how it abides and where it goes when it subsides. Every thought is an opportunity to see through the illusion and discover the ultimate nature of ourselves and everything in the universe.

The form of Vipashana that Padmasambhava is talking about is from the Nyingma tradition. When he says, *If one wonders, 'Is it nothing?' like haze in the heat of the sun, it still shimmers and flashes forth*, he is referring to an aspect of mind very important to bardo practice. The words used here are not random, they are chosen for a specific reason. The words *haze, shimmer*, and *flashes forth* refer to the luminous quality of the mind and thought. When we have been meditating consistently for some time and our thinking has started to diminish, there is sometimes a sense of dimness or darkness in the absence of thought, particularly if we meditate with our eyes closed. Then when thought comes there's this sense of light. It is a very interesting thing. Padmasambhava is using these words to indicate that when we achieve realization all thought, emotions and sensations become the luminous manifestation of our true nature. This is quite different to how we are experiencing thought and emotion now, as that which obscures our true nature, a shadow on our true nature.

The last part of this verse reads: *But if one wonders, 'Is it something?' it has no color or shape to identify it but is utterly empty and completely awake—that is the nature of your mind*. This is a very condensed nature of the mind teaching. In this tradition of practice we explore the mind—the mind that thinks, emotes, feels and senses—with a series of questions that help us to discover its true nature. We ask these questions in tandem with our daily meditation session, just before we sit in stillness or in-between sessions. Padmasambhava is giving us some of these questions here. After we ask ourselves these questions we sit in meditation with the mind itself as the object.

So what does it mean to place our awareness on the mind? It means to place our awareness on thoughts and emotions themselves. Placing our awareness on thinking doesn't mean to entertain it or follow it. It means to be aware as thought rises. We let it rise and then let it dissipate. By being aware of the coming and going of thought, we learn of its nature. Thoughts rise, crest or peak, and then dissolve of their own accord. We need not do anything to them for them to do that, for them to dissolve into emptiness, because emptiness is their nature. The same is true of emotions. Emotions rise because of an external trigger. This trigger might be our memory, but memories most often rise in response to an external stimulus. Something in our life or world prompts these memories to come to the forefront of our mind. In insight meditation we place our awareness on how these thoughts and emotions rise, how they abide, or what they do, and then where they go. To understand the nature of thoughts and emotions more deeply we ask a series of questions like the ones Padmasambhava posed above.

As we do Shamata and Vipashana together, we begin our meditation sitting in stillness, then we ask ourselves the insight questions, then return to simple sitting. One of the main questions is: *Where does thought come from?* Once we've asked the question, we pause and we wait for an answer. Sometimes the dualistic mind will throw up answers, but the really interesting thing is that mostly our mind responds with silence. Those without much meditational ability or experience in Shamata will miss this moment of silence, their minds will start chattering away very quickly. This is a shame because the answer is in the silence. The answer is non-verbal. Spoiler alert – the answer is that thoughts don't come from anywhere. We need to feel this directly. Knowing the answer intellectually does nothing for us. This is not like a quiz show where if you have the answer you win. We really need to *feel* the truth of this. To feel it we need to actually investigate it for ourselves and experience it. We need to sit in our meditation posture, rest and relax, do a little bit of Shamata, then ask: *Where does thought come from?* and then just wait, do nothing, go back into Shamata. For those with even a small amount of meditation experience, the response to that question is a deafening silence. That silence might not last long, maybe a few seconds. For someone with more meditation practice that silence will be elongated. On meeting that silence we often think, 'Oh, there's no answer'. But actually, that *is* the answer. There is no answer because thought doesn't come from anywhere. The absence of answer is the answer. It is important that we abide or rest in that answer – rest in the silence. In this way we can confirm that thoughts, in fact, don't come from anywhere. When we try to find where thought comes from we come up with nothing.

In the West we might say that thought is a neurological process, and it comes from a specific part of the brain. In fact, if we take the brain apart we can't find exactly where the thoughts are. If we examine each component of the neurological process, each aspect of the system, we will not find thought there. Thoughts do not reside in just one part of the brain. We need to keep inquiring until we feel in our heart and know with certainty in our intellect that thought doesn't come from anywhere. It is just a bunch of triggered reactions, dependent arisings. It has no real base or ground. We then continue to our other insight questions: *Where does thought abide?* and *Where does thought go?* We examine these in the same way until we have certainty that thought has no inherent, independent, permanent reality. Thought and the thinking mind are empty. Whatever verbal answers the dualistic mind throws up in response to these questions are all deception. The dualistic mind cannot abide the idea of emptiness, that things can be empty; that they don't come from anywhere, stay anywhere or go anywhere, that they don't have any solid state. So the dualistic mind will throw up all kinds of answers. Just treat this like a little child trying to convince you that unicorns are real. If we stay with the silence we will encounter the truth.

How to Begin and How to Continue

We begin meditating in the same way for both Shamata and Vipashana. We begin with short sessions so that we can ease ourselves in. Going in too hard and too fast might lead to abandoning the practice before we experience any benefit. As Dilgo Khyenste Rinpoche once taught:

> When we begin to meditate on the nature of mind, it is preferable to make short sessions of meditation, several times per day. With perseverance, we will progressively realize the nature of our mind, and that realization will become more stable. At this stage, thoughts will have lost their power to disturb and subdue us.[222]

We can start with as little as two sessions of five minutes each, separated by a short break of a minute or so. In the breaks we drop our meditation posture, including our object of attention, but remain mindful, remain aware of our awareness. These breaks help us to take our mindfulness into the times we are not in formal meditation, what is referred to as post-meditation. Eventually this will make our whole lives part of our practice. As Jetsun Khandro Rinpoche makes clear:

> People take meditation as the actual practice, post-meditation as something that's just going back to their normal lives. Whereas, the actual interpretation is that meditation is just a preliminary to the mindfulness that has to be practiced ... the actual meditation begins when you get off the cushion.[223]

---

[222] 'Dilgo Khyentse Rimpoche On Dzogchen Meditation', KeithDowman.net: http://keithdowman.net/dzogchen/dilgo-khyentse-dzogchen-meditation.html

[223] See the full discussion by Jetsun Khandro Rinpoche on YouTube: https://youtu.be/sFAQUgdd828

After a week or two practicing in this way we add another five minute session, and two weeks after that another session, so that we build up to 20 or 30 minutes a day with a number of breaks. In time, we can reduce the number of breaks, to say one every 15 minutes and then one every half hour or hour.

The most important thing with meditation practice is that we do it regularly, each and every day, and that we accept that some meditation sessions will be pleasant and others difficult. Whether a meditation session is pleasant or unpleasant doesn't matter, every session helps familiarize us with the nature and workings of our mind. In that sense there is no wasted or bad meditation session, no matter how we feel about it.

How to Continue – Dealing with Experiences in Meditation

The Tibetan word for meditation is 'gom'. It means 'familiarization', to become familiar. What are we becoming familiar with? On one hand, we are becoming familiar with the dualistic mind, with how the conceptual mind works. On the other hand, we are becoming familiar with our natural state, which is unadorned, self-perfected awareness. In meditation we are shifting our focus away from the stuff of the dualistic mind—thoughts, emotions and sensations—toward our natural awareness. This shift of focus causes many things to happen in the mind, many changes. As we deepen in our practice of meditation we need to learn how to deal with the many and varied experiences that arise in our practice. If we don't adopt the right attitude towards these experiences then we will stall or plateau.

According to the traditional teachings, meditation has two aspects: the essence and the effects or experience. The essence of meditation is what we call awareness, the simple ability to know, to be aware of things. This simple knowing is the focus or point of meditation – to become increasingly familiar with this ground of awareness that is our true nature. The effects or experiences of meditation can be interpreted as either positive or negative, but are in fact completely neutral. Positive experiences can include feeling peaceful or calm, feeling joyful or having experiences of clarity or thoughtlessness. Negative experiences can be things like feeling bored, feeling that our mind is racing with thoughts, feeling overwhelmed with emotion or feeling uncomfortable in some way. These experiences we have in meditation, whether we categorize them as positive or negative, fall under the category of becoming familiar with the dualistic mind.

We need to recognize that these experiences, both pleasant and unpleasant, are nothing more than the fabrications of the deluded mind. It's all just more stuff for us to observe dispassionately in order to become familiar with how the dualistic mind works. When we are beginner meditators we have a tendency to think our positive experiences in meditation are important, that they signify the practice is working or that they prove we are somehow special. For the most part, they are not important at all nor do they indicate that we are special. Conversely, we have a tendency to think our negative experiences in meditation are a problem with the practice or some external thing rather than just more shenanigans of the monkey mind. Both attitudes are inaccurate and not helpful. In the following poetic passage from *The Awakening Heart: Contemplations on the Buddhist Path* Jamyang Tenphel succinctly describes the attitude we should have to meditative experiences when he writes:

> Remember that no matter what experiences you have, they can never be reproduced. You can never retrace your steps to remake or reproduce any experience. They are truly like fireworks, once they have made their sparkling pretty flashes, they are gone forever. Gone. Gone for good. So, don't dwell on the past. Continue with your meditation as if it were the first time. Fresh and free from expectations or any echoes of the past. Remain in the timeless now. This very present unfathomable moment. Freedom only exists in this inexplicable now. Not dwelling on

past events, or in anticipation of future ones. Surrender entirely to the unfindable now. Let go, and let it all be. No past. No future. No present. No you.[224]

The way to deepen in our meditation practice is to continue with regular sitting sessions that we maintain irrespective of positive or negative experiences and to adopt an attitude of impartiality about those experiences, recognizing that these things are just part of the dualistic mind's near limitless ability to fabricate thoughts, feelings, sensations and illusions. Furthermore, so long as we are having so-called meditative experiences we have not attained realization. Indeed, those experiences are evidence that we are still trapped in duality. Worse, attachment to those experiences blocks our full realization. As the Ninth Karmapa, Wangchuk Dorje (1556-1603), explains:

> ... if you are obsessed with and attached to whatever experiences and insights you have, you will destroy them. Be detached from them and remain steadily in a non-compulsive state of being unattracted.[225]

This means that no matter how profound our experiences and realizations, we need to be diligent about treating them as no big deal. That's what the Ninth Karmapa means when he says to remain steadily in a non-compulsive state of being unattracted. It just means to not think our experiences are anything special, to actively remind ourselves that we are all utterly equal, with none of us more special than any other. If we think the point of meditation is positive or exalted experiences then when those experiences do not arise, or negative ones arise, we will lose our ability to practice, to keep becoming familiar with the mind. As I've already mentioned, the real point of meditation is to shift

---

[224] Jamyang Tenphel, *The Awakening Heart: Contemplations on the Buddhist Path*, Timeless Awareness Publications, 2023, no page, Kindle Edition.

[225] Wangchuk Dorje, the Ninth Karmapa, *The Mahamudra: Eliminating the Darkness of Ignorance with Oral Commentary Given by Beru Khyentse Rinpoche*, translated by Alexander Berzin Library of Tibetan Works and Archives, 1989, p. 63.

our focus and identification away from experiences, and away from thoughts, feelings and sensations, to our fundamental awareness. Whatever arises in the mind, whether supposedly good or supposedly bad, we simply maintain our awareness of what is happening without being swept up. It's not about how we feel. Our awareness of what is happening is the point. As the great Kagyu master Gampopa makes clear:

> When meditators are learning to stabilize the mind, they should not regard meditative equipoise as something good. If they fail to have an experience of meditative equipoise, they should not regard that as a failure. The important point is not whether meditative equipoise is present, but whether you can maintain awareness in both a settled and a disturbed state of mind. If disturbing thoughts arise, you should use them with awareness to recognize that thoughts are transient — they arise, persist for a while, and then disperse. The transience of a thought is revealed by its elusiveness. Before you can get hold of a thought, it is already gone, and another one has appeared in its place.[226]

Meditative experiences, good or bad, are just waves on the surface of the ocean, they are not its deep nature. None of the things we might experience in meditation have anything to do with our true nature, with enlightenment. Our true nature is fundamental *unadorned* and non-dual awareness, which is there no matter what we are experiencing, thinking or feeling.

When significant obstacles to our meditation arise—such as wild thoughts, overwhelming sensations, boredom or experiences of drowsiness or dullness—we apply a method to settle or reinvigorate our practice. That method can be as simple as adapting our posture or repeating a mantra or

---

[226] Gampopa quoted in the book "The Ninth Karmapa, Wangchuk Dorje's Ocean of Certainty" ISBN: 978-1934608203 - https://amzn.to/387QJ01

aphorism (see thee section on Dream Yoga for useful aphorisms). Kyabje Dudjom Rinpoche provides excellent advice for when we feel drowsy in practice or our meditation is dull:

> In meditation practice, you might experience a muddy, semi-conscious, drifting state, like having a hood over your head: a dreamy dullness. This is really nothing more than a kind of blurred and mindless stagnation. How do you get out of this state? Alert yourself, straighten your back, breathe the stale air out of your lungs, and direct your awareness into clear space to freshen your mind. If you remain in this stagnant state you will not evolve, so whenever this setback arises, clear it again and again. It is important to be as watchful as possible, and to stay as vigilant as you can.

This is one of the reasons we build regular short breaks into our meditation session – to guard against dullness and drowsiness. In those breaks we can stretch, have a sip of water, adjust our posture and refresh our gaze by looking out a window. In time, the breaks also help us to bring our meditation into daily life, making every aspect of our lives a practice of awareness. When we do this everything that happens, in both the mind and in our experience of the world, becomes fuel for abiding in rigpa. Another very powerful, yet quite unexpected, method for shifting obstacles in our meditation is devotion. There is nothing better for invigorating our practice than opening our hearts to the guru. This is eloquently described by Kyabje Dudjom Rinpoche when he explains:

> The best way to eliminate obstacles in our meditation is through devotion to our enlightened teacher. It is not a matter of mixing one thing with another thing, but rather of pouring water into water. Just as space enclosed by the hands becomes identical to the space outside once the hands are parted, so there is no difference between our mind and

that of our teacher. The Lama's mind is not better, nor is ours impure. Such differences simply do not exist. This is the secret to meditation.[227]

Here Dudjom Rinpoche is suggesting that we engage in Guru Yoga, merging our minds with the guru's mind, to stabilize our meditation practice. In my own experience, this is profoundly effective.

Finally, it is important to remember that meditation, in this case silent sitting practiced in tandem with insight, is an authentic method for recognizing the true nature of mind, which is also the true nature of everything. That recognition leads to full awakening, to enlightenment. Therefore, we must maintain a consistent daily meditation practice no matter what happens. I will close this discussion of how to continue in our meditation practice with a short quote from Dudjom Sangye Pema Shepa Rinpoche that succinctly states the fruit of our efforts:

Eventually, through familiarity in meditation practice, an experience of the infinite purity of all that exists wells forth from within.[228]

---

[227] Kyabje Dudjom Rinpoche, *The Pay of Thoughts,* for full text see: https://www.bodhicharya-london.org.uk/Kent/PDF/Dudjom-Rinpoche-The-Play-of-Thought.pdf

[228] Dudjom Sangye Pema Shepa Rinpoche, Dudjom International Foundation website: https://www.dudjominternationalfoundation.com/

CHAPTER THIRTEEN

PRACTICING GURU YOGA

Becoming one with Buddha-mind is not a new attainment;
it is how you have always been.

Guru Yoga or Lamai Naljor is about the bardo between sense of self and sense of other, or between subject and object, between here and there, now and then, this and that. It is also about the gap between distorted (or impure) perception and pure view. In this gap is found timeless, non-dual awareness. This timeless, non-dual awareness is, of course, rigpa, the true nature of mind. Guru Yoga, then, awakens us to the Dharmakaya aspect of our true nature, the fact that our nature is perfect, unbound openness, as vast as space, empty yet cognizant. Combining our sitting meditation with Guru Yoga is a powerful method for recognizing the true nature of mind. Remember, we discussed earlier that Guru Yoga is the merging of subject and object, the collapse of the dualistic view and the dualistic mind. In essence it is about becoming familiar with our true nature. As Ngakchang Rinpoche explains:

> Lamai Naljor [Guru Yoga] is very important as a method of practice because we seem to find some difficulty in trusting or believing directly in our own enlightened nature. It's easier to trust in the enlightened nature of the teacher since it is he or she who has inspired us to practice. In this sense, the teacher's enlightened nature is a reflection of our own

enlightened nature. So Lamai Naljor is really a way of coming to trust your own enlightened nature.[229]

It should by now be abundantly clear to us that Guru Yoga is not about becoming a groupie to spiritual teachers and doing whatever they say. Guru Yoga is a precise meditative method that brings profound, and very swift, benefits. All Buddhist meditative techniques require an object, something on which we place our awareness until our awareness and the object are one and all duality between observer and observed collapses. In Guru Yoga the object is not the teacher per se but devotion; the physical and emotional experience of it. This devotion can be for the teacher or for the Dharma itself. Eventually that devotion brings about a profound unity that cannot be described in words. The mind/heart of the teacher and the mind/heart of the student merge. This happens surprisingly quickly. In this sense it is superior to many other practices.

The superiority of Guru Yoga as a technique of awakening is described in detail by Drubwang Penor Rinpoche when he explains:

In fact, there are many practitioners who have realized the nature of mind and attained perfect enlightenment just by doing Guru Yoga. Being introduced to the nature of one's mind can happen only through the master's blessings, and without the blessings nothing will happen. This is not something that can be bought, and no matter how learned a scholar you may become, without a qualified master it's not possible to recognize the true nature of our mind. As this is the root of the practice, without blessings there is no way to attain enlightenment, and the path to Buddhahood is blocked. There is no other way to discover the nature of your mind; you can't buy it or find it anywhere other than through the

---

[229] 'Interview with Ngakchang Rinpoche', *Arobuddhism*, https://arobuddhism.org/q-and-a/lamai-naljor.html

blessings of a qualified master. That is why the single most important practice in Dharma is Guru Yoga.[230]

When Penor Rinpoche refers to blessings (*jinlap* in Tibetan) he is not talking about something magical, but rather very specific qualities of heart and mind that arise in the practitioner as a direct result of devotion – open-heartedness, surrender, selflessness, love and profound ease or rest. In that state our true nature is revealed without effort or striving. Technically, these blessings are not given by the master but rather are innate to us and are awakened by our devotion to the master, which means it is totally up to us. It also means that the focus of our devotion need not be physically present. It doesn't matter if our teacher is close to us or far away. Time, space and location do not matter. What matters is the state of our hearts. We already know from Togden Shakya Shri that if we have devotion and faith toward the master, 'there is not even a hair tip's difference if the master is alive or not'.[231] The practice of Guru Yoga is about our own hearts, not about anything or anyone else. It is also the most effective way to recognize the true nature of the mind and the ultimate nature of the universe.

But how do we actually *do* Guru Yoga? Dudjom Rinpoche described it succinctly when he wrote:

Pray to Guru Rinpoche, then settle within the state of your mind and the guru's mind inseparable.

In the relaxed openness of your mind's uncontrived state of naturalness,

Do not stop, cultivate, accept, or reject thoughts.

Relax without grasping; whatever arises will be self-liberated.

---

[230] Drubwang Penor Rinpoche, *An Ocean of Blessings: Heart Teachings of Drubwang Penor Rinpoche*, translated by Ani Jinba Palmo, Snow Lion, 2017, p. 7.

[231] *Togden Shakya Shri: The Life and Liberation of a Tibetan Yogin*, by Kathog Situ Chokyi Gyatso, translated by Elio Guarisco, Shang Shung Publications, 2011, p. 159.

This is the ultimate guru. Abide in that natural state!

It is not a new attainment; it has never been separate from you.[232]

There are some actions here unique to Guru Yoga that we need to understand how to do – praying to the guru, merging our mind with the guru's mind, relaxing in an uncontrived state of naturalness. We will discuss these actions as they apply to informal Guru Yoga and formal Guru Yoga. This next section on informal Guru Yoga is excerpted from *Resting in Stillness*, the book I co-authored with Jamyang Tenphel. It was written by Jamyang and arose from his decades-long experience in Guru Yoga practice.[233]

Informal Guru Yoga

Firstly, it's important to feel like you can really relate to your Lama in a fundamental, basic way. It's good to feel that you have things in common, however superficial this may sound. You need to relate to their personality, life story, lifestyle, and external form manifestation. This is a way of approaching the guru psychologically, and helps your mind develop a type of trust, as flimsy as this may sound. It's like building the foundations for your Guru Yoga. You need to like them, because they represent the enlightened version of yourself. You should feel like they are just like you, except completely awakened. Read about them, watch videos of their homeland, and learn about their culture and daily lives. Learn all the details you can to flesh out your understanding of them from the ground up. Begin with their outer lives, then learn about their inner lives and their spiritual practices. Read stories about them written by their students. Really get as much of a picture of them as you can. You should develop a great respect for them and an ever-growing trust in their methods and accomplishments. The beauty of this practice is

[232] Dudjom Rinpoche, *Wisdom Nectar: Dudjom Rinpoche's Heart Advice*, Snow Lion, 2005, p.118.
[233] Martin Jamyang Tenphel & Pema Düddul, *Resting in Stillness*, 2020, pp. 65 -67.

that it does not rely on your Lama actually being alive, which gives hope to those of us whose Lamas have departed this world.

Next, sit in meditation and visualize them in front of you. Visualize and recall all the details you have learnt about them. Recall all the inspiring stories about them, and that they truly were enlightened. Then, imagine them coming towards you and merging with your heart. You may want to recite a mantra, like the Vajra Guru Mantra, *Om Ah Hung Benza Guru Padma Siddhi Hung*, while visualizing this merging. Repeat this merging over and over, at your own pace, feeling all the inspiration that you have gained from your investigation into their life. Feel respect and faith in their practice, and their path, and its fruition, and call upon them over and over to merge with you. Eventually you will experience the Lama merge with your heart and he/she will never leave it again. You'll feel a great joy and bliss with the certainty of this knowledge. Your heart/mind will feel expansive and free and full of compassion. You will know, with unshakeable certainty, that you and the guru are now inseparable. At this point you'll realize, or deeply understand, that you no longer need to visualize the guru externally, because he/she is now inseparably entwined with your heart. Along with this feeling comes the certain knowledge that you truly have Buddha Nature, and that you can absolutely achieve realization in this lifetime. As sure as you are that the sun will rise and set each day, you will feel inseparable from the Lama and convinced that realization is possible in this life.

Formal Guru Yoga

We can see from Jamyang's advice about informal Guru Yoga in the section above that the Lamai Naljor method does not need to be overly complicated, time-consuming or stuffy and has nothing to do with being subservient to someone else. Informal Guru Yoga works wonderfully if you have natural devotion for a teacher, whether a contemporary, living master or a master from the historical past. If you don't have natural devotion for a teacher, the way to develop it is to use a more formal Guru Yoga practice that relies on a fully enlightened being such as Shakyamuni Buddha, Padmasambhava or Khandro Yeshe Tsogyal. There are Guru Yoga practices associated with all Tibetan Buddhist lineages. There is a beautiful and concise practice in the Dudjom Tersar, the lineage descending from Dudjom Lingpa and Dudjom Rinpoche, that is presented in the form of a foundational practice or "ngondro" that can be undertaken as a daily practice rather than an accumulation or preliminary practice.[234] In fact, Guru Yoga should never be seen as a preliminary practice but as the main practice, if not the whole path. Thinley Norbu Rinpoche (1931 – 2011), one of Dudjom Rinpoche's children and a Dudjom lineage holder, puts it this way:

> Without anticipating another actual practice in the future, holding the actual practice of Lamai Naljor as the life of the main practice, if one is able to practice like the unceasing flow of a river, it is like one hundred rivers flowing under a single bridge. By arriving at this essential point, one's practice will be greatly enhanced.[235]

As with all things in Vajrayana Buddhism, there are different levels of practice. There are outer, inner and secret approaches to Guru Yoga. Dilgo Khyentse Rinpoche explains:

> The outer method is to visualize the guru dwelling above our head and to pray to him ardently, with fierce devotion. The inner method is to realize, through the practice, that our own body, speech, and mind are inseparable from the wisdom body, speech, and mind of the guru. The secret method is to meditate upon the guru in his sambhogakaya form,

---

[234] The full ngondro text can be found here: https://www.lotsawahouse.org/tibetan-masters/dudjom-rinpoche/dudjom-tersar-ngondro

[235] Thinley Norbu, *A Cascading Waterfall of Nectar*, Shambhala Publications, 2006, p. 166.

the body of divine enjoyment. The most secret method introduces us to the natural state of awareness.[236]

Although there are these different levels to Guru Yoga, we need only be concerned with the outer level, as the inner and secret levels unfold naturally as our heart fills with devotion. Devotion dissolves our sense of self, breaking down the false boundaries we have constructed between ourselves and others, between ourselves and the guru. This leads to a natural realization that our body, speech and mind are in fact the body, speech and mind of awakened nature (the kayas). That recognition then leads effortlessly to abiding in the natural state of awareness.

The basic method of all formal, outer Guru Yoga practice is described by Khenchen Palden Sherab Rinpoche and Khenpo Tsewang Dongyal Rinpoche in this way:

> ... in the sky in front of you, or if you prefer above your head, feel the presence of your teacher in the form of Guru Padmasambhava. Guru Padmasambhava is the embodiment of all Buddhas and teachers of the three times and ten directions. Feel strong devotion to him and then recite the Seven Line Prayer, as well as the prayers to the lineage masters and root teacher. Then, after praying, visualize that blessing lights come from Guru Padmasambhava, which cleanse and purify all your negativities, obscurations, and habitual patterns. Doubt, hesitation, dullness, weakness in meditation—these and all other hindrances to your realization are completely removed. Feel this very vividly. Then Guru Padmasambhava dissolves into light. This light enters your crown chakra, moves down your central channel, and enters your heart center where it merges with your awareness. At that moment let your mind look

---

[236] Dilgo Khyentse Rinpoche quoted in Reginald A. Ray, In the Presence of Masters: Wisdom from 30 Contemporary Tibetan Buddhist Teachers, Shambhala Publications, 2004, p. 191.

at your mind. What happens? The watcher and the watched merge, and there is no longer any subject and object. Now release your muscles and nervous system. Let everything go. Abide in the inexpressible nature of the mind, beyond categories and characteristics.[237]

The letting go of the muscles and nervous system is a very important step. It is a total physical relaxation. This bodily relaxation helps the mind to drop into stillness. When both body and mind are relaxed and still the truth of the non-duality of our own fundamental awareness and that of the guru is luminously evident. Use whichever formal or informal practice works best for you. The main point is to keep it simple and undertake the practice consistently (daily) with open-heartedness and enthusiasm.

The True Guru

Guru Yoga is about the total equality of the guru and student. It is the opposite of the idea of being subservient. It is essentially about the spacious awareness we rest in after the dissolution in the formal practice. That spacious awareness is our true nature. True Guru Yoga is based on the recognition that our true mind is the same as the guru's true mind, which is the same as the Buddha's mind. Our true mind, though currently obscured, is no different from the Buddha. That is the realization of Guru Yoga. The essence of Guru Yoga practice and its value is clearly expressed by Dzongsar Khyentse Rinpoche when he teaches:

> I strongly recommend that you unite your mind with the mind of the guru again and again. Visualize Guru Rinpoche as you chant the vajra guru mantra, then, after every hundred mantras, dissolve Guru Rinpoche into you. The more often you go through this process, the better, so try effecting the dissolution every ten or twenty mantras, then just watch

---

[237] Khenchen Palden Sherab Rinpoche and Khenpo Tsewang Dongyal Rinpoche, *The Nature of Mind: The Dzogchen Instructions of Aro Yeshe Jungne*, Shambhala Publications, 2016, P.102.

the inseparability. Needless to say, the experience will not leave your life unchanged.[238]

As we deepen in our practice of Guru Yoga we realize that the true guru is within. As we've already seen, in Tibetan Buddhism the guru is considered to have multiple aspects – outer, inner and secret. Dzongsar Khyentse Rinpoche puts it this way:

> In the Vajrayana, the guru has three aspects: the outer guru, the inner guru, and the secret guru. It's important to be clear about these before entering a path that uses the guru as a method for awakening. The great Sakyapa master Könchok Lhundrup explained that the outer guru is the physical person you can see and communicate with, from whom you can receive verbal and symbolic teachings and instructions. The outer guru is "as Buddha as it gets." The inner guru is the nature of your mind— in other words, a mind that is not thinking of a "thing" but is simply cognizant and undeniably present. And the secret guru is the emptiness of all phenomena.[239]

Ngakpa Karma Lhundup Rinpoche often says: 'In the beginning rely on the human guru. In the middle rely on the Dharma as guru. In the end rely on your true nature as guru'. When we say rely on the Dharma as guru we mean rely on the texts, the teachings and the liturgies or sadhanas, but also on the application of those texts in practice. In this way our own practice, our meditation, becomes our inner guru. Through our practice we encounter wisdom and true compassion. That experience is a wonderful teacher. Through applying the teachings given to us by the outer guru, the human

---

[238] Dzongsar Khyentse Rinpoche, *Not for Happiness: A Guide to the So-Called Preliminary Practices*, Shambhala Publishing, 2012, p. 181.

[239] Dzongsar Khyentse Rinpoche, *The Guru Drinks Bourbon*, Shambhala Publishing, 2016, pp. 26-27.

master, we encounter the inner guru as our own practice and eventually the secret guru (our true nature). As Dzongsar Khyentse Rinpoche explains:

> The whole purpose of the outer guru is to fish out the inner guru, to teach us how to tap into the space between past thoughts and future thoughts and, if possible, remain there. That moment is the inner and secret gurus.[240]

Recognizing the Mind as Guru, a poem by Shangpa Kagyu master Kyergongpa (1154 – 1217), makes this explicit:

> Oh, mind that is my guru,
>
> I meet you by recognizing what I am.
>
> I pray to you by letting go of doubt and hesitation.
>
> I revere you by letting go and settling naturally.
>
> I serve you by resting continuously in the nature of things.
>
> I provide you with food by resting without strain in empty clarity.
>
> I provide you with drink by knowing attention and distraction make no difference.
>
> I clothe you by knowing appearance and sound as illusory displays.[241]

Once we have recognized the true nature of mind, the ultimate nature itself becomes our teacher. At this point we realize with certainty that the human guru is a manifestation or embodiment of that ultimate nature and that there is no separation between us and the master, never was and never will be. There can never be such a separation. As the true guru is our own nature

---

[240] Dzongsar Khyentse Rinpoche, *The Guru Drinks Bourbon*, Shambhala Publishing, 2016, p. 76.

[241] See the whole poem here: http://unfetteredmind.org/recognizing-mind-as-the-guru/

from which we can never be parted, all we need do is relax into that nature and rest. This is expressed beautifully by Dudjom Rinpoche when he writes:

Since pure awareness of nowness is the real Buddha,

In openness and contentment I found the Lama in my heart.

When we realize this unending natural mind is the very nature of the Lama,

Then there is no need for attached, grasping, or weeping prayers or artificial complaints.

By simply relaxing in this uncontrived, open, and natural state,

We obtain the blessing of aimless self-liberation of whatever arises.[242]

In time our Guru Yoga practice will deepen to the point that we let go of the teacher as the focus of our devotion. Our devotion becomes boundless and non-referential. It becomes like the sun, shining on everything equally. At first we may feel resistant to relinquishing our teacher as the focus of our practice, because we don't want to let go of our love and gratitude for them. The things is, once we let go of the teacher as a method our love and respect for them not only doesn't diminish, it flowers even more. Our attachment to the outer form of our teachers is actually an obstacle to full awakening. I will close this section with a pith instruction from the great Drukpa Kagyu yogi Togden Amtrin which, among other things, encourages us to let go of our attachment to the outer form of our gurus:

Do not cling to the external face or form of the guru;

Your own mind is the true face of the greatest guru.

Do not be superstitious and admire magical powers;

---

[242] Dudjom Rinpoche, *Wisdom Nectar: Dudjom Rinpoche's Heart Advice*, Snow Lion, 2005, p197 – 198.

Real change in the mind is the greatest magical power.

Do not rely on receiving blessings;

Continual mindfulness of the true nature is the greatest blessing.[243]

Practicing Guru Yoga at the Time of Death

The experience of the non-dual nature of all beings, of the non-dual reality that the Buddhas are inseparable from sentient beings, from ourselves, is powerfully transformative and is a great support in the bardos, especially the Bardo of Dying. The significance of Guru Yoga to practicing the bardo teachings is made clear by Tsele Natsok Rangdrol:

> … the person who has realized whatever appears to be the display of the guru and also to be the great equal taste inseparable from self-cognizance, will indeed never depart from the dharmata realm of great bliss either in this life, the bardo or the next life.[244]

The open-heartedness, surrender and awe-filled devotion we feel for the Buddhas and our teachers as a result of practicing Guru Yoga becomes the rocket fuel we need to get us swiftly to a recognition of our own nature. As we discovered in our discussion of the Bardo of Dying, one potent method for achieving liberation at the time of death, of enabling us to recognize the Mother Luminosity as it dawns, is to rely on our trust, respect and devotion to the guru. Below is a pith instruction from Jetsunma Tenzin Palmo about how to practice Guru Yoga at the time of death:

> Relax. Concentrate on the object of one's devotion—either the lama or Tara or Chenrezig, whoever you have devotion for—and go towards the light. Then let go. It's very important to let go. No more attachment

---

[243] Quoted in Jamyang Tenphel, *The Awakening Heart: Contemplations on the Buddhist Path*, Timeless Awareness Publications, 2023, no page, Kindle Edition.

[244] Tsele Natsok Rangdrol, *Mirror of Mindfulness*, Rangjung Yeshe Publications, 1987, p. 63.

to this lifetime, to this body, this mind, to one's relationships, to one's wealth or status. Let it all go … If we have devotion and we keep our mind solely on our object of devotion as much as we can, then that is all we have to worry about. Keep an openness of mind, let go and go towards the object of our devotion. That is enough.[245]

We can see by this pith instruction that memorizing all the details of the dissolving elements (earth, fire water etc.) and all the different types of visions that might appear is unnecessary. So too are elaborate tantric practices such as Phowa. All we need is some meditative stability and devotion. Devotion is not only the fuel of our practice, it makes our practice rich and joyful. As Jamyang Tenphel makes clear:

> The path of devotion is the path of tremendous joy, tremendous wonder and tremendous profundity, resulting in nothing less than the Great Perfection.[246]

If we do not have devotion and are resistant to developing it then meditative stability becomes even more important. Without devotion meditative stability and clear insight into the illusory nature of our perception is our only hope at the time of death.

---

[245] New Year's Retreat: A session with Jetsunma Tenzin Palmo (teaching video). See: https://youtu.be/-qgy707_mKw

[246] Jamyang Tenphel, *The Awakening Heart: Contemplations on the Buddhist Path*, Timeless Awareness Publications, 2023, no page, Kindle Edition.

CHAPTER FOURTEEN

PRACTICING DREAM YOGA

This is a dream-like illusion, a mere mirage, a fleeting fabrication. Let it go and rest.

Dream Yoga seizes the opportunity in the bardo between deep sleep and waking in which we dream. It is about developing clear insight into the nature of reality and the illusory and distorted nature of our perception. It has three parts: Wake-up practice, daytime practice and night-time practice, which includes what happens while we sleep. To a Buddhist, the things we perceive when we are awake and the things we perceive when we are dreaming are of the same nature, they are all illusory and empty. As Pema Khandro Rinpoche notes:

> If we think about it, we see that our lives are consumed by a series of dreamlike states: memories, daydreams, fantasies, future plans, emotional states, imagination, fears. Like nighttime dreams, all these mental states are partially based on "reality" and partially based on our interpretations, projections, and extrapolations.[247]

Waking life is as much a dream as the dream state. All is illusion fabricated by the dualistic mind. One of the Tibetan words for the dualistic mind (sprul pa'i sems) translates loosely as 'the mind that is like a magician creating

---

[247] 'You're Caught in a Dream. Wake Up!', *Lion's Roar*, February 8 2019, https://www.lionsroar.com/youre-caught-in-a-dream-wake-up/

illusions'.[248] In our so-called waking life we are as much a victim of mirages and illusions as we are when we are asleep and dreaming. The only way out is to recognize the illusion. And what do we discover about the illusion when we recognize it for what it is? We discover that everything that we perceive, whether we are awake or dreaming, is all the luminosity, the radiance, of the ultimate nature. The only way to recognize the illusion and realize the truth of the luminous nature of all is through meditation, contemplation of the view, and practices like Dream Yoga and Guru Yoga which, all together, tame and disempower the mind as illusion-making magician. Pema Khandro Rinpoche makes this quite clear when she writes:

> We practice meditation to unravel the root of suffering by discovering our mental afflictions are also like dreams. If we aren't familiar with mind's dreamlike propensities, we make our afflictions into our reality. If our habit is aggression, we can read anger into everything. If our habit is insecurity, we can read self-loathing into anything. We project our own emotions onto others. Acting on these misperceptions is how we produce negative karma. When we live caught in a dream that we don't know we're dreaming, we suffer tremendously.[249]

The point of Dream Yoga is to understand or recognize the illusory and empty quality of all things. This is done by remaining aware whist dreaming, in effect entering into a lucid dream state and recognizing that we are dreaming. According to the Dream Yoga teachings there are three types of dreams:

1. Ordinary dreams. These are dualistic and arise or are triggered by the activities of our waking life including thoughts, emotions, memories and experiences.

---

[248] Ibid
[249] Ibid.

2. Clear light dreams. These are spiritual visions, blessings from our teachers and manifestations of our practice on the path.

3. Lucid dreams. These usually begin as ordinary dreams before being transformed by the realization that we are dreaming.

In Dream Yoga we aim to transform ordinary dreams into lucid ones, to recognize we are experiencing an illusion projected by our own minds, an illusion that in its true nature is the Ground or Mother Luminosity. Karma Lingpa, who discovered *Self-Liberation through Seeing with Naked Awareness* and the *Bardo Thodol*, explicitly links discovering the luminous nature of all and the practice of Dream Yoga when he writes:

> When the dream bardo is dawning upon me, abandoning carelessly and stupidly lying like a corpse, enter in the natural sphere of unwavering attentiveness, recognizing your dreams, practice transforming illusion into luminosity. Don't sleep like an animal! Do the practice which mixes sleep and true reality.[250]

Once we have apprehended the dream, that is, we are aware inside the dream that we are dreaming, we manipulate the content of the dream to directly experience the illusory and hollow nature of all things. We turn a blue sky red, we turn green grass blue. We turn a dog into an elephant and a stone into a diamond. We change our body shape, our gender and our skin color. We fly through the sky, we meditate under water. We visit other worlds. By transforming the dream we convince ourselves that it is mere illusion, all a fabrication of the dualistic mind. We gain certainty that the mind is the source of everything we experience. We then bring that understanding of the illusory nature of things into our waking life, learning to see everything we perceive as just another mirage generated by the dualistic mind. Dream

---

[250] Karma Lignpa, '*Root Prayer of the Six Bardos*', translated by Adam Peacey, 2016. For full text: https://www.lotsawahouse.org/tibetan-masters/karma-lingpa/root-verses-six-bardos

Yoga is *always* done in tandem with a daytime meditation practice in which we remain mindful of the dream-like nature of reality. We see all things as the rainbow-like display of the mind (more on this in the next section).

As I mentioned earlier, the traditional form of Dream Yoga is an advanced practice that requires thousands of hours of meditation as a preliminary. It involves putting the body into specific postures and performing a tantric visualization. This form of Dream Yoga also requires initiation or empowerment and the completion of thousands of repetitions of the ngondro or foundational tantric practice. To give you a sense of what is entailed in traditional Dream Yoga, here is Gyatrul Rinpoche describing the physical postures required:

> The meditation posture is called the seven-point posture of Buddha Vairocana and requires legs crossed right over left in the full or half lotus position, a straight spine, relaxed arms, hands right over left in your lap, chin tucked in slightly, eyes gazing out over the tip of your nose and the tip of the tongue touching the roof of your mouth. This posture is to be maintained until you naturally fall asleep; and if thereafter the posture shifts, it is no longer relevant. The rishi posture is to sit with knees up parallel to the chest, right leg crossed in front of left with crossed arms (right over left) and elbows touching knees with fingertips touching opposite shoulders. Feet are flat on the ground. The third, most popular option is the sleeping snow lion posture. Here you are on your right side with right hand under your head (or pillow), knees tucked in slightly with left arm extended down the side of the body. This is the posture assumed by Lord Buddha Shakyamuni when he passed into parinirvana.[251]

---

[251] Gyatrul Rinpoche, *Meditation, Transformation, and Dream Yoga*, Shambhala Publications, 2002, P. 106.

According to tradition, when you adopt these postures before sleep, your head should be pointing to the north and your face toward the west. Then there is the visualization, which Gyatrul Rinpoche describes as:

> In terms of the mind, you should consider that, in the center of the physical location of your heart, a clear, empty syllable AH appears which is clear white and luminous. Do not forget to maintain pure awareness of self-nature as the embodiment of primordial wisdom (the deity). You should allow your mind to remain in equipoise upon this stainless white syllable AH. At this point, once again you may invoke the blessings of the lama by recalling his or her kindness. Inspired by pure faith and devotion, once again state your aspiration to recall and apprehend your dreams. With that as your final thought, from the syllable AH, five-colored rainbow light rays radiate to encompass all of phenomenal existence. Imagine that there is no place where the rays do not pervade. All appearances become like five-colored rainbow light. Consider that all appearances are just like a dream and that all the light rays and patterns are but a dream. Then consider that all the light rays dissolve all appearances of samsara and nirvana into shimmers of light which are also like a dream. Imagine then all appearances as shimmering light being drawn back to reabsorb and dissolve into the AH in your heart. Then focus solely upon the syllable AH appearing lucidly like a radiant image of the moon rising in a clear sky. At this point the mind is concentrating solely upon AH, without grasping, simply remaining aware.[252]

Once we have stabilized the visualization (can do it without distraction) we will have developed the capacity to transform objects in our dreams. If these passages from Gyatrul Rinpoche inspire you then certainly you should pursue formal training in Dream Yoga. There is however a way of practicing

---

[252] Ibid.

Dream Yoga that does not require complex postures or visualizations or empowerment. This form of Dream Yoga relies on Guru Yoga and is, in comparison, quite effortless.

To practice Dream Yoga in this effortless way is quite simple. Each night when we go to sleep we look at a picture of our teacher, our Heart Lama. I have a framed picture of Dudjom Rinpoche and Dudjom Lingpa by my bed. First, we set our intention – which is to turn our sleep and dreams into Dharma practice for the sake of sentient beings. We ask our teacher: "Please, precious Guru, empower me to recognize dreams and waking life as illusory display in order to benefit sentient beings" or something similar. It's important to use our own words. We then make an offering to our teacher. I usually offer everything in all the known universes and everything beautiful within them, all the celestial delights. I visualize beautiful galaxies, beautiful stars, beautiful landscapes, mountains of precious gems, piles of precious metals and all works of art, music and literature. I also offer all merit and wisdom accumulated in the three times (past, present and future). Finally, I offer my body, speech and mind, my very life. We each need to make offerings that are meaningful to us. After making our offerings, we make our request again: "Please, precious Guru, empower me to recognize dreams and waking life as illusory display in order to benefit sentient beings". We then do some informal Guru Yoga, which is to visualize our teacher in front of us as we recite our chosen mantra. After we've recited the mantra (3, 7, 21 or 108 times or more) we dissolve the image of our guru into our heart. This is the most important thing – we need to *feel* the Lama dissolving into our heart. Then we simply rest in equanimity and go to sleep.

Dudjom Rinpoche provides very clear guidance on another approach to practicing Dream Yoga in this devotional way, as a form of Guru Yoga:

When you go to sleep at night, after praying to be able to recognize luminosity, consider that the teacher on the crown of your head passes through the crown opening [chakra] and comes to rest in your heart, which is now in the form of a four-petaled lotus. Concentrate on the light from the teacher's body filling your body and the house with light, like a lamp held up in a dark room. Dissolving into the radiant, naked state of awareness-emptiness, fall asleep in this state without mental dullness and without being interrupted by other thoughts. If you wake up, stop the flow of thoughts and reflections—distraction, wildness, stupefaction, and so on— and concentrate solely on the teacher in your heart; then maintain the radiant state of luminosity. By doing so, you will gradually be able to recognize the luminosity of deep sleep and recognize your dreams.[253]

In my personal experience, practicing in this way is profoundly beneficial. It also leads to a general quietening of the mind, so that we cease having ordinary dreams and only have dharma-related ones or none at all (having no dreams is a good sign sometimes). Practicing in this way is also a form of letting go, allowing our dream practice to unfold according to the Lama's blessings. Dzongsar Khyentse Rinpoche offers this version of Dream Yoga as Guru Yoga:

... aspire to perceive and experience the luminosity of simple cognizance. As the process of falling asleep offers an excellent opportunity for recognizing this luminosity, make strong aspirations to simply 'cognize'. At death, all your sensory mechanisms will dissolve, which means this 'simple cognizance' will be entirely unbothered by your senses or your reaction to sense objects. All that will be left is your mind. So ... visualize a lotus at the center of your heart on which sits your guru, who is the embodiment of all the Buddhas. Then, as you fall asleep, just think about your guru.[254]

---

[253] Dudjom Rinpoche, *A Torch Lighting the Way to Freedom,* Shambhala Publications, 2016, p. 270-271.

[254] Dzongsar Jamyang Khyentse, *Living Is Dying: How to Prepare for Death, Dying and Beyond,* Shambhala Publications, 2020, P. 46.

This form of Dream Yoga, in which we simply think of our guru and make the wish that we recognize the luminosity that is our fundamental awareness and the true nature of our dreams, is a method without striving and without expectation. Sometimes we will dream and know we are dreaming, sometimes we will have very auspicious dreams, sometimes we will not dream at all. Whatever happens in our dreams, we just let it happen with as little attachment as possible. We are not trying to be dream yogis and yoginis, we're not trying to be anything at all. We are just relaxing into open-hearted devotion. Nothing we can do ourselves surpasses the transformative power of the blessing waves of the Lama. It is always my preference to rely on that. But, to each their own way.

Daytime Dream Yoga Practice

To support our Dream Yoga there is a simple practice or contemplation we can do during the day. This contemplation is part of what is commonly known as 'Illusory Form Yoga'. As with all practices we need to understand why we might engage in Illusory Form Yoga rather than just do it because we are told to or think we should. We practice Illusory Form Yoga because it alleviates suffering for ourselves and others. It's that simple. It corrects our perception. It awakens us to the profound reality that subject and object are not separate, that we and all other beings are deeply interconnected, that our world and the mind are one. Once we understand this our sense of freedom increases and our negative emotions and behaviors subside. Dudjom Lingpa puts it this way:

> Sentient beings apprehend appearances as being something other than themselves and thus they remain bewildered. Buddhas perceive those same appearances as being mere displays of their own primordial consciousness and are thus enlightened.[255]

---

[255] Dudjom Lingpa, *Buddhahood Without Meditation*, translated by Richard Barron, Padma Publishing, 2002.

Andrew Holecek, an experienced Dream Yoga practitioner and teacher, suggests that Illusory Form Yoga is about learning to discern the difference between how our deluded senses perceive things to be and how they actually are.[256] He explains that illusory form practice is:

> ... all about separating appearance, how things seem to be, from reality, how things actually are. We think things are solid, lasting, and independent, but that's just a mere appearance. In reality, they are illusory, or dreamlike. It's a simple practice with massive liberating results. It's also very practical.[257]

I like to call this kind of practice Rainbow Yoga, which aptly describes both Dream Yoga and Illusory Form Yoga. Rainbow Yoga awakens us to reality, specifically to the fact that all things, especially thoughts and feelings, are the rainbow-like display of the mind. Let me unpack this idea a little. What is meant by the idea that everything in the mind and in the universe is the display of the mind, its appearances, is that everything we perceive with our senses and interpret with the dualistic mind is not at all what those senses and our deluded mind tells us it is. Our senses and mind give us an exact opposite impression of our experiences, ourselves and the universe: that they are permanent, fixed, solid, contained and independent, with their own inherent existence. Rainbow Yoga liberates us of this delusion and reveals our mind, ourselves and the universe as vast, open, dynamic, fluid and deeply interconnected. That being said, these appearances or displays are just misperceptions of what is truly there, and because they arise from the ground of being they have the same taste of that ground — perfection and purity. Longchenpa, the great Nyingma master of fourteenth century Tibet, explained it this way:

---

[256] Andrew Holecek, Dream Yoga: Illuminating Your Life Through Lucid Dreaming and the Tibetan Yogas of Sleep, SoundsTrue, 2016, no page number, Kindle Edition.

[257] Andrew Holecek, Dream Yoga: Illuminating Your Life Through Lucid Dreaming and the Tibetan Yogas of Sleep, SoundsTrue, 2016, no page number, Kindle Edition.

Naturally occurring timeless awareness – utterly lucid awakened mind – is something marvelous and superb, primordially and spontaneously present. It is the treasury from which comes the universe of appearances and possibilities, whether samsara or nirvana.[258]

So even though our perception is profoundly distorted it nevertheless has the same nature as enlightenment – luminosity. It is not only Buddhism that asserts that everything we experience is dream-like and illusory, a kind of lightshow. The greatest physicists the world has ever known agree. Albert Einstein (1879–1955) once said:

Concerning matter, we have been all wrong. What we have called matter is energy, whose vibration has been so lowered as to be perceptible to the senses. There is no matter.[259]

The lauded physicist David Bohm (1917 – 1992) echoed this when he suggested that:

Matter, as it were, is condensed or frozen light ... all matter is a condensation of light into patterns moving back and forth at average speeds which are less than the speed of light ... You could say that when we come to light we are coming to the fundamental activity in which existence has its ground, or at least coming close to it.[260]

In other words, all matter in the universe is frozen light. But how does light solidify in this way? Who or what freezes it? It is our perception that freezes it, making the luminosity of the universe and ourselves seem solid and fixed when it is not at all. Dudjom Lingpa captures this notion of reality being

---

[258] Longchen Rabjam, *A Treasure Trove of Scriptural Transmission: A Commentary on The Precious Treasury of the Basic Space of Phenomena*, Richard Barron (trans), Padma Publishing, 2001.

[259] Albert Einstein quoted in Sreechinth C, *Einstein Wisdom: Quotes from an Extraordinary Brain*, UB Tech, 2016, p. 326.

[260] David Bohm quoted in Lee Nichol (ed.) *The Essential David Bohm*, Taylor & Francis, 2005, pp. 152 – 153.

fluid until our deluded perception tricks us into believing that is solid or fixed when he writes that:

> This is like water in its natural, fluid state freezing in a cold wind. It is due to dualistic grasping onto subjects and objects that the ground, which is naturally free, becomes frozen into the appearances of things.[261]

Our dualistic, self-grasping minds are the cold wind that tricks us into perceiving light and luminosity as solid objects, as permanent and lasting things. To understand and experience our luminous nature, and the luminous nature of the whole universe, is profoundly transformative. Thus the need for Rainbow Yoga.

Rainbow Yoga (Illusory Form and Dream Yoga) is about the bardo between moments of perception. Although we seem to experience the world in a continuous, unbroken stream of perception, in reality our perception is a series of singular moments separated by a gap (bardo). That gap is very brief, a mere $1/64^{th}$ of a second according to traditional Buddhist reckoning. Though brief, that gap is nevertheless profoundly important, because in that bardo between moments of perception is a more direct experience of reality as it is – dynamic, pervasive, unified, and luminous. This reality is a manifestation or display of the non-dual awareness that is the ultimate nature of all things. In other words, Rainbow Yoga awakens us to the Sambhogakaya aspect of our true nature, the way our minds creatively produce the magical display of reality.

This is how our perception works: our sense organs receive "information" about the world in the form of light waves and soundwaves etc. That information is sent to the brain where it is processed (interpreted) and used to build (fabricate) our sense of the world, our experience of reality. Let's

---

[261] Dudjom Lingpa quoted in B. Alan Wallace, *Mind in the Balance: Meditation in Science, Buddhism, and Christianity*, Columbia University Press, 2014, p. 180.

take the pervasive phenomenon of light as our example to unpack this a little more. When light hits our eyes, it stimulates sense receptors that are each attuned to different wavelengths of light to send information to our brain. In the brain that information is used to create a sense of color, depth, perspective and thus a sense of separate objects. All this is interpreted or perceived by our dualistic mind, which is predisposed to see things as fixed, solid, separate and lasting. It is this fabrication of a world of solid and separate things that we "see". In effect, our eyes are not seeing anything, they are just sensing light, it's our brain and dualistic mind that is doing the seeing, and it sees only what it wants to see; or rather what it is preconditioned to see.

From the moment the raw experience of light is registered by the eye to the moment the dualistic mind has interpreted this experience, and constructed a false vision of reality, is much less than a second. It is less than $1/64^{th}$ of a second to be precise. And immediately after that moment of perception another follows, then another and another and another, so that the false vision seems continuous and real – like the screening or streaming of a film.

In that $1/64^{th}$ of a second gap we are in fact experiencing reality (the world, the universe and ourselves) more directly, more purely. It just whips by so quickly we don't notice it, especially because our attention is on the false vision, which we self-identify with as "our experience" and are deeply attached to. This is a tragedy because in that bardo between moments of perception there is a direct experience of phenomena in which all is luminosity, all is fluid and dynamic, all is devoid of inherent lasting substance. In other words, all is Shunyata, which is primordial wisdom. Rainbow Yoga, supported by simple meditation, helps us to find that gap and rest there in the unmediated or naked experience of life.

Although Illusory Form Yoga is normally teamed with Dream Yoga it can be approached as a practice in its own right. On its own it can radically transform our perception and our minds. The point of Illusory Form Yoga is not that there is no reality, that the phenomenal world doesn't exist. The point is that our perception is an illusion, a mirage, a fabrication. Our perception tells us things about the world and our existence that are not true, that are complete fictions. These fictions cause us a great deal of suffering. It's important that we get this distinction – the Buddha Dharma does not say that things do not exist. The Dharma says they exist but not as our perception implies they do. Most importantly, sentient beings exist. They are real. Their suffering is all too real. Their need of us is very real as well. But our perception of them is distorted. The things of the mind—thoughts, feelings, emotions, sense perception and our sense of self—these are real, but they are not what we think they are. In fact, even though these are the things we identify with most strongly they are the most illusory of all. They are true fabrications. They do not reflect the truth whatsoever. Our sense of self— which is the sense that our thoughts, feelings, perceptions, wants, likes and dislikes constitute a separate, unchanging entity—is a delusion; a profound and harmful delusion. The truth of the illusory nature of all things was first expounded by the Buddha and is recorded in the Diamond-Cutter Sutra:

> A shooting star, a clouding of the sight, a lamp, an illusion, a drop of dew, a bubble, a dream, a lightning's flash, a thunder cloud – this is the way one should see conditioned phenomena.[262]

To say that we should understand all that we experience as like a dream, like a bubble, an illusion of light, is not to say that nothing is real. Dreams are real. Illusions are real. They are, however, not accurate reflections of reality. They are completely of the mind. They are also insubstantial and fleeting. Dzongsar Khyentse Rinpoche explains the illusory nature of our perception of the world when he writes:

---

[262] *Diamond-Cutter Sutra*, Chapter 32. See: https://diamond-sutra.com/read-the-diamond-sutra-here/diamond-sutra-chapter-32/

From a Buddhist point of view, each aspect and moment of our lives is an illusion. According to the Buddha, it's like seeing a black spot in the sky that you are unable to make sense of, then concentrating on it intensely until finally you are able to make out a flock of birds; or hearing a perfect echo that sounds exactly like a real person shouting back at you. Life is nothing more than a continuous stream of sensory illusions, from the obvious ones, like fame and power, to those less easy to discern, like death, nosebleeds and headaches. Tragically, though, most human beings believe in what they see, and so the truth Buddha exposed about the illusory nature of life can be a little hard to swallow.[263]

Kyabje Dilgo Khyentse Rinpoche makes the same point about the illusory nature of our experience with respect to our thoughts, feelings and sensations:

Do your thoughts appear like luminous rainbows? When a rainbow appears vividly in the sky, you can see its beautiful colors, yet you could not wear it as clothing, or put it on as an ornament. It arises through the conjunction of various factors, but there is nothing about it that can be grasped. Likewise, thoughts that arise in the mind have no tangible existence or intrinsic solidity. There is no logical reason why thoughts, which have no substance, should have so much power over you, nor is there any reason why you should become their slave.[264]

So much of our suffering arises from believing our thoughts and feelings to be true, to be accurate reflections of the world and ourselves. This suffering is the result of confusion about what is at the heart of our experience.

---

[263] Dzongsar Khyentse Rinpoche, *Not for Happiness: A Guide to the So-Called Preliminary Practices*, Shambhala Publications, 2012, p. 25.

[264] Dilgo Khyentse Rinpoche, *The Heart of Compassion: The Thirty-seven Verses on the Practice of a Bodhisattva*, translated by the Padmakara Translation Group, Shambhala Publications, 2007, p. 141.

Buddhist practitioner and translator Cortland Dahl explains that the root of our confusion is a:

> ... deeply ingrained tendency to believe that the "external" objects that populate our experience exist independent of our consciousness. This reified split between perceiving subject and perceived object sets off a chain reaction of confusion and destructive emotions, a process that perpetuates the cycle of suffering. Inquiring into the nature of this apparently dualistic experience, however, allows us to see that this is, in fact, a false distinction.[265]

In other words, the things we perceive or experience are not separate from the mind. When we get this truth—when we get it on a level beyond mere intellectual understanding—our whole experience of the world and ourselves radically transforms. The most important aspect of that transformation is a profound change to our sense of what we are. We currently think our thoughts, perception, feelings and especially our sense of self are substantial, separate from everything else and lasting. The real truth is that they are not. Our sense of self and our thoughts and feelings are completely illusory. Even our bodies are illusory. We think our bodies are solid, separate, independent and permanent and this is how we experience them. In fact our bodies are permeable, interconnected with all other things, dependent on all other things and highly ephemeral. Ironically, the only way in which our thoughts, sense of self and sense of embodiment reflect so-called reality is in that they too are like rainbows; ephemeral, a deceptive trick of the mind, dream-like, and a result of misperception. In the *Phenapindupama Sutra* the Buddha teaches that physical form is like 'a lump of foam', something that we perceive as solid but that is made up mainly by space, and that feelings are like water-bubbles,

---

[265] *Distinguishing Phenomena from Their Intrinsic Nature: Maitreya's Dharmadharmatavibhanga with Commentaries by Khenpo Shenga and Ju Mipham*, translated by the Dharmachakra Translation Committee, Snow Lion Publications, 2021, p. xii.

which are also mostly space. The same sutra describes perception as like a mirage and the dualistic mind as like an illusion.[266]

Our thoughts and feelings and our sense of self are the result of the mind creating a perception of substantial, lasting form that is not truly there. One of my teachers, Ngakpa Karma Lhundup Rinpoche, explained the notion of the dualistic mind as a magician creating illusions in this way: 'All of our thoughts are magical illusions created by our mind. We get trapped, carried away by our own illusions. We forget that we are the magician in the first place!'[267] As Niguma, the great yogini and co-founder of the Shangpa Kagyu lineage, has taught:

> This variety of desirous and hateful thoughts that strands us in the ocean of cyclic existence once realized to be without intrinsic nature, makes everything a golden land … If you meditate on the illusion-like nature of illusion-like phenomena, actual illusion-like Buddhahood will occur through the power of devotion.[268]

In this quote Niguma is making it very clear that the only difference between samsara and 'the golden land' or nirvana, and between delusion and Buddhahood, is the way we perceive our reality.

The heart message of illusory form practice is this: The universe and its contents are dream-like illusions. Nothing is truly substantial or solid. Everything is luminous space. Nothing exists independently, everything is interconnected and interdependent. On a certain level, every single thing

---

[266] See:http://bhantesuddhaso.com/teachings/sutta/sn-22-95-phe%e1%b9%87apindupama-sutta/

[267] Ngakpa Karma Lhundup Rinpoche quoted in Pema Düddul, 'Freedom from Illusion: Simple Steps to Awakening to the True Face of Reality' in *Tricycle: The Buddhist Review* (November 2021), https://tricycle.org/magazine/reality-in-buddhism/.

[268] Quoted in *Lady of Illusion*, translated by Sarah Harding, Shambhala Publishing, 2011. No page number – Kindle version.

is permeated by every other thing. Everything is impermanent, nothing remains the same for long. Everything is in a perpetual state of change. From moment to moment the things that we think are stable and solid are being altered by natural forces. The second we sense or perceive something, it has already changed, even if only at the atomic or sub-atomic level. The thing we perceived is gone. In fact, it was never truly there. Our perception is more accurately defined as *misperception*. As Khetsun Sangpo Rinpoche points out:

> Wherever we go, wherever we are, whatever food we eat, whatever conversation we make, whatever thoughts proliferate, whatever activities we take up, and whatever appearances might dawn for us, all these are actually, in that very moment, the stuff of dreams. The essence of dreams is untruth, and there is no holding on to an untrue nature.[269]

We see, hear, smell and even touch things that are not really there. This is delusion, this is suffering, yet we don't recognize it as suffering because we think it is our normal and natural state, but to be so disconnected from realty is indeed a form of suffering. What we sense or perceive as solid things, as separate, lasting entities, as our reality, is in fact a dream-like illusion, an illusion that in essence is nothing more or less than pure luminous space or Shunyata.

What is the benefit of understanding things this way? Firstly, seeing all as an illusion undermines our misperception of reality and weakens delusion. Secondly, illusory form practice cuts off attachment and aversion. What is the point of desiring things that are nothing more than insubstantial apparitions? Why be averse to mere mirages? Why act on a thought when that thought is a dream-like fabrication? Why invest in or dwell on emotions that are temporary and insubstantial? None of the tricks of the dualistic mind are

---

[269] *Strand of Jewels: My Teachers' Essential Guidance on Dzogchen*, translated by Anne Carolyn Klein, Snow Lion, 2015, p.25.

worth our time. Rainbow Yoga helps us to treat this trickery as the gaudy, deceptive lightshow that it is. As Tsoknyi Rinpoche notes:

> Illusion immediately becomes more workable when we acknowledge it as simply an illusion. The Western habit is to work against the grain and to try and organize the illusory into something solid and structured. In the stressful attempt to nail down the illusory nature of things, our chance to be at ease, spacious, awake, and free, which already exists within ourselves, gets lost.[270]

Recognizing the fabricated and illusory nature of reality and ourselves gives rise to fearlessness around suffering and death. This "entity" we think of ourselves is a fabricated construction that casts a shadow over the truth – our luminous nature or undying primordial awareness. When we recognize that what we are identifying with is a mere shadow we no longer fear its demise. We no longer fear death. As Dzongsar Khyentse Rinpoche suggests:

> None of your assumptions about who you are, who you make-believe you are, or the labels you attach to yourself, is the real 'you'; it's all guesswork. And it is this very guesswork—assumption, make-believe, labelling and so on—that creates the illusion of samsara. Although the world around you and the beings within it 'appear', none of it 'exists'; it's all a fabricated illusion. Once you fully accept this truth—not just intellectually but practically —you will become fearless. You will see that just as life is an illusion, so is death. Even if you cannot fully realize this view, becoming familiar with it will reduce your fear of death exponentially.[271]

Thirdly, illusory form practice will help us in the Bardos of Dying and Becoming – enabling us to recognize everything that manifests there

---

[270] *Fearless Simplicity: The Dzogchen Way of Living Freely in a Complex World*, Rangjung Yeshe Publications, 2003, p. 51.

[271] Dzongsar Jamyang Khyentse Rinpoche, *Living Is Dying: How to Prepare for Death, Dying and Beyond*, Shambhala Publications, 2020, p. 7.

as dream-like appearances cast by the mind, as illusions. Just as when we are watching movies or television we remind ourselves, 'This is all just a projection. None of it is truly real. Relax,' so too when we are dying or find ourselves in the Bardo of Becoming (rebirth) we simply remind ourselves that it is all a projection, like a movie, and then just rest. We will be able to do this because we have developed the habit of not getting swept up in our reactions, of recognizing everything that appears to our perception as an illusion cast by the mind.

Finally, recognizing the illusory nature of all things, including our sense of self and our body, brings us much closer to recognizing the true nature of the mind and the absolute or ultimate nature of all. To see the illusory nature of things is to be released from our ignorance and our perpetual yearning and fear into a state of relief and joy. If we truly recognize that our experience is already a self-perfected display of the ultimate nature then we have no need to strive, nothing to do but rest in that perfection. This famous verse by Longchenpa illustrates this point:

> Since everything is but an apparition, perfect in being what it is, having nothing to do with good or bad, acceptance or rejection, one may well burst out in laughter.[272]

When our ignorance about the true nature of ourselves and the world dissolves, we are literally released from a delusion and freed from all the tension, stress and worry that this delusion produces. In the recognition of the empty and illusory nature of all things, including ourselves, there is nothing but profound relief, total freedom and unshakeable rest. Free of all those afflictive mind states, our hearts naturally open. As Kyabje Dilgo Khyentse Rinpoche notes:

---

[272] Longchen Rabjam, 'The Natural Freedom of Mind', in *Crystal Mirror* (trans. Herbert Guenther), Dharma Publishing, 1975, p. 124-125.

When you recognize the empty nature of "I," you simultaneously recognize the empty nature of "other." When ignorance disappears, so too does the distinction between self and other. You stop treating people as adversaries to be overcome, and perceive friends and relatives as dream-like magical illusions.[273]

To recognize the illusory nature of things means to feel it deeply or directly know or experience it. How is it achieved, this recognition, this deep knowing of the true, illusory and dream-like nature of all things? It is achieved through our ongoing meditation practice in tandem with simple contemplation supported by daily reminders (more below). To contemplate illusory form is to contemplate impermanence and Shunyata (emptiness) but also to reflect on the ways that our sense perception and our interpretation of our sense experience profoundly misleads us. Once again, let's take as an example our perception of color.

Color is an illusion created by the brain. In reality, physical matter has no color – the sky is not truly blue, grass is not green and water is translucent but often appears otherwise to us, either blue or green. Our eyes and brain cooperate to create the perception of color where there is none, by interpreting the wavelengths of light bouncing off various objects. Of course light itself has no color either. Color is a complete fabrication and yet look at how dominant it is in our world and in our life. Just look out the window. All that color out there is an illusion, a fabrication. Our perception of the world on this level is a fabrication of the brain. This is true of our perception in general. Everything we experience is a fabrication of the brain or the dualistic, thinking mind or both. It is very helpful to contemplate

---

[273] Dilgo Khyentse Rinpoche, *The Heart of Compassion: The Thirty-seven Verses on the Practice of a Bodhisattva*, translated by the Padmakara Translation Group, Shambhala Publications, 2007, p. 189.

this regularly, to understand how we come to see color and shapes, to hear sounds, to taste sweetness or bitterness.

It's important to think about all the other things that the brain and the dualistic mind fabricate to create some sense of this reality. Science—physics and chemistry especially—is our friend in this space. Science proves what the Buddha said 2600 years ago. The brain fabricates this reality. This is not how things really are. And yet we cling to it. We believe this is how it is; that this is all real. We believe that the tree outside our window is solid and lasting. But it isn't. It really isn't. We need to remind ourselves of these things. Contemplating the way our senses and brain fabricate our experience reveals the dream-like quality of it all.

One of the profound things that happens when we start to really feel, rather than just intellectually believe in, the illusory nature of things, including our own self and our thoughts and emotions, is that attachment and aversion are cut. What's the point of desiring or wanting mirages? There's no point. So grasping, clinging, chasing after stuff, it all starts to fall away. So too with our fears and aversions. Why be afraid of a mirage? Why be afraid of a fabrication, especially our own thinking, our own feelings and emotions or memories? We start to let it all go. Once we let go we are released into a state of relief. When we do this practice the intensity of our reactions takes a nose dive. We are much more even. And that doesn't mean cold or detached. It means content and connected.

Have you ever been really anxious? We all have anxiety triggers. Public speaking is a common one. When the source of that anxiety has been removed there's a deep relief. For those afraid of public speaking, their heart palpitates, their palms sweat and they really freak out. Then it's over, they've delivered their speech, and they feel this tremendous relief. They realize they were never in any real danger. There was no need for the palpitations, no need for the sweaty palms, no need for the dry mouth.

There was no need for any of that reaction. There was no danger. It was all a fabrication. As we start to see the illusory nature of our perception, and then start to truly feel it, all of the thoughts and reactions and emotions triggered by the illusion weaken and there is a profound relief. It's a burden lifted. There is a lightness that is a very good thing. And then joy arises, we start to feel quite joyful.

As noted elsewhere in this book, we always undertake contemplation in tandem with meditation. The same is true when contemplating illusory form. Shamata meditation helps clarify our contemplations and bring them home, to the heart. Likewise, the contemplations deepen our meditation. It is also helpful to regularly remind ourselves of the illusory nature of things by using a simple aphorism. The aphorism that I use comes from one of my own poems:

This is a dream-like illusion, a mere mirage, a fleeting fabrication. Let it go and rest.

I repeat this aphorism to myself many times a day, especially at times when I'm feeling emotionally reactive or experiencing strong attraction or aversion. When repeating this aphorism it's good to remember that the point of Illusory Form Yoga is not to discount the reality of things but to free us from the grip of our misperception. I repeat a slightly different version of it when I notice myself swept up in thought: *Thoughts and emotions are dream-like illusions, mere fleeting fabrications.* Then I let the thoughts or emotions go by connecting with the breath and resting for a moment. It is a good idea to write or print out these aphorisms and place them prominently in our home and workplace – on our desk, on the fridge, on the bathroom mirror, on our favorite tree in the backyard. It's especially helpful to put them somewhere near our bed so that we will see them on waking and going to sleep. If you like you can print out my poem as your daily reminder:

Everything we experience or perceive is a dream-like illusion, a temporary mirage, a fleeting fabrication. Let it all go and rest.

Likewise, thoughts and emotions are dream-like illusions, mere fleeting fabrications. Let them go and let yourself rest.

At the time of dying all that appears is a dream-like manifestation of mind, a temporary mirage. Recognize this and rest.

After everything we held dear has fallen away, the ultimate luminosity dawns; take refuge in that simple clarity and abide in the infinite rest that is our true nature.[274]

By contemplating the misleading nature of perception and dualistic thinking, and using an aphorism to remind us of the rainbow-like quality of everything, there will come a time when our very perception changes. We will no longer be hoodwinked by the mirage. The veil of fabrication obscuring the ultimate nature will drop away and we will experience reality directly, as it is, in all its luminous perfection. As I have written elsewhere:

Everything in the mind and the universe is the magical emanation of the ultimate nature; pervasive and pristine awareness, rigpa.

All thought and emotion, all objects of the senses, all existent things, are mirages and dreams, rainbow-like illusions, luminous and effervescent, yet impermanent and empty; all arising from the clear light of rigpa and inseparable from it, like the warmth of a fire or the rays of the sun.

When we look, we see only rigpa. When we listen, we hear only rigpa. We cannot taste without tasting rigpa itself. We cannot touch without touching the face of pristine awareness. There is no scent but the fragrance of rigpa. When we think or feel, we are experiencing no less than the radiant dance of the ultimate nature.

Everything is rigpa's vast display. There is nothing else. No you, no me, no this, no that, no here, no there, no then and no now. There is simply

---

[274] *Here We Settle: Dawntime Poems from the Heart,* Timeless Awareness Publications, 2022, p.44.

the oneness of the natural state of emptiness, the ultimate nature and its myriad reflections.

As there is only pervasive and pristine awareness – and nothing further worth pursuing or experiencing – why not settle into the great simplicity of the natural state right now?[275]

The above is my poetic response to a pith instruction from Padmasambhava known as *The Three Pith Instructions of Maha Guru Padmasambhava*.[276] This Pith Instruction encourage us to see all phenomena as a dream-like illusion, a rainbow-like trick of the mind that, even though illusory, arises from the ultimate nature, arises from Shunyata or emptiness. As the illusion arises from emptiness it is, though ungraspable, completely pure and perfect as it is, as is the non-dual awareness that is our true nature. I will close this discussion of Rainbow Yoga with a pith instruction from Khandro Yeshe Tsogyal:

What we understand to be phenomena

are but the magical projections of the mind.

In the hollow vastness of the sky

there is nothing to fear:

All this is but the self-glowing light of clarity.

There is no other cause at all.

All that happens is but the mind's adornment;

Better, then, to stay in silent meditation.[277]

---

[275] *Resting in Stillness*, Timeless Awareness Publications, 2020, p. 136. This poem arose in my mind years after receiving this pith instruction. It was triggered by an informal Guru Yoga session focused on Dudjom Rinpoche and my Dudjom lineage teachers, principally His Eminence Namgyal Dawa Rinpoche and Khandro Semo Lhanzey Wangmo.

[276] I received teaching and transmission for *The Three Pith Instructions of MahaGuru Padmasambhava* from Ngakpa Karma Lhundup Rinpoche at my home in Australia in 2008.

[277] Quoted by Ngakpa Karma Lhundup Rinpoche, personal communication, 16 August 2021.

CHAPTER FIFTEEN

PUTTING IT ALL TOGETHER: APPLYING THE BARDO PRACTICES TO EVERYDAY LIFE

Every single moment is the seed of your awakening.

In this chapter I will bring everything we've discussed in this book into a daily practice formula. By applying this simple formula we can transform our lives into one of deep Dharma practice so that every moment becomes movement towards realization and liberation, without having to change the actual content or day-to-day itinerary of our lives. Everything about our lives can stay more or less the same, it will all be used as fuel for recognizing the true nature. We don't need to go to isolated hermitages, we don't need to go into retreat. We don't have to wait until that is possible. We can start right now. Of course, retreat and solitude are good, and we should try to do that when it's possible, but we can start practicing deeply without having to go anywhere. The formula I'm presenting here is one of many possible ways to apply the bardo teachings. I have focused on simplicity, accessibility and achievability. You can, however, apply the teachings in many other ways. Use the formula that suits you. This discussion about how to make every moment of our life into transformative practice will be divided into the following sections:

- What to do when we are waking up in the morning
- What to do in our daily practice session
- What to do as we go about our daily lives
- What to do when we are going to bed
- What to do when we are dreaming

What to do when we are waking up in the morning

As we wake we do a few simple things. First, if we are able to, we look to the gap between sleeping and being awake and recognize what is there. This recognition will take time and relies on having a consistent meditation practice. Without the space that meditation provides, we will never notice what is in the gap as we will be constantly under fire from thoughts, feelings and sensations.

The next step takes a little preparation. We need to print out and prominently display the aphorisms I mentioned in the sections on Buddha Nature and Illusory Form Yoga. Once we are properly awake, we glance at the aphorisms that we have placed by our bedside and contemplate them, really take them in. This means to read them and then connect with our breathing as we allow our understanding of the aphorisms to rise in our heart-mind.

This is a dream-like illusion, a mere mirage, a fleeting fabrication. Let it go and rest.

All beings, in their fundamental nature, are exactly the same as the Buddha, pure and perfect, as am I.

The use of the aphorisms takes the striving out of our contemplation. We can write them out on little post-it notes or print them out on a full page as visual reminders. There's no striving in reading these reminders, they're just there – by the bed, on the fridge, in a notebook, on a desk, wherever it is. We see them and we remember, it's quite simple. Over time we really start to recognize the illusory nature of things and to feel confidence in our Buddha Nature, which we now know is essential to Dharma practice. We also start to recognize that all other sentient beings are both precious and equal to us. We start to *feel* equal rather than merely believe we are equal. Not superior, not inferior, actually equal.

When we feel truly equal to all others our experience of the world is completely different. While we still feel either inferior or superior, which are both self grasping and both toxic by the way, we do not experience the world as it is. Once we start to equalize and see ourselves as utterly equal to all human beings, to all kitty cats, puppy dogs, cows, birdies, all beings, a profound thing happens: we feel free of inadequacy and insecurity, free of competition and judgement, and all our fears, biases and prejudices melt away. The equalizing of ourselves with all other sentient beings, and at the same time recognizing that they and ourselves are, in our nature, no different to the Buddha, is a deeply transformative thing. This understanding leads directly to recognizing our true nature. Likewise, recognizing that our perception is a mirage, that the things we desire and fear are all impermanent, illusory fabrications and not worth our time, leads to a profound contentment and relief. There is no stress or worry when we understand that all of our emotional reactions are mirages on top of mirages, fabrications on top of fabrications. Only then can we truly relax in the now and open the space for our true nature to shine through.

After we have contemplated these two aphorisms we then, if Guru Yoga is our main practice, think of our teachers. We can imagine our guru rising out of our heart to float in space in front of us, radiating light that carries peace, wellbeing, joy, compassion and love. We bathe in that radiance and rest in ease a moment. After dedicating the positive energy of our waking practice to the wellbeing of all sentient beings we get up and begin our day.

What to do in our daily practice session

Our daily practice session should include simple meditation teamed with either Guru Yoga or joy practice. That's it. Nothing more is needed. Our practice sessions should be at least thirty minutes long, but we can build up to that rather than dive straight in. If we are new to meditation, it's better to go slowly and gently than go fast. You will remember that in our tradition we take little breaks between short meditation sessions. The breaks are important, they help us to bring the same gentle awareness we have in meditation into our daily lives. If we have a guru, whether a living teacher or a master from the past who inspires us, then Guru Yoga followed by meditation is a tried and tested method for recognizing the true nature of mind. If we don't have a guru, or are uncomfortable with the very idea, then the Path of Joy is a subtle yet powerful alternative. Instructions on how to meditate, how to do Guru Yoga and how to use joy as a practice can be found in Chapters Twelve and Thirteen respectively.

It is a good idea to begin each practice session with contemplation of the *Four Thoughts that Turn the Mind to Dharma*. These four thoughts encapsulate the universal fundamentals of all Buddhist traditions and are essential. They are:

1. The preciousness of human life;
2. The truth of impermanence and the inevitability of death;
3. The irrefutability of cause and effect or karma;
4. The disadvantages of samsara and dualistic existence.

It is a good idea to consider these every day. The point of them is not to be glum and morbid. The point of the first one is to be grateful for what we have, mainly our opportunity to practice Dharma. The point of the second one is to not waste time. Time is the most precious resource in the universe. For a true Dharma practitioner any time spent on worldly things is a tragic waste. The third thought is about understanding that even the smallest action can have profound consequences, so we must avoid harming others and ourselves at all costs. The fourth and final thought helps us to understand that there is nothing of value at all in samsara, in mundane existence. In all the universe with all its so-called treasures there is nothing that is of any real value. Not a single speck of it is worth anything to us. Certainly there is nothing more valuable than practicing the Dharma. And why is this the case? Because everything in the universe is devoid of true substance and empty of inherent existence. Therefore it cannot bring us any lasting happiness. Only the Dharma brings real happiness, true joy. The Four Thoughts help us to internalize this truth. Kyabje Dudjom Rinpoche summarized the Four Thoughts when he wrote:

> A physical support such as this [human life], adorned with the abundant qualities of the freedoms and advantages, is extremely difficult to obtain. This body that I have now obtained, like everything else that is born, will not last forever, and is bound to die. At that time, this body will be left behind, but the mind will continue, directed by whatever beneficial and harmful actions I have accumulated, and, as a result, I will experience conditions of happiness or suffering, according to the inevitable laws of cause and effect. No matter where I might be reborn, whether in a high state or a low state, wherever I am among the three realms of samsara, I will be forever beset by the turbulent waves of this vast ocean of suffering. As I recognize the reality of this situation, may my mind turn towards the sacred Dharma![278]

When we deeply contemplate these four thoughts they manifest as: 1. gratitude for our life and its opportunities, especially the opportunity to practice Dharma; 2. A lack of clinging to insubstantial things, an acceptance

---

[278] Dudjom Rinpoche, *Brief Notes on the Visualization for the Concise Recitation of the Pure Vision Preliminary Practice*, Translated by Adam Pearcey, Lotsawa House, 2006, https://www. lotsawahouse.org/tibetan-masters/dudjom-rinpoche/dudjom-tersar-ngondro-notes

of death and an imperturbable motivation to practice while we can; 3. A commitment to living ethically and lovingly and a carefulness with our every action; 4. A renunciation of worldly things and a determination to live a life of spiritual purpose. There is a very short verse from the Dudjom lineage ngondro that can be repeated at the start of each practice session in order to help us contemplate these four irrefutable facts of existence:

This free and endowed human birth is very difficult to obtain.

Everything that is born is by its nature impermanent and bound to die.

Beneficial and harmful actions bring their inevitable results.

The three realms of samsara are an ocean of suffering.

Recognizing this, may my mind turn towards the Dharma.[279]

The most important thing is to keep our daily practice session simple and to be consistent. A little regular practice (as in each and every day) is better than occasional marathon efforts. Below are two short Guru Yoga practices for those new to the practice.

Guru Yoga

Use whichever of the following practices works best for you or you can use one from your own lineage. I composed these concise Guru Yoga texts for my own practice. They will do the trick despite being very short. Simply recite the text and do the visualizations as instructed in the italics.

Concise Dakini Guru Yoga

First, contemplate the Four Thoughts that Turn the Mind to Dharma:

This human life of mine is a precious opportunity:

---

[279] Dudjom Rinpoche quoted in Thinley Norbu, *A Cascading Waterfall of Nectar*, Shambhala Publications, 2006, pp: 32-45.

To take to heart the truth of impermanence and death and heed the irrefutable fact of cause and effect

To embrace that which leads to liberation and abandon all worldly pursuits that lead only to misery.

Therefore, may my mind be one with the Dharma and may I know with certainty that I can never be separated from the ultimate guru.

After rousing compassion for all sentient beings recite:

For the sake of all beings including myself,

I go to refuge to the Heart Lama,

Embodiment of the Triple Gem of Buddha, Dharma and Sangha.

I offer to you, precious Lama, my body, speech, mind and heart,

With no reservations and nothing held back.

One's true Lama emerges from the chakra at your heart and takes form in space as Yeshe Tsogyal. Then recite with feeling:

Above me in space on a blossoming lotus throne

My true Lama appears as Dakini Guru Yeshe Tsogyal, the Queen of Great Bliss;

Embodiment of all the Victorious Ones, Equal to all the Buddhas of past, present and future.

Guru Dakini, queen of all siddhis,

Dancer with Emptiness, dispeller of all obstacles,

Vanquisher of delusions and obscurations,

To you I pray: Inspire me with your example and grant your blessings,

So that all obstacles to enlightenment are dispelled,

And my compassionate aspirations are all spontaneously fulfilled.

Guru Dakini, from the four energy centres on your body of pristine light,

Send luminous beams of perfection and healing

To dissolve into the centres at my crown, throat, heart and navel.

Through this generous blessing my body is transformed into rainbow light and I know

That all barriers to full awakening have dissolved.

Dakini Guru, Yeshe Tsogyal, now please dissolve into light and become one with me,

So that I may rest in the inseparable unity of your ultimate nature and my own mind.

The dakini guru dissolves into your heart.

AH, AH, AH!

Now rest in perfect evenness for as long as possible. Afterwards, dedicate the merit.

Concise Dudjom Guru Yoga

First, contemplate the Four Thoughts that Turn the Mind to Dharma:

This human life of mine is a precious opportunity:

To take to heart the truth of impermanence and death and heed the irrefutable fact of cause and effect

To embrace that which leads to liberation and abandon all worldly pursuits that lead only to misery

Therefore, may my mind be one with the Dharma and may I know with certainty that I can never be separated from the ultimate guru.

After arousing compassion for all sentient beings recite:

For the sake of all beings including myself,

I go for refuge with the Heart Lama,

Embodiment of the Triple Gem of Buddha, Dharma and Sangha.

I offer to you, precious Lama, all the delights of all the universes in existence

As well as my body, speech, mind and heart, my very life

With no reservations and nothing held back.

The Incomparable Guru, Dudjom Rinpoche, Jigdral Yeshe Dorje[280] *arises as a body of light from your own heart. In the space in front and above you he takes the form of Padmakara, embodiment of all the Buddhas of past, present and future. After rousing compassion for all sentient beings and devotion for the guru recite with feeling:*

Incomparable Guru,

Radiant in the form of Padmakara,

Embrace me in unwavering refuge.

Accept my offering of all that exists and all that I am.

Shine your blessings on me and make me a conduit

Of your perfect wisdom and limitless compassion,

So that I might benefit others.

---

[280] If you do not feel a connection with Dudjom Rinpoche you can insert the name of any fully realized being.

May your radiance dissolve the dualistic mind and release

The blazing wonder of spacious awareness and boundless compassion

That is the heart of all beings.

Dudjom Rinpoche as Padmakara bathes you in rainbow-colored light rays that enter your five chakras and transform your body into one of rainbow light as you recite:

OM AH HUNG BENZAR GURU PEMA SIDDHI HUNG (21 times or more)

Then dissolve the guru into light which pours into your heart. After a moment, dissolve your own body of light into spacious awareness and rest in Shamata, recognizing that the Guru's mind and your own mind are one and the same – both of the perfect nature of Shunyata.

AH, AH, AH!

Now rest in perfect evenness for as long as possible. Afterwards, dedicate the merit.

At the end of our Guru Yoga session there should always be a period of silent sitting. This is, in fact, one of the most important aspects of Guru Yoga – resting in evenness. We then dedicate our efforts to the wellbeing of all sentient beings, so that our altruistic intention is always at the forefront of our minds. The dedication I penned for myself is below and repeated at the close of this book:

By this humble effort

May all beings be free of fear, sorrow and pain

May all beings know wellness, tranquility and love

May all beings abide in the perfect bliss and equanimity of their true nature

OM AH HUNG

The simplest dedication we can do is to repeat the mantra OM AH HUNG, to offer the positive energy of our practice to the body (OM), speech (AH) and mind (HUNG) of the Buddhas on behalf of all sentient beings. In traditional Tibetan Buddhism, the OM AH HUNG mantra is believed to transform our perception of the world. OM is believed to be the essence of form, AH the essence of sound, and HUM the essence of mind. OM reveals the true nature of our perception, AH the true nature of all sounds, and HUM reveals the pure nature of the mind (thoughts, emotions and sensations). By reciting this mantra we are recognizing the pure nature of all things and simultaneously offering them to the Buddhas on behalf of sentient beings. Alternatively, you can just dedicate and offer in your own words. After dedicating the positive energy of our practice session to the wellbeing of all sentient beings we proceed with our day.

What to do as we go about our daily lives

What can we do as we go about our lives to make ourselves true practitioners? What do we do when we're in the car stuck in traffic? What do we do when we're on a crowded bus or train, crammed in like sardines? What do we do when we're at work, swamped with seemingly endless and meaningless tasks? What do we do when we're doing the grocery shopping? How are we practicing when we're answering the phone? When we're dealing with someone difficult? When we're feeding our pets or when we're gardening? What do we do to make all that mundane and routine stuff part of our practice in an achievable way?

The answer is surprisingly simple. As I said earlier, we actually don't need to change anything much at all. We don't need to stop doing any of the things that we're doing, unless they are harmful. We don't need to go live in a cave, or go to the Himalayas, or anything like that. We can make our everyday lives our practice without moving house or travelling across the globe, in fact without changing our routines or the principal details of our lives. To make our life our practice we need only do three simple things:

1. Remember the illusory and impermanent nature of our existence;

2. Remember that all beings, in their nature, are no different to the Buddha, and therefore;

3. To the best of our ability live ethically and be kind, generous, loving and compassionate to all beings at all times.

This means that as we go about our day we stop every now and then to repeat our aphorisms and connect with the breath:

This is a dream-like illusion, a mere mirage, a fleeting fabrication. Let it go and rest.

All beings, in their fundamental nature, are exactly the same as the Buddha, pure and perfect, as am I.

We don't need to repeat both aphorisms at the same time. We can repeat the Rainbow Yoga aphorism when we notice something we are particularly attracted to or averse to, when we are having strong emotional reactions to something, or just when we are looking out the window. We can repeat the Buddha Nature aphorism when we are dealing with people, especially difficult ones, or encounter animals or other non-human beings, even mosquitoes and fleas. Each time we repeat our aphorisms and connect with the breath, we allow our natural compassion and love for sentient beings to rise, even if just for a moment. If we find that we have a habit of getting swept up in a particular emotion and the aphorisms and our other practices have not yet weakened it we can apply some "mind training" (*lojong* in Tibetan). Jetsunma Tenzin Palmo defines lojong in this way:

The Tibetan word *lojong* literally means "mind training," but the practice really has more to do with training our attitude, training us out of the habitual ways that we respond to situations that happen to us, especially adverse circumstances.[281]

---

[281] Jetsunma Tenzin Palmo, *The Heroic Heart: Awakening Unbound Compassion*, Shambhala Publications, 2022, p. 2.

Furthermore, Jetsunma explains that the lojong teachings are 'about how to take everything, especially adverse circumstances, onto the path. How to use everything that happens to us as a means of inwardly maturing and becoming spiritually strong is the essence of lojong practice'.[282] Lojong practice involves applying slogans or aphorisms to every situation of our daily lives. If you have emotions or negative behaviors (including attachments) that are particularly "sticky" or unmoveable, the lojong teachings are a very good way of dealing with them. To learn about lojong, Jetsunma's book *The Heroic Heart* is a very good place to start (see the Further Reading section at the end of this book). In the same vein of bringing everything in our lives onto the path, we can also think of the Dharma in every mundane action we do, as Kyabje Dudjom Rinpoche suggests:

> In a sense everything is dreamlike and illusory, but even so, humorously you go on doing things. For example, if you are walking, without unnecessary solemnity or self-consciousness, light-heartedly walk toward the open space of truth. When you sit, be the stronghold of truth. As you eat, feed your negativities and illusions into the belly of emptiness, dissolving them into all-pervading space. And when you go to the toilet, consider all your obscurations and blockages are being cleansed and washed away.[283]

This is quite a profound practice that quickly transforms every moment of our lives into the path towards lasting freedom. Kyabje Dilgo Khyentse Rinpoche provides more examples of this kind of practice:

> At all times, again and again, we should make vast prayers for the sake of all beings. When falling asleep we should think, "May all beings achieve the absolute state"; when waking up, "May all beings awake into the

---

[282] Ibid

[283] Dudjom Rinpoche quoted in *The Tibetan Book of Living and Dying* by Sogyal Lakar, Rider, 2002, p. 83.

enlightened state"; when getting up, "May all beings obtain the body of a Buddha"; when putting on clothes, "May all beings have modesty and a sense of shame"; when lighting a fire, "May all beings burn the wood of disturbing emotions"; when eating, "May all beings eat the food of concentration"; when opening a door, "May all beings open the door to the city of liberation"; when closing a door, "May all beings close the door to the lower realms"; when going outside, "May I set out on the path to free all beings"; when walking uphill, "May I take all beings to the higher realms"; when walking downhill, "May I go to free beings from the lower realms"; when seeing happiness, "May all beings achieve the happiness of Buddhahood"; when seeing suffering, "May the suffering of all beings be pacified."[284]

In my own practice, as well as making an offering on behalf of all sentient beings of everything positive that comes my way, I make use of all the negative things as well. If I'm hungry I think, 'May I take on the hunger of all sentient beings so that they are always nourished'. If I have a headache I think, 'May I take on the pain of all sentient beings so that they are free of pain and always at ease'. Finally, I would add to this list of prayers a brief one for when we are watching television or seeing a movie: 'This is all just a projection. None of it is truly real. May all beings recognize the illusory nature of their existence and rest in their true nature.' If we want to employ these strategies it's a good idea to start with just a few activities – walking, sitting and eating, say. To help support this type of practice we can print out the quotation from Dudjom Rinpoche above and post it in prominent places in our home or workplace.

---

[284] Dilgo Khyentse Rinpoche quoted in Reginald A. Ray, *In the Presence of Masters: Wisdom from 30 Contemporary Tibetan Buddhist Teachers*, Shambhala Publications, 2004, p. 93.

Buddhist Ethics

Living ethically is also a profoundly transformative practice. Everyone needs to develop their own sense of ethics as it is a deeply personal thing. Having said that, for Buddhists living ethically means to live without causing harm or causing the least harm possible. We don't need to be Buddhists to understand that no being wishes to suffer and that all beings wish to be content or happy. We know this because this is what we want ourselves and we are no different from any other being. The five Buddhist Refuge Precepts are a good ethical foundation to begin with. They are:

1. To abstain from killing. We all understand that to kill a fellow human being is always wrong and indefensible. We need to extend this understanding to all beings without exception. The fullest interpretation of this vow is to be vegetarian or vegan. In today's capitalist world the purchase of meat and animal products is equivalent to killing as it funds the ongoing slaughter, torture and abuse of animals. We certainly should abstain from hunting and fishing, from swatting mosquitoes, from using mouse traps and bug zappers etc.

2. To abstain from deceiving oneself or others. Essentially, don't lie or mislead for our own gain or avoid facing the true state of our minds. It's especially important we don't mislead ourselves or others about our spiritual progress. We don't fool ourselves into believing we are a holy or special being or aspire to be a spiritual teacher when we are still victim to negative emotions.

3. To abstain from taking what is not freely offered. Essentially, don't con, cheat, finagle or steal. This is about weakening greed and selfishness.

4. To abstain from sexual misconduct. The main point of this precept is to not use sex to harm others or ourselves, as with rape and sexual

abuse. In our modern age there is ample scientific evidence that sexual acts once considered misconduct, such as masturbation, oral sex and same-sex activity, should no longer be categorized as such. Of course, monks and nuns avoid sexual contact of any kind.

5. To abstain from alcohol or intoxicants. Essentially this is so that we don't break the other four precepts while under the influence and also so that our mind remains clear enough for us to practice Dharma (specifically meditation). The exception to this rule is if alcohol or intoxicants are ingredients of an essential medication (such as cannabis for chronic pain or epilepsy).

The main point about these precepts is to not get too hung up or uptight about them. We just do our best. We are simply mindful of our thoughts and behavior. We certainly don't judge ourselves if we aren't able to keep them. If we like to get tipsy now and then there's no need to think it's the end of the world or we are bad people. If others get tipsy or eat meat or are promiscuous it's frankly none of our business. Certainly we should not judge. Judgement is a form of violence and it has no place in Dharma. Love does not judge.

No matter how advanced we think we are as practitioners, these ethical precepts are essential. As Padmasambhava taught: 'Though the view should be as vast as the sky, keep your conduct as fine as sifted barley flour'. This instruction means that no matter how non-dual our view becomes, we can never ignore or break the fundamental Buddhist precepts.

More than merely abstaining from unethical behavior such as killing, we need to actively connect with others in a kind, loving and compassionate way. We need to make an effort for others, to listen to them, to understand them, to open our hearts to them. We should provide whatever we can provide if they are in need, protect them if they need protection, raise our voices against hatred, discrimination and prejudice wherever we find it. Most importantly, we should speak to the transformative power of kindness, compassion and love whenever we get the chance. Buddhist ethics is as much about acting with love as it is about refraining from doing harm. Another aspect of Buddhist ethics is our responsibility to share the benefits of the Dharma with others, especially those who are suffering. If we have medicine and someone is sick it is cruel to withhold it. Everyone who has taken refuge as a Buddhist has the obligation to share the Dharma according to their capacity. This is not about trying to convert others to Buddhism, but about sharing the value and benefits of self-awareness and compassion to daily life with those who are in need. This can be done in a completely secular way. It is also important that we share the Dharma in a way that is culturally appropriate for us. As Dungse Shenphen Dawa Rinpoche once advised:

> … you must acknowledge the importance of your commitment to spread the precious Dharma in your language and your culture. To practice Tibetan Buddhism is not to exchange a religion or a culture for another one coming from Asia, but to continue to develop the awakening of one's mind.[285]

If we do share the Dharma we must do so from a motivation of kindness and with humility. If we are unable to share the Dharma with kindness and humility, then perhaps we should not. We certainly shouldn't share Dharma in order to show off our knowledge, or pretend we have accomplished more than we have. This would be a breach of the second refuge precept. The Buddha himself described the five essential attitudes for those teaching Dharma:

---

[285] Teaching transcript, excerpt shared as a Facebook post, October 18 2022. Available at: https://www.facebook.com/photo/?fbid=1349957609074756&set=gm.2468097100012104 &idorvanity=521780201310480 (Accessed: 14 November 2022)

The Dharma should be taught with the thought, 'I will speak step-by-step'.

The Dharma should be taught with the thought, 'I will speak explaining the sequence'.

The Dharma should be taught with the thought, 'I will speak out of compassion'.

The Dharma should be taught with the thought, 'I will speak not for the purpose of material reward'.

The Dharma should be taught with the thought, 'I will speak without hurting myself or others'.

It's not easy to teach the Dhamma to others, Ananda. The Dhamma should be taught to others only when these five qualities are established within the person teaching.[286]

You will note that the Buddha does not require the teacher to be highly accomplished or realized, or even an expert in Buddhist philosophy. What is required is long term commitment to the Dharma and open-heartedness. At the time of the Buddha it was expected that those with more experience on the path would share their knowledge and experience with those who were new to the path. Generally, those who had been fully ordained as monks or nuns for ten years or more were considered "elders" and taught others. The non-monastic, white robe wearers, such as Buddha's close disciple Vimalakirti, tended to teach after a slightly longer period of time. The expectation that those teaching any kind of Dharma be realized or highly accomplished is unique to Vajrayana and is, in part, an aspect of Tibet's extremely hierarchical feudal society. In reality, it is only Vajrayana throne-holders who need to be be realized, as those are the teachers we take on as the object of our devotion in Guru Yoga.

---

[286] *Udayi Sutta: About Udayin*, AN 5.159, translated from the Pali by Thanissaro Bhikkhu, 1997. Full sutra is here: https://www.accesstoinsight.org/tipitaka/an/an05.159.than.html

That being said, these five attitudes and the tradition of appointing elders after a decade or more of serious and sincere practice—that includes at least some solitary retreat each year—clearly shows that some knowledge and experience is essential. More than that, they show that a compassionate motivation and a mind relatively free of egotism or arrogance is necessary. The final verse, in which the Buddha tells his disciple Ananda that these five attitudes should be 'established within the person teaching' indicates that we ourselves, the disciples or students, need to determine if the person teaching has these qualities. This is more easily done of the person comes recommended by someone we trust (another teacher, say) but we can in fact make this assessment ourselves. There is an old saying in the Dharma: 'It is the student who makes the teacher.'

The fifth attitude needed by a teacher has been traditionally understood to mean that a person teaching Dharma hurts themselves if they exalt themselves, or think they are somehow superior to others or see themselves as an important spiritual being. There's a quick test to see if we're ready to teach. If we think we are, we are not. Generally, it's best not to teach until we are asked to do so by our own teachers.

The hurting of others has traditionally been interpreted to mean to put others down and make them feel inferior or "less than". This fifth attitude or principle strongly demands a democratic environment for Dharma teaching to be successful. Each one of us needs to keep this in mind every time we open our mouths to talk about or share the Dharma. The Dharma should always be shared in a spirit of kindness, fairness and total equality. Anything else is just the play of the self-centered ego. This seems in contradiction to the practice of Guru Yoga, in which we do in fact exalt our gurus. This is why we should be very careful when we choose our teachers. They need to be impervious to our pure view of them. No matter how much we revere them, the guru should remain unaffected by our high regard of them; always humble, always seeing us as perfectly equal to them. The best teachers do not see us as disciples or students but as friends, as loved ones. My own teachers are all like this.

As with our daily practice session, we need to keep our practice in the everyday world simple and, as often as we can throughout the day, dedicate whatever Dharma practice we do to the wellbeing of all sentient beings by simply reciting OM AH HUNG, which is offering our practice and any benefit it creates to the body, speech and mind of the Buddha on behalf of all sentient beings.

What to do when we are going to bed

Each night when we are going to bed we do three simple things:

1. Write in a dream and gratitude journal
2. Remember our Buddha Nature and contemplate the illusory nature of all things
3. Do our Dream Yoga set up

We discussed the importance of gratitude in Chapter Eight. Here I will briefly outline how to keep a dream and gratitude journal. We keep the journal by the bed so that we can jot down any dreams we have and keep a record of how our Dream Yoga is going. As we write in the journal, we are creating a habit of paying attention to dreams in our waking life, which flows into our dream state. The more we write down our dreams the more we remember our dreams and the more aware we become as we are dreaming that we are, in fact, dreaming. To strengthen the habit of keeping a journal we write in it whenever we have a dream and document our gratitude each and every night before we go to sleep. It's important that we create a record of our gratitude practice that we can review as time passes to remember all the things that have benefitted us and all the times we have felt grateful. This deepens our gratitude and our awareness of the positive aspects of our lives. Doing it in our heads is not as potent.

So how do we keep a gratitude journal? We spend a few minutes each night writing down between three and five things for which we feel grateful as well as why we are grateful for these things. For example, if we write that we are grateful for our precious human body we also jot down some specific details about the benefits our body brings – the ability to go for relaxing walks, the ability to hug the ones we love, the ability to experience nature, the ability to do Tai Chi or yoga, the ability to eat delicious food, whatever it might be. It's important that our gratitude journaling isn't just a list of things, but also a record of precisely why these things or events make us feel grateful. When we are writing down why we are grateful we need to add enough detail that it is very clear how we felt, so that when we review it we will have a fuller sense of how we were feeling at the time; what the emotions and sensations were. As well as things and events, we try to include people on our gratitude list, those who have supported us, been kind to us, loved us. It can also be helpful to consider what our lives would be like without these people and things. That can really strengthen our gratitude. Apart from positive things, we can also be grateful for the negative things and unfavorable things we managed to deal with, or at least avoid making worse. For example, if someone at work was angry towards us we could write that we were grateful we didn't react by being angry in return because anger makes us feel terrible and makes every situation worse. Traditionally, Buddhists see everything positive that occurs to them as a gift from the Buddhas and Bodhisattvas, or from our gurus. Seeing things as a gift ensures we don't take them for granted and helps us to appreciate them more. This is especially true when unexpected things happen, such as we win a raffle or someone does something kind out of the blue. The element of surprise can heighten our gratitude quite considerably. The most important thing about the gratitude journal is to allow a feeling to arise in connection with the things we are writing about. Gratitude is a heart awareness, not an intellectual understanding.

After we have written in our journal we look at our Buddha Nature and Rainbow Yoga aphorisms, connect with the breath, and rest with the truth of them for just a few moments (or longer if desired).

All beings, in their fundamental nature, are exactly the same as the Buddha, pure and perfect, as am I.

This is a dream-like illusion, a mere mirage, a fleeting fabrication. Let it go and rest.

Now we'll go over the Dream Yoga set up that we do as we are preparing to go to sleep. As we just covered Dream Yoga in the previous chapter, this discussion will be brief. The first thing I'd like to discuss is the idea of a wearable Dream Yoga reminder. The wearable reminder is something we can look at as we are going about our lives that reminds us that everything we perceive or experience, everything we think and feel, everything we believe and every action we take, is all the dream-like display of mind. This wearable reminder is something we need to plan ahead for, so it is wise to decide what our reminder will be first, before we begin our Dream Yoga practice. Nearly twenty years ago I got a tattoo on my hand of the Tibetan seed syllable AH. Every time I see it as I go about my daily life I am reminded that this is all a dream-like manifestation of mind. Then, when I'm dreaming, I make a point of looking down at my hand and when I see that tattoo, I know I'm dreaming. The minute I have that understanding the dream becomes a lucid one, one I can transform into practice (see next section). It doesn't matter what we choose as our wearable reminder, a ring, a bracelet, it just needs to be something we wear each day and see whenever we look at our hands. Something I have suggested in the past is that Rainbow Yoga practitioners paint their fingernails in rainbow colors, or paint just the thumbnail a dark blue. This is an inexpensive way to have a reminder that doesn't require us to remember to put on a piece of jewelry. The reminder is always there, helping us to remember that everything is a dream-like display of mind.

Now, when we are in bed and ready for sleep, we follow these simple steps:

- We look at a picture of our teacher and feel the gratitude and love we have for their contribution to our spiritual progress

- We set our intention, which is an altruistic one, to turn our sleep and dreams into dharma practice for the sake of sentient beings.

- We make a mental offering to our teacher (especially of our own body, speech and mind)

- Then we recite: *Precious Guru, empower me to recognize dreams and waking life as illusory display in order to benefit sentient beings.* We recite this a few times so that we are clear in our mind what we are requesting.

- We remind ourselves to look at our hand if we have a dream.

- We perform Guru Yoga. That is, we visualize our teacher in front of us as we recite our chosen mantra. After we've recited the mantra (3, 7, 21 or 108 times or more) we dissolve the image of our guru into our heart. Then the guru dwells in our heart, radiating blessings. At that point, we simply rest in equanimity and allow ourselves to fall asleep.

- If we wake throughout the night we gently place our awareness on our heart where the lama dwells, radiating light and love, and then go back to sleep.

The general vibe of this form of Dream Yoga is to feel the compassion and protection bestowed by the guru, to rest in a feeling of love (tsewa in Tibetan), devotion (mögü) and joy (gawa) that dissolves grasping and allows us to simply rest as we are. In that state of contented rest we are much more likely to become lucid in our dreams and be able to turn the dream state into meditation on luminosity or the true nature of mind.

What to do when we are dreaming

This section will focus on how to do Dream Yoga while we are actually dreaming. Dream Yoga has four aspects or steps:

1. Recognizing
2. Transforming
3. Multiplying
4. Unifying

The first step is becoming lucid or *recognizing* that the dream is a dream. This step relies on the foundation of our daily meditation practice, on having repeated our illusory form aphorism throughout the day, on having made our aspirations as we were falling asleep, on keeping a dream journal and on our wearable reminder. Without these, the likelihood of realizing that we are dreaming is slim. This step has a flow-through benefit in the Bardo of Dying – it helps us to realize that we have died. Many people enter the Bardo of Dying without knowing they have died. Learning to recognize everything as a dream helps us to realize when we have entered the Bardo of Dying, because dreams and the after-death states have the same taste.

When we are falling asleep we remember to look at our hand if we have a dream. Then, when we do look at our hand in the dream, and because we have done all the groundwork, we will realize we are dreaming. Once we know we are dreaming we need to maintain our awareness that we are dreaming without waking. We simply observe the dream. Once we are able to become lucid in our dreams and able to observe the dreams without waking, we engage in the three activities of transforming, multiplying and unifying.

The second step is *transforming* the contents of the dream, including ourselves. We do this to learn that everything is a projection of mind; that nothing is fixed as it is, that everything changes, and indeed that nothing has an inherent essence or lasting substance. We transform ourselves to loosen our clinging to the categories or labels we cling to, and indeed to our sense of self itself. We can really have fun with this and be creative. There is nothing wrong with embracing the openness and freedom this practice brings. We can transform our familiar world into an alien one full of vibrant and unusual things. In fact, why not visit other worlds? Time and distance mean nothing to the dreaming mind. We can be in another galaxy instantly, spend decades there and then be back in our bed when we wake in the morning. We can change the colors and shape of things. Why not make the sky purple and clouds perfect cubes? We can change our skin color and features, change our gender and age, we can shape-shift into animals, birds and even into a goldfish if we want. We can live as a cow, deer or rabbit and truly know what it is to be a vulnerable being. As Khenchen Palden Sherab has taught:

> In the reality of the dream you can transform anything, including yourself. If you want to be a lion, you'll immediately experience yourself as a lion and know how that feels. You can also be transformed into a mountain, a tree, the earth, water, a man or woman, a child, or any of the beings in the six realms. You're not bound by physical circumstances. You can be free and independent and do whatever you like. There are no barriers here. You can be anything.[287]

While we are having fun, it's important to challenge our deeply held beliefs about ourselves by changing the things we cling to most. This practice is about seeing through our preconceptions to the truth of things. If we are most attached to our gender, change that first, or abandon gender altogether and become a truly non-binary being. If we have a deep sense of our personality, who we are, change into someone else, someone you admire and then someone you detest. Literally live in other people's shoes for a while. If you have a strong sense of your national or ethnic identity, become someone from a different place and background. Tibetan? Become an American. American? Become Ethiopian. Chinese? Become an Inuit

---

[287] Venerable Khenchen Palden Sherab Rinpoche, 'A Modern Commentary on Karma Lingpa's Zhi-Khro teachings on the peaceful and wrathful deities', transcript by the Venerable Khenpo Tsewang Dongyal Rinpoche. Full text here: https://holybooks-lichtenbergpress. netdna-ssl.com/wp-content/uploads/A-Modern-Commentary-on-Karma-Lingpas-Zhi-Kro-Teachings-on-the-peaceful-and-wrathfull-deities.pdf

person. Anglo-Australian? Become Chinese. We can literally become anything, experience anything. If we suffer from racist fear, we can become a member of the race that most terrifies us. We make the most of the transforming practice by uprooting our dearest held identifications, facing our fears and dissolving our biases; whilst simultaneously recognizing the illusory and empty nature of everything.

The third step is *multiplying* the contents of our dreams, including ourselves. Like the transforming practice, the multiplying practice teaches us that everything is a projection of mind, empty and impermanent. The goal of this practice is to multiply things as much as we can, beginning by merely duplicating things to multiplying them by tens, then thousands, then millions. In particular, we multiply ourselves, whichever self we decide to be in the dream. As Khenchen Palden Sherab Rinpoche explains:

> You might take a hundred forms, or become ten different things at once. You could be various gods, a few Buddhas, a naga, three Bodhisattvas, a dozen human beings, many types of animals and a grove of trees, all at the same time. You can multiply yourself in millions of forms. Increase the variety and open yourself to the way that you embody the whole cosmic system. Understand that this is all you. The inconceivable vastness of our nature is what is revealed by this practice.[288]

Traditionally, accomplishing this stage of Dream Yoga enables the practitioner to visit all the pure lands of the Buddhas and receive teachings from them all at once. This is said to supercharge practice exponentially. It also means there can be a million versions of ourselves all meditating at once, taking us

---

[288] Venerable Khenchen Palden Sherab Rinpoche, 'A Modern Commentary on Karma Lingpa's Zhi-Khro teachings on the peaceful and wrathful deities', transcript by the Venerable Khenpo Tsewang Dongyal Rinpoche. Full text here: https://holybooks-lichtenbergpress. netdna-ssl.com/wp-content/uploads/A-Modern-Commentary-on-Karma-Lingpas-Zhi-Kro-Teachings-on-the-peaceful-and-wrathfull-deities.pdf

with lightning speed towards the recognition of the true nature of mind and enlightenment.

The fourth step is *unifying* the dream and the dreaming mind with luminosity, or the clear light, which means to merge with or become one with the true nature of mind and everything. This is the most important aspect of Dream Yoga. In fact, if we can do this, if we can embrace the luminosity of the true nature like a child climbing into its parent's lap, then we don't need to do the transforming or multiplying. Usually, however, the ability to merge with the luminosity of the true nature depends on having accomplished the other steps first. This step is about dissolving the sense of the dreamer and the dream as separate into basic awareness itself. In other words, this step is the dissolution of the dualistic split between subject and object, knower and known. Clearly, this step mirrors the merging of mind process of Guru Yoga. The ability this step develops is nothing less than the ability to recognize the ground luminosity, the true nature of all, at the time of dying. This step is becoming one with the source of all.

So how do we do this? It is impossible without having done many hundreds of hours of meditation first. Having said that, with a stable meditation practice of some duration under our belt collapsing the dualistic separation between dreamer and dream and merging with the inherent luminosity of all is as simple as relaxing and letting everything go. It's about surrendering, not grasping, not holding onto anything. It's about dropping the sense of the self as separate and independent. It's about resting, leaning into our true nature and letting everything be exactly as it is. This attitude of rest and letting go is the fruition of the practice, but also should be the attitude we begin with. Khenchen Palden Sherab Rinpoche explains:

Clear light or primordial luminosity has many different aspects, but the most important is the complete absence of clinging and freedom from attachment. The best way to do Dream Yoga is to not cling to the dream, not be attached to recognizing the dream, not hold onto the results of multiplying or transforming, and in general, to not cling to any of these practices. If you don't cling, dreams themselves take on a radiant, transformed quality, becoming almost transparent to the clear light.[289]

This echoes what I said earlier about entering into Dream Yoga without any desire to be some kind of dream yogi or yogini, to just surrender and allow the blessings of the Buddhas and our teachers, which are already and always flowing, to penetrate our being. I will close this discussion of how to apply the bardo practices to everyday life and our dreams with a quote from Kyabje Dilgo Khyenste Rinpoche:

> Your first thought in the morning should be to dedicate the coming day to the happiness of all beings. Throughout the day, put the teachings into practice. In the evening examine what you have done, said, and thought during the day. Whatever was positive, dedicate the merit to all beings and vow to improve on it the next day. Whatever was negative, confess and promise to repair it. In this way, the best practitioners progress from day to day, the middling practitioners from month to month, and the least capable from year to year.[290]

What to do when we are dying

The most important thing to do as we are dying is to remember that everything we are experiencing in that state or bardo is a projection of mind,

---

[289] Venerable Khenchen Palden Sherab Rinpoche, 'A Modern Commentary on Karma Lingpa's Zhi-Khro teachings on the peaceful and wrathful deities', transcript by the Venerable Khenpo Tsewang Dongyal Rinpoche. Full text here: https://holybooks-lichtenbergpress. netdna-ssl.com/wp-content/uploads/A-Modern-Commentary-on-Karma-Lingpas-Zhi-Kro-Teachings-on-the-peaceful-and-wrathfull-deities.pdf

[290] Dilgo Khyentse Rinpoche, *The Hundred Verses of Advice: Tibetan Buddhist Teachings on What Matters Most*, Shambhala Publications, 2006, p.155.

like a dream or movie. Khenchen Palden Sherab Rinpoche, the Dudjom lineage yogi-monk, makes this clear when he says:

> All perception and conscious experience is nothing other than the expression of your mind. Everything you see, hear, feel, taste, smell and touch is mind. What does mind really refer to? Mind is open, empty and pure from the beginning. Mind is also the embodiment of the three kayas. Our practice is to discover and express the true nature of the mind. We must study, contemplate, meditate on and ultimately actualize the trikaya realization[291]. If we are devoted and one-pointed in our efforts, all phenomena reveal the trikaya. When the moment of death comes, we will recognize this event as a lucid display of the three kayas, another design of the true nature.[292]

Everything that arises, including the black, white and red "appearances" or visions, is a play of the mind. We just need to wait calmly and patiently until these appearances pass and the clear light dawns. Apart from recognizing the illusory and dream-like nature of things all we have to do is relax. To relax means to release grasping, release clinging. We simply relax and wait for the luminosity which is the radiance of the true nature of all to rise. As that radiance dawns, we merge with it, embrace it, become one with it. And how is that done? We don't need to do anything. It happens naturally. To be one with all is our natural state and so all we need do is let go and relax

---

[291] Remember that Kaya means "body" and trikaya means "triple body". This refers to the three inseparable aspects of the Buddha mind: Dharmakaya (mind), sambhogakaya (speech or energy) and nirmanakaya (body). They are also the three aspects of the true nature of mind: spacious awareness, luminosity or compassion, and movement or thought respectively.

[292] Venerable Khenchen Palden Sherab Rinpoche, 'A Modern Commentary on Karma Lingpa's Zhi-Khro teachings on the peaceful and wrathful deities', transcript by the Venerable Khenpo Tsewang Dongyal Rinpoche. Full text here: https://holybooks-lichtenbergpress. netdna-ssl.com/wp-content/uploads/A-Modern-Commentary-on-Karma-Lingpas-Zhi-Kro-Teachings-on-the-peaceful-and-wrathfull-deities.pdf

into that state. Our Guru Yoga practice of relaxing our muscles and nerves helps here as it shows us how to let go and simply allow the natural process of merging with the Mother Luminosity to occur. Once we have relaxed into that state we are free, liberated from all suffering. That state is Bodhicitta, the awakened mind of compassion, enlightenment. Of course, we can only reach this state of true freedom if we have practiced diligently while we were alive.

If we haven't practiced diligently and we can't relax into the luminosity of all at the time of death then our back-up plan is to think of our guru and fill our hearts and minds with devotion. From that place of deep, heart-felt devotion we call out to the lama to help us to traverse the bardos safely. As I explained in Chapter Five, the presence of unshakeable devotion means that none of the projections of the bardos, none of the visions or appearances, will occur. If we have such deep devotion that our sense of self completely dissolves as soon as we call on the guru, then the ground luminosity will rise almost instantly. This is quite simply because the self is not there to project anything. There is no dualistic mind, which is what creates all of the experiences of the bardos except the rising of the ground or Mother Luminosity. A truly devoted person has merged completely with the guru, become one with the ground luminosity. This is the swiftest and safest journey through the bardos of all. If our devotion is not so unshakeable then, at the very least, we will be reborn as a practitioner in a place free of suffering permeated with the Buddha Dharma, in other words a Pure Land. The Pure Land most bardo practitioners seek to travel to is Zangdok Palri, the abode of Padmasambhava known as the Glorious Copper-Colored Mountain. Zangdok Palri is an emanation of Padmasambhava's compassionate mind and a state where all beings can achieve enlightenment without obstacles. Zangdok Palri is not some place somewhere else, some celestial heaven, it is an aspect of our very own mind and heart. As such, it is open to all of us as a safe haven of final accomplishment.

If we do not have a teacher, a truly enlightened guide, then we can rely on Bodhicitta itself as our guru. The great Kadampa sage Gyalse Tokme Zangpo (1295 – 1369) describes how to do this when he wrote:

> The particular conduct is to lie on one's right side, with the right hand supporting the right cheek. With the little finger of that hand, close the right nostril and breathe through the left. Then, with love and compassion as a preliminary, train in giving and taking as you breathe in and out.[293] After this, consider that everything within samsara and nirvana including birth and death is only a mental projection while mind itself is not truly existent in any way. Then rest in this state of understanding, without clinging to anything at all. Thus, one passes away while combining and meditating upon the two types of Bodhicitta. It is said that although there are a great many instructions for the moment of death, none is more wonderful than this.[294]

It is profoundly important that we always remember, especially as we are dying, that in our true nature we are all perfect; exactly as we are. We are no different to the Buddha, pure and flawless. Beyond the chatter of our ordinary mind, that we wrongly believe to be ourselves, there is something greater – our true nature, which is none other than Bodhicitta, the awakened compassionate mind. How marvelous! I will close this discussion of how to integrate the bardo practices into our daily life with a quote from Ngakpa Karma Lhundup Rinpoche:

> Emaho! Both life and Death are like movies, magical illusions created by our mind. We simply forgot that we are the magician in the first

---

[293] This refers to the practice of Tonglen. For instruction on this practice see Jetsunma Tenzin Palmo, *The Heroic Heart: Awakening Unbound Compassion*, Shambhala Publications, 2022, p. 77.
[294] Gyalse Tokme Zangpo, *Commentary on the Seven Points of Mind Training*, Translated by Adam Pearcey, 2018. For full text see: https://www.lotsawahouse.org/tibetan-masters/gyalse-thogme-zangpo/commentary-on-seven-points-mind-training

place. We are lost in our own day dreams and night dreams. Let the thoughts and feelings arise, acknowledging them without judgment. They get effortlessly self-liberated. Rangshar-Rangdöl (Naturally arising – Naturally liberated).[295]

---

[295] Ngakpa Karma Lhundup Rinpoche, Facebook post, October 18 2022. Available at: https://www.facebook.com/karma.lhundup.39 (Accessed: 19 October 2022)

CHAPTER SIXTEEN

LUMINOUS AWARENESS ARE WE, NOT THIS CRUDE MATTER

Your very own mind is the gateway to Buddhahood.

A major theme of this book is the notion that bardo practice does not require elaborate tantric methods, rituals or esoteric yogic breathing and postures. Nor should it. Bardo practice should be democratic, accessible, simple and palatable to the modern mind. The bardo teachings are for everyone, irrespective of any label or category that might be applied to them. It doesn't matter what bodies we are in, what gender we perform, what our sexuality is. The color of our skin, our bank balance and the level of education we have or don't have don't matter at all either. It doesn't even matter what religion we are. By virtue of our enlightened inner nature these teachings are our birthright. Our Buddha Nature qualifies us to receive and practice the bardo teachings. Our very own mind is the gateway to Buddhahood.

To be a bardo practitioner we need only a simple meditation practice teamed with pared back or essentialized forms of Rainbow Yoga and Guru Yoga. None of these practices (as presented in this book) require empowerment and none have precursor practices or require tantric preliminaries. Importantly, these practices are not only powerful but also safe and risk-free. It is well-known that all tantric practice (including visualizing oneself as a deity) comes with risks, whereas simple meditation infused with joy, love, compassion and devotion does not. As the great master Patrul Rinpoche (1808–1887) warned:

> Some practitioners, though they have studied and understood a bit about emptiness, and they have visualized a deity and recited its mantras for many months and years, may take rebirth as harmful spirits because they deviate from the teachings and fall under the spell of malicious intent. However, practitioners whose main practice is compassion will never run those risks.[296]

Despite the common tendency to chase so-called higher practices, there are actually no higher practices than those emphasized in this book (meditation, Rainbow Yoga and Guru Yoga). These three simple practices all lead to the natural arising of boundless love, compassion and devotion. More to the point, these practices on their own can take us all the way to enlightenment. I am not alone in saying this – we've already seen that the greatest masters of our age, such as Kyabje Dilgo Khyentse Rinpoche and Kyabje Dudjom Rinpoche, have said exactly this. Dilgo Khyentse Rinpoche made it clear that the realizations of higher practices such as Dzogchen Trekcho and Togyal dawn naturally with devotion.[297] Likewise, Dudjom Rinpoche said that those with devotion will achieve realization without relying on any other methods.[298]

I've also made it very clear throughout this book that bardo practice is a complete path in itself, with no need for anything else. When these three

---

[296] Dza Patrul Rinpoche, *Enlightened Vagabond: The Life and Teachings of Patrul Rinpoche*, translated and compiled by Matthieu Ricard, Shambhala Publications, 2017, P. 164.

[297] Dilgo Khyentse Rinpoche, *The Wish-Fulfilling Jewel*, Shambhala Publishing, 1999, pp. 92-93.

[298] Dudjom Rinpoche, *A Torch Lighting the Way to Freedom*, Shambhala Publications, 2016, P. 260.

methods of silent sitting, Rainbow Yoga and Guru Yoga are the heart of our daily practice they form a seamless unity that turns each and every day into a sacred experience. If we practice meditation with heart we will awaken to the Nirmanakaya aspect of our true nature, its movement and activity, its boundless compassion. If we practice Rainbow Yoga with heart, we will awaken to the Sambhogakaya aspect of our true nature, the way our minds creatively produce the magical display of reality. If we practice Guru Yoga with real devotion we will awaken to the Dharmakaya aspect of our true nature, the fact that our essence is perfect, unbound openness, as vast as space, empty and timeless yet vividly aware. Once we have awakened to our nature there is no need for further striving. As Karma Tsultrim, the revered retreat master of Thrangu Monastery, once said:

> No matter what I do, whether walking, sitting, standing or lying down, I never stray from luminosity. This is very convenient, since I have no need for any additional, effortful practice.[299]

Of course, to reach this state we need to have an understanding of the universal fundamentals – cause and effect, impermanence and Shunyata or emptiness and non-self (anatta). These are encapsulated by the Four Thoughts that Turn the Mind to Dharma which we contemplate at the beginning of every practice session. We also need to cultivate renunciation, ethics and compassion. These things form the foundation of every Buddhist path. As noted in the first chapter of this book, all authentic spiritual practice begins with Bodhicitta. Bodhicitta is the ground, or starting point, of the Buddhist path in that it is our true nature. It is the essence of the practice itself in that it awakens our heart, and it is also the fruit. Bodhicitta is the awakened state. Furthermore, we will not progress on the path without confidence in our own enlightened nature and the Buddha Nature of all sentient beings. Indeed, Longchenpa

---

[299] Karma Tsultrim quoted in Lama Karma Drodhul, *Siddhas of Ga*, translated by Lama Yeshe Gyamtso, KTD Publications, 2020, no page, eBook edition.

tells us that confidence in our Buddha Nature dissolves obscurations and negative karma. It is essential. Other than these fundamental things, our path to awakening can be joyously simple.

The most important thing we need to remember about the bardos is that in the gap between the shenanigans of dualistic mind there is already the ultimate nature, rigpa, our Buddha Nature. It is already there. It does not need to be created, cultivated or refined. It is right there, right now, closer than our own hearts. All we need do is recognize it, feel it, and remain with it. Our Buddha Nature is the same now as it was when we were born and will remain unchanged even after a lifetime of practice. It is already perfect. Time spent on the path is not the measure of a Dharma practitioner's value. The measure is the degree to which we allow our true nature to shine. The measure is sincerity, love and kindness. The measure is openness, evenness and uninhibited joy. The measure is selflessness, in every sense of that word. The bardos reveal this to be true. The gap between one thought, emotion or perception and another is literally a break in delusion, a break in the painful illusion of samsara. In that gap is the ground of nirvana, enlightenment. In that gap is Bodhicitta, which is selfless love, compassion and joy.

To paraphrase Yoda from *Star Wars*: Luminous awareness are we, not this crude matter of our bodies. To awaken to the truth of our enlightened nature, we need to apply the teachings in daily practice. We need to sit in meditation. We need to practice Guru Yoga and Rainbow Yoga in direct, simple and personally meaningful ways. We need to recognize the true nature of our mind, which is non-dual spacious awareness. In Guru Yoga, recognition of the ultimate nature of everything or the absolute truth is fueled by devotion. In Rainbow Yoga recognition of the ultimate nature of everything or absolute truth is fueled by compassion. Devotion and compassion are both of the heart. Devotion, compassion, joy and love are all of the same perfect taste. Not just because they all arise from Dharmadhatu (the sphere or space of

Shunyata) but because they are all the natural radiance of our true nature, of the awakened mind/heart. It is clear therefore that the true heart—the heart of total openness and boundless compassion, the heart of Bodhicitta—is the foundation, means and fruition of the Buddhist path.

If we can recognize our true nature while we are alive then, if we do not awaken as Buddhas in the bardo of this life, we will awaken as Buddhas in the Bardo of Luminosity that arises as we die. Death, then, should not be seen as fearful or awful, but as an opportunity for total liberation that will benefit ourselves and all other sentient beings. Death should not be taken lightly, nor underestimated. Only a fool takes death lightly. Even so, there is no benefit in fearing it. It is a gateway to Buddhahood, a sacred moment in every sentient being's existence. That being said, let's not wait for death to awaken to our ultimate nature. Let's do everything in our power to awaken right here and right now. Bodhicitta, the enlightened mind, is not in some distant time or place. It is right here with us in this very moment. Just sit down in silent meditation and deeply relax and you will know this to be true. In that quiet ease we understand the great mystery of life and death, which is that rest and ease are our sole purpose and that our true nature is as vast and uninhibited as the sky. Resting in that boundless state and embodying the love and compassion it inspires is all we are meant to do.

By this humble effort

May all beings be free of fear, sorrow and pain

May all beings know wellness, tranquility and love

May all beings abide in the perfect bliss and equanimity of their true nature

Om Ah Hung

APPENDIX ONE

Table 3: The Eight Stages or Cycles of Dissolution in the Death Process

STAGE	FACTOR DISSOLVING	EXTERNAL SIGN	INTERNAL SIGN
1	**Earth element**	Body becomes very thin, limbs loose; sense that body is sinking under the earth	**Mirage-like vision**
	Aggregate of form	Limbs become smaller, body becomes weak and powerless, sight becomes unclear and dark	
	Basic mirror-like wisdom	One is no longer able to clearly perceive forms	
	Eye sense	**One cannot open or close eyes**	
	Colors and shapes	Luster of body diminishes; one's strength is consumed	

STAGE	FACTOR DISSOLVING	EXTERNAL SIGN	INTERNAL SIGN
2	Water element	**Saliva, sweat, urine, blood and regenerative fluid dry greatly**	Smoke-like vision
	Aggregate of feelings	Body consciousness can no longer experience the three types of feelings accompanying he mental consciousness	
	Basic wisdom of equality	One is no longer mindful of the three types of feelings accompanying the mental consciousness	
	Ear sense	**One no longer hears external or internal sounds**	
	Sounds	"Ur" sound in ears no longer arises	
3	Fire element	One cannot digest food and drink	**Spark-like vision**
	Aggregate of discrimination	One is no longer mindful of the affairs of close persons	
	Basic wisdom of analysis	One can no longer remember the names of close persons	
	Nose sense	Inhalation weak, exhalation strong and lengthy	
	Odors	**One cannot smell**	

STAGE	FACTOR DISSOLVING	EXTERNAL SIGN	INTERNAL SIGN
4	Wind element	The ten energies move to the heart; breathing ceases	**Dull light**
	Aggregate of compositional factors	One cannot perform physical actions	
	Basic wisdom of achieving activities	One is no longer mindful of external worldly activities, purposes and so forth	
	Tongue sense	Tongue becomes thick and short, root of tongue becomes blue	
	Tastes	**One cannot experience tastes**	
	Body sense and tangible objects	One cannot experience smoothness and roughness	
5	Eighty conceptions	Energy in right and left channels above heart enter central channel at top of head	**Clear vacuity (space) filled with white light**
6	Mind of white appearance	Energy in right and left channels below heart enter central channel at base of spine	**Very clear vacuity (space) filled with red light**

STAGE	FACTOR DISSOLVING	EXTERNAL SIGN	INTERNAL SIGN
7	Mind of red increase	Upper and lower energies gather at heart; then energy enters drop at heart	**Vacuity (space) filled with thick darkness; then, as if swooning unconsciously**
8	Mind of black near-attainment	All energies dissolve into the very subtle life bearing energy or force in the indestructible drop at the heart	**Very clear vacuity (space), the mind of the clear light or luminosity (rigpa)**

*This table is adapted from one in the book *Death, Intermediate State and Rebirth in Tibetan Buddhism* (Snow Lion, 1981) by Lati Rinbochay and Jeffrey Hopkins.

FURTHER READING

Bardo states, death and dying

Chokyi Nyima Rinpoche (1991) *The Bardo Guidebook*, Rangjung Yeshe Publications.

Dzogchen Ponlop Rinpoche (2008) *Mind Beyond Death*, Snow Lion Publications.

Joan Halifax (2019) *Being with Dying: Cultivating Compassion and Fearlessness in the Presence of Death*, Shambhala Publications.

Judith L. Lief (2001) *Making Friends with Death: A Buddhist Guide to Encountering Mortality*, Shambhala Publications.

Yongey Mingyur Rinpoche with Helen Tworkov (2021) *In Love With the World: A Monk's Journey Through the Bardos of Living and Dying*, Random House Publishing Group.

Robert A. F. Thurman, (translator) (1994) *The Tibetan Book of the Dead*, Bantam Books.

Tsele Natsok Rangdrol (2010) *Mirror of Mindfulness: The Cycle of the Four Bardos*, Rangjung Yeshe Publications.

Dudjom Rinpoche

Dudjom Rinpoche (2003) *Counsels from My Heart*, Shambhala Publications.

Dudjom Rinpoche (2005) *Wisdom Nectar: Dudjom Rinpoche's Heart Advice*, Snow Lion Publications.

Khenpo Tsewang Dongyal (2012) Light of Fearless Indestructible Wisdom: The Life and Legacy of His Holiness Dudjom Rinpoche, Snow Lion Publications.

Guru Yoga

Dilgo Khyentse Rinpoche (1999) *The Wish-Fulfilling Jewel*, Shambhala Publications, Boston.

Shenpen Hookham (2021) *The Guru Principle: A Guide to the Teacher-Student Relationship in Buddhism*, Shambhala Publications.

Meditation

Tenphel, Martin Jamyang & Düddul, Pema (2020) *Resting in Stillness*, Timeless Awareness Publications.

Traleg Kyabgon Rinpoche (2015) *Moonbeams of Mahamudra: The Classic Meditation Manual*, Shogam Publications.

Universal Foundations

Dudjom Rinpoche (2011) *A Torch Lighting the Way to Freedom*, Shambhala Publications, Boston.

Jetsunma Tenzin Palmo (2022) *The Heroic Heart: Awakening Unbound Compassion*, Shambhala Publications.

Jigme Lingpa (2018) *Steps to the Great Perfection: The Mind-Training Tradition of the Dzogchen Masters*, translated by Cortland Dahl, Snow Lion Publications.

Traleg Kyabgon Rinpoche (2014) *The Essence of Buddhism: An Introduction to Its Philosophy and Practice*, Shambhala Publications

Traleg Kyabgon Rinpoche (2015) *Karma: What It Is, What It Isn't, Why It Matters*, Shambhala Publications

ABOUT THE AUTHOR

Pema Düddul describes himself as a simple Buddhist disciple. He doesn't see himself as a Dharma teacher but as a writer whose main topic is Buddhist practice. He doesn't have or want students. For Pema, writing about Dharma is one of the ways he reflects on the teachings he's received, how he deepens his understanding, how he learns to apply the Dharma to everyday life. It is also how he shares his love for the Buddha's teachings with others. Pema is the Buddhist Chaplain in the University of Southern Queensland's Multi-Faith Service and the Co-Director of Jalü Centre for Buddhist Practice. Pema has been a Buddhist for forty years, discovering at the age of eleven that his personal worldview and the tenets of Buddhism were in perfect accordance. Pema first engaged with the Chan tradition but is now mainly focused on Tibetan Buddhism. Pema considers Dudjom Rinpoche, Jigdral Yeshe Dorje (1904-1987), to be his Heart Teacher. Over the years Pema has received teachings from masters in all four schools of Tibetan Buddhism. Like many thousands of others he has attended teachings with the great masters of our age, notably His Holiness Dalai Lama, Kyabje Sakya Trizin and Jetsunma Tenzin Palmo. In 2005 he received the vows of a white robe wearer. He received these vows from one of his principle teachers, Ngakpa Karma Lhundup Rinpoche. It was around this time that he was given the Dharma name Pema Düddul. More recently, Namgay Dawa Rimpoche, one of Dudjom Rinpoche's grandchildren and Dharma heirs, kindly agreed to be Pema's Dudjom lineage guru. Pema has decades of experience as a Buddhist practitioner and has taught mindfulness and meditation in Buddhist, educational and other settings since 2007. Pema has a doctorate (PhD) in Creative Writing and is co-author, along with Jamyang Tenphel, of *Resting in Stillness*, a book about meditation, compassion and the nature of the mind. His book of contemplative poetry *Here We Settle* was published by Timeless Awareness Publications in 2022.

GETTING IN TOUCH

Connect with Pema on Facebook: https://www.facebook.com/JaluMeditation/

Visit Jalü Centre for Buddhist Practice online: www.jalumeditation.org

Watch videos on the Jalü Centre for Buddhist Practice YouTube channel: https://www.youtube.com/channel/UCzexKfjNQZ-70RN5w7EcsHQ

Made in United States
Orlando, FL
03 February 2023

29430418R00173